THE WHITE KNIGHT

THE WHITE KNIGHT

A Study
of
C. L. Dodgson
(Lewis Carroll)
by
ALEXANDER L. TAYLOR, M.A.

OLIVER & BOYD
EDINBURGH: TWEEDDALE COURT
LONDON: 98 GREAT RUSSELL STREET, W.C.

First published 1952

Printed in Great Britain
by W. S. Cowell Ltd, at the Butter Market, Ipswich
for Oliver & Boyd Ltd, Edinburgh

Preface

In *The White Knight* two assumptions are made: that C. L. Dodgson was a normal, though peculiarly retiring and secretive individual; and that it is impossible to write a sustained book of 'nonsense', taking that word at its face-value.

It may seem a pity to destroy the Carroll legend, the beautiful story of the brilliant mathematician who revealed his heart only to little children. Nevertheless, I feel that the man is more interesting than the myth, the truth, or what I have seen of it, better than the fairy-tale.

The facts have been difficult to come by, for the family biographer, Stuart Dodgson Collingwood, suppressed all those which might have given offence to people then living, and conspired with Dodgson himself to bury the secret of the 'disappointment', which clouded the life of 'Lewis Carroll'. Dodgson's diary has now been edited by Roger Greene and, it is hoped, will shortly be made available to the public. To Miss F. Menella Dodgson, Lewis Carroll's niece, I owe a great debt of gratitude for having supplied me with extracts and summaries from the unpublished diaries. These throw some light on Dodgson's very strained relations with the formidable Dean of Christ Church and the beautiful Mrs Liddell. There is no doubt in my mind that Dodgson was in some sense in love with his heroine or that the breakdown in their relationship which occurred as Alice grew up was the real disappointment of his life.

Alice Liddell acted upon this Mathematical Tutor and free-lance journalist as a powerful stimulus and catalyst, fusing all his powers in the effort to charm and amuse. At her feet he laid his mathematics and his adult interests, decked out in cap-and-bells, as Kingsley had wrapped his up in 'Tom-fooleries'. When he lost her, his powers disintegrated, and in this there is gain as well as loss. His most dynamic writings are his most obscure. As inspiration declined he became more explicit. We may work back from *Sylvie and Bruno* and his letters to the *Pall Mall Gazette* and see what he was doing in the 'sixties when he gave nothing away.

That this is important may need emphasis because of another Carrollian fallacy: that mid-Victorian Oxford was a quiet backwater where nothing ever happened. The truth is that Oxford in the 'forties and 'sixties was the intellectual storm-centre of England. There the 'Oxford Movement' provoked the cry of 'No Popery'—forgotten since the days of James II. There, too, reason and dogma clashed in the *Essays and Reviews* controversy and the Huxley-Wilberforce debate on Darwin's *Origin of Species*. It is of the greatest importance that Dodgson had views of his own on all these matters and that he used his folly as a stalking horse. *Alice's Adventures* in part and *Through the Looking-glass* almost in its entirety are books for children in much the same sense as *Gulliver's Travels* is a book for children. Carrollian 'nonsense' is in fact a branch of allegory and satire. 'Children of all ages', who wish to preserve their illusions, are advised not to read this book.

And yet, need any illusions be lost? The *Alice* books are great and wonderful works of art. They can survive dissection as they will outlive commentary. My hope is that the new discoveries will enrich enjoyment for some and spoil it for nobody.

Grateful acknowledgement is hereby made:

for help, advice and encouragement at all stages of the research to Professor Peter Alexander, Professor of English Literature in the University of Glasgow;

for submitting to continual Carroll-talk over a period of years and for many valuable suggestions to my friends, Mr William Montgomerie, M.A., B.A., and Mr John Campbell, M.A.;

for permission to quote from and criticize 'Lewis Carroll and the Oxford Movement,' which, in a way, provoked this book, to 'Shane Leslie, M.A.'; and to Sir John Squire, editor and proprietor of the *London Mercury*;

for permission to quote from 'Alice's Recollections of Carrollian Days', a most valuable source, to Wing-Commander Caryl Hargreaves and the editor of the *Cornhill Magazine*;

for help in the solution of the scales of notation problem to Mr James Cassells, M.A., B.Sc.;

for help in the Mad Hatter's Watch problem to Professor L. J. Russell, Professor of Philosophy in Birmingham University;

for help with the translation of Gustav Theodor Fechner's

Vier Paradoxe, No. 4, 'Space Has Four Dimensions', to Mr David Penman, M.A.;

for private letters to Mr Sidney Herbert Williams, Mr Walter de la Mare, General Sir Bernard Paget, Sir Frederick Francis Liddell, Miss Rhoda Liddell, Miss F. Menella Dodgson and Wing-Commander Hargreaves;

for assistance in tracing many obscure and out-of-the-way works to the librarians and staffs of the University Library, Glasgow, the Mitchell Library, Glasgow, the Carnegie Library, Ayr, and the Bodleian, Oxford;

for permission to quote from copyright works to Miss F. Menella Dodgson, Messrs Macmillan and Co., Messrs Cassell & Co., the executors of Mrs Alice Wilson Fox and the Editor of *The Times*;

for financial backing to the Carnegie Trust;

for more help than could be reasonably expected to Messrs Oliver and Boyd, Ltd;

for help of all kinds to my wife.

For all opinions expressed, for all matters of fact, for anything which in any way is done amiss, I alone am responsible.

A. L. TAYLOR

June 1952

Contents

CHAPTER ONE

Before Alice

ON 27 January, 1832, Charles Lutwidge Dodson was born at Daresbury, near Warrington. His father and mother were full cousins and he was the eldest son, the third of eleven children, all of whom stammered.

His mother was a quiet, gentle person, whose influence, though life-long, was mild, and the dominant personality in the Rectory was that of his father.

Charles Dodgson the elder was a very remarkable father to have. The son of a captain in the 4th Dragoon Guards, he was born at Hamilton in Lanarkshire and educated at Westminster and Christ Church, Oxford, where he took a double first in Classics and Mathematics. His father, the Captain, was the first break in a long line of churchmen, and Charles Dodgson reverted to the family profession. In 1830 he married his first cousin, Frances Jane Lutwidge, and settled at Daresbury as Rector of that quiet, sleepy little place. It was thirteen years before Sir Robert Peel's influence obtained for him the Crown living at Croft in Yorkshire. Soon afterwards, he was examining chaplain to the Bishop of Ripon; later he became Archdeacon of Richmond and in 1853 a Canon of Ripon Cathedral. That was his limit. He was comfortably off but never rich, a man of strong views, on the fringe of the important events which happened in the Church during his lifetime, a brilliant but never an eminent mathematician, a ripe classical scholar, a reader of *The Times*, a wit.

Of his qualifications to be the father of 'Lewis Carroll', the two most important were his mathematics and his strong (but not extreme) views on Church affairs. In both of these, whether deliberately or inadvertently, he interested Charles at an early age, whereas the boy showed little aptitude for Latin, in which his father had taken a first.

Charles had a natural aptitude for mathematics. As a mere child he found a book of logarithms and took it to his father with the request: 'Please explain'. His father smilingly told him he was much too young to understand so difficult a subject. 'But,' said young Dodgson, with devastating simplicity, 'please explain.'

He was educated entirely at home in the years he spent at Daresbury and for a year after that at Croft. During this period the *Tracts for the Times* were appearing and being read by his father, whose theological position, as he later revealed it in his sermon *Ritual Worship* of 1852, was that of Keble and even of Newman up to the *Tract XC* period. Young Charles saw his father at work on his translation of Tertullian for the Library of the Fathers. He knew that Dr Pusey was writing footnotes for it. Here were mysteries: logarithms and the Primitive Church, numbers arranged according to some unfathomable system and a great incomprehensible Church controversy in which his own father was somehow involved.

The boy would seek refuge in the garden, where he made pets of snails and toads and tried to understand their ways of thought—with about equal success. He tried to interest earthworms in fighting but with no success at all. These were the early days of the railways and Charles must have been one of the first children in the world to play trains. He had a model railway in the garden at Croft and, displaying a practical streak no doubt transmitted from his Yorkshire ancestors, sold tickets and refreshments to the passengers. He was always extremely conscious of the value of money and, though generous with it in his later affluence, neither careless himself nor inclined to condone carelessness in others. In this the child was father of the man.

He was also a born entertainer, and found an audience ready to hand in his numerous brothers and sisters. He enjoyed mystifying them, and here again displayed a trait which remained with him throughout his life. One of his amusements was amateur conjuring; another was marionettes. For the latter he wrote his own plays, but while this shows his bent towards writing, it is still more important that he liked doing things behind a screen, manipulating wires and making puppets dance, disguising his voice, producing things out of nowhere. Abracadabra!

One winter he constructed a maze in the snow; all his life he enjoyed setting puzzles.

At the age of twelve Charles was sent to a private school at Richmond, where he wrote his first parody, sent to his brother Skeffington, aged six:

My dear Skeff—
    Roar not lest thou be abolished.
        Yours, etc.—

All his life he was a parodist.

In his first report upon him, Mr Tate remarks upon his re-markable prowess in mathematics—but the prowess is scarcely surprising when one considers that few children of his age are coached by a first-class mathematician; nevertheless, it does prove his mathematical bent, for his progress in Latin is less satisfactory and he had been coached by a first-class classical scholar. Mr Tate does not hesitate to credit him with genius, but advises his parents to conceal from him his 'superiority over other boys'.

His reports from Rugby, to which he proceeded in 1846, confirm his mathematical precociousness and for the first time we have direct evidence of his interest in theology. 'His mathe-matical knowledge,' writes Dr Tait, 'is great for his age.' He does not say that his knowledge of the classics is great for his age but only 'and I doubt not he will do himself credit in classics'. If he had already done himself credit, Dr Tait would doubtless have said so. 'As I believe I mentioned to you before, his ex-amination for the Divinity prize was one of the most creditable exhibitions I have ever seen.' Now Dr Tait, a future Arch-bishop of Canterbury, was one of the Four Tutors who protested against Newman's *Tract XC*.

'My dear father,' Dodgson wrote to a friend in the 1880's, 'was what is called a "High Churchman" and I naturally adopted these views.' Before he left Rugby he was evidently deeply interested in Church affairs and in mathematics; he continued to be deeply interested in both as long as he lived.

Charles was not happy at Rugby. 'I cannot say,' he after-wards wrote, 'that I look back upon my life at a Public School with any sensation of pleasure, or that any earthly consider-ations could induce me to go through my three years again.' To begin with, he was no good at games; nor had he that all-round brilliance in scholarship which the wondering schoolboy accepts as a substitute for powerful physique, brute courage and acts of skill. He made, he later supposes, 'some progress in learning of various kinds, but none of it was done *con amore*', and he spent 'an incalculable time in writing out impositions'. Again, he complains of the lack of privacy, particularly at night, and one cannot help wondering if his later prudishness was not another trait in his character which showed itself early. He was a bad mixer, an odd fish. Not for him the adoration of the House and the 'three times three'; for him, rather, the apple-pie bed, the 'de-bagging', the feeling of insufficiently recognized merit.[1]

How sweet to return to the Rectory in the holidays and at the end of schooldays, to his mother's affection, to talks with his father on subjects of which probably not one of his schoolfellows, or for that matter many of his masters, knew anything whatever, and above all to the worship of the ever-increasing tribe of brothers and sisters, all inferior in knowledge and experience, all granting him unquestioned leadership! As early as 1845 he began editing, and in the main writing, what Collingwood calls happily enough 'very local magazines', their circulation being confined to the inmates of Croft Rectory. In the preface to *Misch-Masch*, 1855, he supplies a bibliography. Apart from *Misch-Masch* itself, which was a private anthology or scrapbook added to until 1862, there were seven of these magazines. The first was 'Useful and Instructive Poetry', in 1845. There followed the only one to which the family contributed with any enthusiasm, 'The Rectory Magazine', which was not bound until 1848. Then came (and went) 'The Comet', 'The Rosebud', 'The Star' and 'The Will o' the Wisp', of all of which he had a low opinion. Nevertheless, they show him hard at work creating a world of fantasy into which he could escape and from which he could peep out at the larger and steadily widening prospect around him.

The case of *The Rectory Umbrella* is rather different. Charles had left Rugby after the winter term of 1848 and spent the next two years at home. Perhaps his father thought he would prepare for Oxford better under his own eye; or perhaps he realized that Charles was a misfit at Rugby and felt that he had

---

[1] Stuart Dodgson Collingwood's *Life and Letters of Charles Lutwidge Dodgson* is the authority for these early days.

stuck it long enough. At all events there is no doubt that he was at Croft during the whole time that *The Rectory Umbrella* was being produced and that this magazine was the most important result of the unusually long interval between school and university. It is, in fact, Charles Dodgson's first book and he is at some pains to make it clear that no one helped him in its pages 'even with a single word'.

'This we started, we believe, in 1849 or 1850, in a ready-bound square volume. It was admired at the time, but wholly unsupported, and it took us a year or more to fill the volume by our own unaided efforts. The volume exists and in good preservation, and therefore any further account of it is needless.'[1] The 'we' is Royal or editorial, and in the valedictory poem he insists on his sole authorship of all the contents:

> But in thee—let future ages
> Mark the fact which I record,
> No one helped me in thy pages,
> Even with a single word.

It was his own little world, made by himself, and despite the fact that he was entertaining his brothers and sisters, and perhaps his parents also, one feels that he made it chiefly for himself. It is a world in which the events of the Rectory, his reading and his mathematics appear whimsically distorted, and embellished with footnotes which burlesque those in the learned tomes of his father's library.

Moreover, he is his own illustrator, and while his drawings have no real artistic merit, they have the same impish quality as his prose and verse and are in their crude way extremely effective. Apart from illustrations there is a series of drawings which parody well-known pictures; the best of them substitutes an engaging young hippopotamus for the child in the yellow frock of Sir Joshua Reynolds' 'Age of Innocence'. A prose commentary accompanies each drawing.

The peculiar genius which produced the Mock Turtle is already evident in the Zoological Papers: 'Pixies', 'The Lory', 'Fishs' (not Fishes) and 'The One-winged Dove'. The 'Lory', which was later to reappear in *Alice's Adventures*, was a stuffed one in the York Museum. It had struck him as so quaint that he thought there could never have been more than one, and he

---

[1] *The Rectory Umbrella and Misch-Masch*, ed. Florence Milner, p. 91.

gave it a mythological background derived from Southey's *Curse of Kehama*. 'Fishs' he found in 'a German book'. Fishs have 'ordinarily angles at them,' he quotes delightedly, 'by which they can be fanged and heaved out of the water'. The geometrical sense of the word 'angles' obtrudes itself and the result is a species of angular fishes. In *The Times* of 22 July, 1850, he found a cryptic advertisement: 'The one-winged Dove must die, unless the Crane returns to be a shield against her enemies'. Here was another new species ready-made for him.

It was in *The Times* too, or so he says, that he read of 'Cuffey, or the Chartist'. In this, the second of a series called 'Representative Men', he reveals the orthodox Tory attitude to the Monster Petition and march on London. A piece of schoolboy wit is not to be taken seriously, but it passed the Archdeacon's censorship, whereas there is no sign of theology or mention of Church matters in *The Umbrella*.

Mathematics, on the other hand, crept back into his fantasy-world in the form of two 'difficulties', both of which concern time. One is merely an ingenious riddle: Which is more useful, a clock which is right only once a year, or a clock which is right twice a day? As the second clock is stopped, the first, surprisingly enough, is the more useful.

The other 'difficulty' is called 'A Hemispherical Problem', or 'Where Does the Day Change its Name?'

Half of the world, or nearly so, is always in the light of the sun: as the world turns round, this hemisphere of light shifts round too, and passes over each part of it in succession.

Supposing on Tuesday it is morning at London; in another hour it would be Tuesday morning at the west of England; if the whole world were land, we might go on tracing Tuesday Morning, Tuesday Morning all the way round, till in twenty-four hours we get to London again. But we *know* that at London, twenty-four hours after Tuesday morning, it is Wednesday morning. Where, then, in its passage round the earth, does the day change its name? Where does it lose its identity?

This is a real problem, the practical answer to which is: 'The International Date-line', though Sandford Fleming did not suggest the 'time zones' we use today until 1878.[1] To young Dodgson it suggested nonsense, a kind of make-believe world with absurd laws of its own. A line might be fixed, on one side

---

[1] See P. W. Wilson: *The Romance of the Calendar*, pp. 305-7.

of which it would be Tuesday and on the other, Wednesday. (The Date Line is now bent to avoid just this farcical state of affairs.) The position of the people on the line he noted as ambiguous and the only other possibility—that everybody should be allowed to choose what day it is for themselves—he dismissed as impracticable.

But there is a query here as to the nature of time which opens up vast fields of speculation. For example, he suggests that unless a line were fixed, 'there would be no distinction at all between each successive day, and no week, month, etc., so that we should have to say, "The Battle of Waterloo happened today, about two million hours ago" '. Note that 'today'. The familiar divisions of time which we take for granted have disappeared and we are in a strange new world, dayless, weekless, monthless, really timeless.

With a sigh, he gives it up, reducing it to the level of a nursery rhyme:

> If all the world were apple pie
> And all the sea were ink
> And all the trees were bread and cheese,
> What should we have to drink?

Here already, the product of a mind only seventeen years of age, is a new approach to reality, the approach he has taught us to regard as nonsense—that is to say, something more profound than the sense of the workaday world.

On 24 January, 1851, Charles took up residence at Christ Church, where his father had been before him. It was only seven years since Oxford had, against its better judgment, been linked to the outside world by railway, and a mediaeval calm still brooded over its spires and quadrangles. Brick had scarcely made its appearance among the ancient stone, rough-cast, wood and plaster of the city. Such shops as there were catered almost exclusively for the University and the meadows came right up to the college buildings.[1] It was, in fact, a little like going into a monastery. Nevertheless, it was a disturbed and shaken Oxford at which Charles Dodgson arrived.

'The least reflecting person,' said Benjamin Jowett, then a mere tutor, 'cannot fail to be aware that during the last twenty years a great change of opinion has taken place in this university

[1] J. W. Mackail: *Life of William Morris*, p. 29.

and almost, it may be said, throughout the country. How far such changes of opinion may be the reawakening of a slumbering past, what reactions they may give birth to, whether they tend to further divisions or separations, to strengthen religion or the contrary, is not necessary to enquire here . . . Happening in this place they must exercise an undue influence over us.'[1]

He was referring to the first Oxford Movement, which had so greatly stirred Charles Dodgson senior during his years at Daresbury and which was still having repercussions, though the main battle had been fought and lost before the younger Charles went to Rugby. It was in a way the result of the Great Reform Bill of 1832, the year of our Charles Dodgson's birth. So long as Members of Parliament were drawn from good Anglican families they were content to leave Church government to the Bishops and Archbishops in the House of Lords. But the Parliament which met in 1833 was a reforming Parliament and it proceeded without delay to reform the Church of England.

Reform was actually needed. Not only were more than half the clergymen in England appointed by lay patrons, but a clergyman could hold a number of livings and put a miserably paid curate into each of the least desirable parishes.[2] Within two years an Ecclesiastical Commission was set up; new bishoprics were created in Manchester and Ripon; it became illegal to hold two benefices more than a mile apart; canonries were suppressed and the funds thus obtained redistributed. When, later, Archdeacon Dodgson became a Canon of Ripon Cathedral, he had to spend three months every year in residence at Ripon, his family moving with him.

The Church did not accept this lay interference without protest. On the contrary, it reacted violently, and from the start Oxford was the source of the resistance movement. On Sunday, 14 July, 1833, John Keble, Fellow of Oriel College and Professor of Poetry in the University of Oxford, preached a sermon in which he pointed out that Parliament, whose members could now be of any denomination, was taking upon itself the right to make laws for the Church. He also denied the implication that 'the Apostolic Church' was merely 'one sect

---

[1] In a sermon preached at Oxford in 1852 or 1853.
[2] J. L. and B. Hammond: *The Age of the Chartists*, p. 220.

among many'.[1] In the same year appeared the first of the *Tracts for the Times* by John Newman. These also insisted on 'Apostolical Descent' and stated plainly, 'We must necessarily consider none to be really ordained who have not *thus* been ordained'—ordained, that is, by the laying on of hands transmitted directly from the Apostles themselves.[2] To this Archdeacon Dodgson subscribed in his sermon of 1852.

For some time, and in some cases all the time, there was no thought of a return to Rome. On the contrary, the claim made by Swift in *A Tale of a Tub*, that the English Church is as old as the Church of Rome, was vigorously re-affirmed. In fact, it might be said that there was much concern about the Church of Rome and speculation as to the exact point at which it had left the original, only-true-begotten Church of England.

But in 1841 Newman carried his interest in the Primitive Church one step too far and attacked the Thirty-nine Articles, subscription to which was still a condition of attendance at both Oxford and Cambridge. He first quoted the words of the article: 'The Romish doctrine concerning purgatory, pardons, etc., is a fond thing (res est futilis) vainly invented and grounded upon no warranty of scripture, but rather repugnant to the Word of God'.[3] Next he pointed out that it was only the Romish doctrine on these points which was condemned in the Articles, not, for instance, the Calvinistic doctrine or the Primitive doctrine.

The way lay open to a return to long-forgotten practices and beliefs. The Thirty-nine Articles, the defence-system of English Protestantism, had been by-passed. Logically the case was unanswerable. As Gladstone wrote to Lord Lyttelton, it was 'an abc truth'.[4]

But the reaction was immediate and violent. Protests within the University led to a sensational press campaign, censure of the Tract and Newman's withdrawal from Oxford. Moreover, *Tract XC* was not merely the last tract but the end of the Tractarian Movement as a single-minded Anglican revival.[5] In future there were two camps: those like Dr Pusey, on whom

---

[1] John Keble: Advertisement to *The National Apostasy considered in a Sermon.*
[2] *Tract No. 1*, p. 2.
[3] *Tract XC*, Section 6.
[4] Morley: *Life of Gladstone*, Vol. I, p. 306.
[5] *Letters of J. H. Newman*, Vol. II, pp. 327–34; *Life of Stanley*, Vol. I, pp. 291–6.

leadership of the High Church party at Oxford devolved, and those like Ward, who openly stated that he himself had subscribed to the Thirty-nine Articles with the mental reservation that he none-the-less considered Rome the true Church. On 13 February, 1845, Ward and Newman appeared before Convocation to answer a charge which amounted to heresy, and though only Ward was censured and 'degraded',[1] both seceded to the Church of Rome and were followed by numerous other converts.

These were the events to which Benjamin Jowett referred in his sermon delivered soon after Dodgson's arrival at Oxford. As he darkly hinted, reactions did take place and Jowett himself was to figure prominently in a new and fierce Oxford Movement in the opposite direction. For twenty years Dodgson, the University and the English Church were to be 'unduly influenced', and yet all three survived to breathe a more tranquil air.

Altogether, Dodgson spent forty-seven years at Christ Church, and this was by no means a record. Christ Church was like that. Meantime he had to find his feet, and whatever may be thought of an upbringing in which all but four years were spent entirely at home, it was certainly a big advantage to follow a distinguished father to Christ Church. One of the canons, Dr Jelf, author of a work on *Confession and Ritualism*, wrote to the Archdeacon expressing his pleasure and that of the Christ Church chapter that Charles was coming among them; and it was no doubt on his father's account that one of the tutors, the Rev. J. Lew, offered him one of his own rooms. Otherwise he would have had to seek lodgings in the town, for the House was full to capacity.

The change from public school to university was much less marked in those days than at present. Dodgson was still in some danger of spending his time writing out impositions, and indeed, if he had been a little earlier, might have had to bend over. The arrangements in the great old Dining Hall, with its portraits of Henry VIII and Wolsey, whose Kitchen adjoins it, were feudal. The undergraduates were divided into Commoners, Gentlemen Commoners and Noblemen, or 'Tufts', who ranked as Doctors by virtue of their blue blood and occupied

---

[1] *Life of Jowett*, Vol. I, pp. 93–4. Wilberforce voted for the degradation of Ward, Gladstone against it. See Ashwell's *Life of Wilberforce*, Vol. I, p. 247.

the High Table on the dais, while their tutors dined at the lower
level.[1] Dodgson was a commoner. He dined in a mess of half a
dozen men who had their own table. Dinner was served at five,
on pewter dishes and plates. He could have as much meat as he
cared to cut off the joint for himself.

Attendance at chapel was compulsory but most undergraduates rose at the last moment and breakfasted after their
devotions. Not so Charles Dodgson. He was in the habit of 'I
will not say getting up, but of being called, at a quarter past six,
and generally managing to be down soon after seven'. He therefore breakfasted before chapel. Moreover, he worked late. One
morning, having been up till after midnight the night before,
he slept in and missed chapel altogether. For this he expected
an imposition, but the Prick-bills must have failed to notice his
absence.

Nor was this surprising, for the state of the cathedral was
ruinous and even scandalous. Most of the building was out of
use, the undergraduates crowded into the choir and the singers,
men and boys, perched in galleries on opposite sides under the
gloomy Norman arches.

During the perfunctory service, when Dean Gaisford's responses drowned all others, the Prick-bills walked about identifying the men on their lists. At the entrance stood Keys, the
verger, armed with a dog-whip to keep dogs out. He actually
lived in the south transept and kept his beer under the Deanery
pew.[2] Big changes were due here and big changes were to take
place, but not till Dodgson's undergraduate days were over.

A few days after he arrived at Christ Church his mother died
suddenly and Charles was called home to attend the funeral.
This was a shattering blow at the outset of new and important
experiences, and though we have no record of the boy's feelings,
none is really necessary. She was a charming and affectionate
mother; home could never be the same again. There was
nothing to do but work hard and carve out a career for himself.

The first rooms of his own were in Peckwater Quadrangle,
'which,' says Collingwood, 'is annually the scene of a great
bonfire on Guy Fawkes' Day, and generally speaking is not the
best place for a reading man to live in'. Dodgson, however, was

---

[1] Thompson: *Life of Dean Liddell*, pp. 135–7.
[2] Ib., pp. 149–50.

a reading man. In November of his second term at Oxford he won a Boulter Scholarship and the following year obtained First Class Honours in Mathematics and a Second in Classical Moderations.

On Christmas Eve, 1852, he became a Student, on Dr Pusey's nomination. This meant that while he held the Studentship he had to remain unmarried and that he would eventually take Holy Orders. Morley tells us that in Gladstone's day 'the Student-designate wrote a theme, read it out before the Chapter, passed a nominal, or even farcical examination in Homer and Virgil, was elected as a matter of course by the Chapter, and after Chapel on the morning of Christmas Eve, having taken several oaths, was formally admitted in the name of the Holy Trinity'.[1] As Dean Gaisford welcomed both Gladstone and Dodgson into their Studentships, the ceremony was probably unchanged.

Archdeacon Dodgson wrote his son a letter of congratulation, in which he quoted Dr Pusey's letter to him. Dr Pusey had great pleasure in nominating Charles for a studentship. Five names had been put forward but it was plain that the Censors like himself thought Charles on the whole the most eligible. In any case it was Dr Pusey's turn to nominate a Student; it was characteristic of the Archdeacon that he had written to Dr Pusey asking him not to nominate Charles unless he deserved it.

No particular work was expected of a Student, but he had certain duties, including that of becoming a 'Prick-bill' in the Chapel. He had to prick his own name in in the mornings, and one October morning in 1853 he forgot to do so. For this omission he and his fellow Prick-bills, seven in number, had to write out two hundred lines apiece.

Dodgson could scarcely be unaware of the important events which had taken place in the city and University so shortly before his time. No doubt he could have identified the spot where Ward measured his length in the snow when he emerged, 'degraded', from the Sheldonian Theatre, 'his papers flying in every direction'.[2] And an event which took place in his first year at Oxford must have given an added zest to the celebrations on Guy Fawkes' Day when the bonfire was lit in Peckwater

[1] *Life of Gladstone*, Vol. I, p. 50.
[2] *Life and Letters of Dean Church*, pp. 55-7.

Quadrangle outside his rather unsuitable chambers. This was the so-called 'Papal Aggression'.

On 7 October, 1850, Dr Wiseman, newly created Cardinal and appointed Archbishop of Westminster, had issued his famous pastoral or manifesto in which he looked forward to the 'restoration of Catholic England to its orbit in the ecclesiastical firmament'. The effect of this document when its contents became known in England was like that of a declaration of war. By the time Wiseman reached England, the country had worked itself into a state in which his life was considered unsafe. Like the Oxford Movement it excited everybody, as Purcell said, 'from the Prime Minister and the Lord Chancellor down to the street-boy, who chalked up "No Popery" on the walls'. *Punch* featured a caricature of the Prime Minister as just such a street-boy who had chalked up 'No popery' and taken to his heels.[1]

Lord John Russell's government introduced the Ecclesiastical Titles Bill to allay public anxiety and Gladstone made one of his most impressive speeches against it at its second reading in March, 1851. He defended the earnest desire of the lay Catholics of this country for diocesan bishops as against vicars apostolic, and was heard by a spell-bound house which nevertheless passed the bill by an overwhelming majority.[2] A month later, Henry Edward Manning, one of the remaining leaders of the High Church party and an old Oxford man, seceded to the Church of Rome.

In the previous July, while Dodgson had been at home, a controversy had arisen which illustrates a tendency in the opposite direction. The Rev. G. C. Gorham had expressed disbelief in one of the principal High Church dogmas, namely 'baptismal regeneration', and the Bishop of Exeter refused to instal him as vicar of Brampton Speke. The Privy Council overturned this decision, and this assertion of the Crown's right to decide Church matters was resented not only by Manning but also by the Rev. Charles Dodgson. The latter preached against it at the time and again in 1852, when he defined his own, and incidentally his son's, attitude to extreme views on both sides.

Instead of being drawn nearer to the rule of the Reformed Church, as the common and rightful arbiter of their differences, the contending

[1] *Life of Manning*, Vol. I, p. 576.
[2] *Life of Gladstone*, Vol. I, p. 410.

parties seemed simultaneously to take a step back from it; and thus necessarily to increase the distance from each other.[1]

This mathematical illustration might well have been accompanied by a graph showing the Rev. Charles Dodgson in a central position and pursuing a straight course, while H. E. Manning diverged to the right and G. C. Gorham to the left.

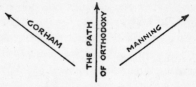

'Romanism,' was the cry of one, 'must be cast out. Our Church retains far too much of its principle.' 'Catholicism,' said the other, 'must be maintained. Our church is far too little imbued with its spirit . . .'

Each desired in his own way to reform the Reformation. And when many on the one side had been drawn away from our communion to that of Rome, and many on the other had become Dissenters in all but the name, it was seen with how much more wisdom and foresight the Church had herself already determined the boundary lines, which they had, by the aid of their own judgment, sought to mark out afresh.[1]

This sermon occasioned some comment and the Archdeacon found himself accused of the 'Romeward tendencies' which had eventually taken Newman and Manning out of the Church of England altogether. In his reply, an open letter to the Lord Bishop of Ripon, he defined his attitude to Baptism, Absolution and, above all, Holy Communion; but the High Church doctrine of the Real Presence is not easily explained. We are not to take the words in their literal sense nor yet are we to regard them as figurative: 'the language both of the Scripture and of the Church is to be regarded as purely *mysterious*, not as metaphorical'.[2] These words are nonsensical. Nevertheless, the Archdeacon knew what he meant by them.

Newman in *Tract XC* had found a weakness not merely in the Thirty-nine Articles but in the whole fabric of common sense, on which had been founded the scientific and mathematical orthodoxy of the nineteenth century. 'The truth is,' he wrote, 'we do not at all know what is meant by distance or intervals absolutely, any more than we know what is meant by absolute time.'

[1] *Ritual Worship*, p. 24.
[2] *Letter to the Lord Bishop of Ripon*, p. 17.

He was not by any means the first to express such doubts. The little problem of 'Achilles and the Tortoise' raises the question of intervals, and Berkeley in his *New Theory of Vision* (1709) had pointed out that we judge size mainly by the sense of touch: 'the judgments we make of the magnitudes of objects by sight are altogether in reference to their tangible extension'. He added that a pure intelligence, with a sense of vision but no sense of touch, would be quite unable to imagine a solid object, or to prove the congruence of triangles, or even, he thought, to imagine a plane figure, since this too involves the idea of distance. In fact he questioned the absolute truth of Euclidean geometry.

Newman, in *Tract XC*, admittedly with an axe to grind, does exactly the same thing: 'Our measure of distance is our hand or our foot; but, as an object a foot off is not called distant, though the interval is indefinitely divisible; neither need it be distant either, after it has been multiplied indefinitely. Why should the perceptions of our eyes or our ears be the standard of presence or distance?'

Like young Dodgson he questioned the nature of time, and it is odd to find him grappling (unconvincingly, it may be said) with 'late discoveries in geology' which he thought 'make it probable that time may under circumstances go indefinitely faster or slower than it does at present; or in other words, that indefinitely more may be accomplished in a given portion of it. What Moses calls a day, geologists wish to prove to be thousands of years.' He concluded that we might be 'close to the throne of God, though we seem far from it', and that in 'things spiritual' a transit through space was not a necessary condition of approach and presence. 'The condition is unknown.' He gives as an example the appearance of Christ to St Paul on his conversion.

Another interesting idea Newman expressed was that man might have more than five senses. He pointed out that a fly might be near a building and yet the building would not be present to the fly because it could not see it, while it would be present to the man who could. Similarly, Newman thought, the soul might be capable of having Christ present to it by the stimulating of dormant, or the development of possible energies.[1]

[1] *Tract XC*, pp. 53–7.

There is no doubt that the Archdeacon had read *Tract XC*,
no doubt that he would be interested in these mathematical or
quasi-mathematical ideas, some of which may well have been
familiar to him already. There is also very little doubt that he
would discuss these ideas with his eldest son, himself a mathematician of promise. To a thoughtful person such questions are
real, in a way more real than business or politics. Charles
Dodgson the elder peered into this no-man's-land between
mathematics and religion but in the long run held to the doc-
trines, Articles and formularies of the Church of England, as
his bishop said of him, 'in their plain, obvious and grammatical
sense'.

Charles Dodgson the younger was extremely unlikely to do
that, and there is proof that later he had opinions of his own on
all these matters. It is impossible to say just when he became interested—the time could have been as early as 1845 when he was
thirteen or as late as 1852 when he was twenty. But it could
scarcely be later than that.

Meantime he was a Prick-bill in the 'Chapel' and no doubt
suitably impressed by the extraordinary powers of Dean
Gaisford. The Christ Church 'Chapel' was the cathedral of the
diocese of Oxford but the Bishop of Oxford had no authority in
it. Young Dodgson must often have seen Bishop Wilberforce
slipping unobtrusively into his stall as if he were an inter-
loper.

Nevertheless, though no match for Dean Gaisford, Samuel
Wilberforce was a great churchman. It was 'Soapy Sam' who
revived the Convocation of the Clergy as a counterblast to the
reforming House of Commons. His idea was to take the affairs
of the Church out of the control of Parliament and set up a
rival constitution with an upper and lower house of its own and,
despite all obstacles and setbacks, that is what he did accomplish.
In 1852 Convocation met for the first time in a century and a
half, and registered a protest against the recent Papal Aggression on the grounds that Cardinal Wiseman had denied the
existence of the English branch of the Catholic Church. The
public suspected nothing, for the Bishop of Oxford took good
care to 'keep all asleep' until, as he wrote in his diary, the stone
he had so hardly rolled uphill had begun to roll over.[1]

[1] Daniel: *Bishop Wilberforce*, p. 123.

What did they think of each other, these two intensely self-centred individuals? Could Dodgson as he pricked in the names know anything of the suave, ubiquitous, really formidable Wilberforce, with his seat in the House of Lords, his meetings with Gladstone and the pundits of the press, his genius for getting his own way? The Bishop could scarcely be expected to notice a slim, good-looking undergraduate with an anxious face and a list of names in his hand.

For the next two years Dodgson worked hard but, in view of the examination results of 1854, must have followed his mathematical bent almost to the exclusion of all other subjects. It is true that for three weeks before 'Greats' he slogged thirteen hours a day at philosophy (mainly Aristotle) and history, and all night before the *viva voce*, but these are the signs of neglect not interest, and he finished as might be expected in the Third Class. How different was the result in the Final Mathematical School when he obtained First Class Honours and topped the list!

It was in preparation for this crucial test that Dodgson went to Whitby in the summer of 1854. The Rev. Bartholomew Price was in charge of this Mathematical Reading Party, when according to Mr Walter de la Mare, who quotes Dr Paget (later Dean of Christ Church and a life-long friend of Dodgson's), the story of *Alice's Adventures* 'was first "incubated" by Dodgson, then only twenty-two, to amuse a circle of eager youngsters of both sexes'.[1]

Neither Mr Walter de la Mare nor I can find the source of this information but the hint is worth examining, were it no more than a guess, and I feel sure that it is much more. Price, author of a massive treatise on the Differential Calculus (published 1849), was then working at a still more monumental work on the Infinitesimal Calculus. No doubt he discussed with his students the Statics and Dynamics of Particles and other fascinating topics and it would be quite like at least one of his pupils to turn this material to account in its amusing aspects when entertaining children on the beach as it was his life-long habit to do. If so, there is one part of *Alice in Wonderland* which may well date from as early as 1854, namely, the Fall of Alice.

Walter de la Mare: *Lewis Carroll*, p. 49.

Dodgson says he sent his heroine down the rabbit-hole without the slightest idea of what was to become of her. It was, however, no ordinary rabbit-hole. It went straight on like a tunnel for some way and then dipped suddenly down.

Down, down, down. Would the fall *never* come to an end? 'I wonder how many miles I've fallen by this time?' she said aloud. 'I must be getting somewhere near the centre of the earth. Let me see; that would be four thousand miles down, I think . . . yes, that's about the right distance—but then I wonder what latitude or longitude I've got to?'

The story passes smoothly on, leaving this odd question unanswered:

'I wonder if I shall fall right through the earth! How funny it'll seem to come out among the people that walk with their heads downwards. The antipathies, I think—'
Down, down, down.

It is, of course, not a real problem in dynamics, but it is suspiciously like one. If there were a shaft right through the centre of the earth and you, a small child on the beach at Whitby, fell down it, what would happen to you? Would you stop at the centre? And if so would you slow down or bounce to a standstill, or would you go right on to the 'antipathies'? Nonsense! There is no such well, could be no such fall, no happy landing at the centre—for that is where he decided Alice must end her fall unharmed: 'thump! thump! down she came upon a heap of dry leaves, and the fall was over'.

This part of the story is not really necessary at the place where it occurs. Alice could perfectly well have followed the White Rabbit down into the long low hall with its glass table, little curtained door and gold key without falling or thinking of falling four thousand miles. But, as will be seen in due course, the Mad Hatter's Watch could not possibly be two days out unless she had accomplished this long and interesting descent. It is at all events a reasonable conjecture that at some time during that Mathematical Reading Party Dodgson found some children on the beach, perhaps digging a deep hole in the sand. He drew them into conversation and, partly for his own amusement, partly for theirs, partly no doubt for that of his companions if any were present, bewildered and charmed them by questions and answers which took them into a world of fantasy and make-believe, the more fascinating because it was more than half serious.

In the following year Alice Liddell arrived at Christ Church, but there is reason to believe that at least one of her adventures was there before her. And, unknown to either story-teller or heroine, others were in preparation.

CHAPTER TWO

The Little Low Door

THE life of an undergraduate who takes examinations seriously is strange, under-surface, self-centred. He is conscious
of the outside world but it has little reality for him. He is rather
like the sick man in 'The Convalescent' by Charles Lamb. 'He
understands not what the callings and occupations of mortals
are; only he has a glimmering conceit of some such thing.' Now
this period of intense activity on planes of thought far removed
from those even of the average undergraduate was coming to an
end for Charles Dodgson. He was finished with examinations.
And, dimly at first, but over an ever widening field, he became
aware of the world in which he had to live and through which he
had to make his way.

On 13 February, 1855, he was made a sub-librarian of Christ
Church, which brought him another £35 a year. A month later
he acquired a Bostock scholarship, of £20 a year, which, he noted
with satisfaction, almost enabled him to dispense with further
help from his father. October brought a new Dean, Dean
Liddell, in whose honour Dodgson was made a Master of the
House—that is, given the privileges of a Master of Arts within
the walls of Christ Church—and by this time he was certain of a
lectureship in the following term and had already begun taking
private pupils.

His thoughts in the closing hours of 1855 were as pleasant as
any he had ever had. He had begun the year as a mere Bachelor
of Arts, still dependent upon home for part of his income. Now
he was Master of Arts, with an income of over £300 a year and
an assured, if scarcely opulent, future as a mathematical tutor.
As the bells rang out the old and in the new he had a moment of
self-abasement. 'Great mercies, great failings, time lost, talents
misapplied,' he wrote in his diary; 'such has been the past year.'
Perhaps he was mentally 'touching wood' in case fortune had
been too good to him.

Apart from his oral invention on the beach at Whitby in
1854, if indeed this incident took place, Dodgson had apparently

contributed a poem and a prose article to *The Whitby Gazette*
and these, together with two lost poems in *The Oxonian Advertiser*,
were the first of a considerable number of such odd pieces which
he sent to various periodicals in the next few years. None of
these is of much intrinsic value, but several are of great interest.
In 1855 Edmund Yates started *The Comic Times*, one of the host
of rivals which *Punch*, though constantly said to be not what it
was, has somehow managed to survive. To this Dodgson contributed his 'Tema con Variazioni', beginning,

> I never loved a dear gazelle
> Nor anything that cost me much,

which is as clever a piece of flippancy as even Oxford has ever
produced. As in his footnotes to *The Rectory Umbrella*, the
humour consists in reading into the words of the original meanings not intended by the author.

In the same year he concocted the famous first verse of
'Jabberwocky', and copied it into *Misch-Masch* with explanations of the 'words' which differ considerably from those offered
by Humpty Dumpty in *Through the Looking-glass*. The title of
the 1855 version is 'Stanza of Anglo-Saxon Poetry' and the
spelling is suitably archaic: "Twas bryllyg and ye slithy toves
. . . '. Some time later he added the remaining stanzas, but the
first verse had to wait sixteen years for publication.

Another of the poems in *Through the Looking-glass*, the White
Knight's mournful ballad, appeared in *The Train*, which Yates
started in 1856 as a successor to *The Comic Times*. It was a
parody on Wordsworth's 'Resolution and Independence' and
much closer to the original than the *Looking-glass* version. For
The Train Dodgson produced his famous pseudonym, 'Lewis
Carroll', out of his own Christian names, Charles Lutwidge.

Dodgson's best work at this time was of the nature of parody
and burlesque. As a serious poet, and some of his poems were
serious, he was never more than a very minor romantic, whereas
in 'Tema con Variazioni' he achieves perfection with no
apparent effort and in "Twas bryllyg' had already composed
his most original verse of poetry. Two further parodies of 1856
deserve to be noticed. 'The Three Voices', a parody on Tennyson's 'The Two Voices', establishes his interest in that great man
whom he was soon to meet, and 'Hiawatha's Photographing'
caricatures his own experiences as an amateur photographer.

The publication in 1949 of *Lewis Carroll, Photographer*, by
Helmut Gernsheim, renders it unnecessary to say much here
about his expensive and at that time almost unknown hobby.
He learned it from his Uncle Skeffington and from a fellow
student at Christ Church, Reginald Southey, but despite the
heart-breaking difficulties and disappointments of the wet-plate
collodion process, he soon left both his instructors far behind.[1]
The very difficulties and complications appealed to him, and it
was characteristic of one who had earlier indulged in amateur
conjuring that he should now be producing pictures out of a
hooded rosewood box. He used his camera as an introduction to
two kinds of people whose acquaintance he valued, celebrities
and children, approaching the former through the latter and
prepared, if necessary, to photograph undistinguished parents
in order to obtain attractive children as models.

It was a period of trial and error, in prose and verse as well as
with collodion and silver-nitrate, for his early professional
writings are by no means all successful. Some are adolescent,
some trivial, some clever-clever. They were addressed to an
adult public with which Dodgson was never entirely at home.
Still, they were not time wasted or talents misapplied. He was
learning how not to write.

Meanwhile, the new Dean had embarked upon that process
of reconstruction which, beginning with the Deanery, was to
transform the entire precincts of Christ Church. For the next
twenty years the 'relentless reformer', as Dodgson called him,
was restoring the Cathedral, rebuilding the belfry and digging
up the drains in Tom Quad. Nor were his reforms entirely
architectural. While still Headmaster of Westminster School,
Liddell had been a member of the first University Commission,
which had recommended sweeping changes at Oxford and
Cambridge. On behalf of Christ Church, Dean Gaisford had
resisted the work of the Commission by the simple process of
not replying to its communications.[2] Now Liddell was Dean
and the old order reluctantly gave way before him.

'I have done what I could towards retaining the old Christ
Church,' wrote Dr Pusey in 1858. '*Fuit Ilium*. The Commissioners with yourself and Dr Jacobson will be responsible for the

---

[1] Helmut Gernsheim: *Lewis Carroll, Photographer*, pp. 35–7.
[2] *Life of Dean Liddell*, p. 128.

new. I shall be very glad if the Commissioners' plan should work better than I hope of it.'[1]

And yet the Ordinance of 1858, beyond reducing the number of Canons from eight to six and abolishing the private nomination of Studentships, changed little. It took a separate Act of Parliament, the Christ Church Oxford Act of 1867, to get the tufts out of the top table and admit the educational staff to a share in the administration of the House. Long before that, however, the Dean had swept old Keys out of the Cathedral, dog-whip, beer and all, and, after extensively altering the building, reopened it to the general public. Dodgson scarcely knew what to make of it all. Many of the Dean's proposals were bound to improve his own standing at Christ Church, and when carried out actually did so. But he had liked things slack and quaint, governed by use and wont rather than by reason. On the whole his sympathies were with the departed Dean Gaisford, with Dr Pusey and the old guard.

His political opinions, after wavering slightly in the year 1856, set permanently Conservative. He had been reading Charles Kingsley's *Alton Locke* and was briefly stirred by the social plight of the industrial masses and even by the possibility of doing something to improve matters. But the task appeared hopeless. 'Each one,' he wrote, 'has his own *nostrum* to propound, and in the Babel of voices nothing is done. I would thankfully spend and be spent so long as I were sure of really effecting something by the sacrifice, and not merely lying down under the wheels of some irresistible Juggernaut.' Dodgson was not of the stuff of which reformers are made and in this he may have been a little unfortunate, for it was the Juggernaut of reform which was now irresistible, and despite the Babel of voices (in which his own can occasionally be distinguished), far more was done than he could have wished.

He was, however, preoccupied with his own progress, financial and academic, for he soon realized that there was no real future in free-lance journalism. His talent was not that of producing facile, readable articles and poems in bulk. On the contrary, everything he wrote bears the mark of careful workmanship, and when success, commercial as well as artistic, did come with *Alice's Adventures*, it came as the result of a long

[1] *Life of Dean Liddell*, p. 143.

process of development, which can be traced in detail. In his first years of independence he was independent and no more.

It was in 1855 that his father had written him a letter full of sound, worldly-wise advice. In it he advised his son to save £150 a year for ten years, investing £100 at 4 per cent, insuring his life for £1,500 and buying books annually to the value of £20/5/-. Should he then obtain 'a living enabling him to settle', he would find himself provided with £1,200 ready cash for furnishing and so on, his life could be insured at a low premium, and he would have the nucleus of a really valuable library. By a 'living', the Archdeacon meant a Vicarage or Rectory like his own.

That Dodgson did consider the Church as an eventual mode of earning a livelihood, to put it no higher than that, there is no doubt. The chief obstacle at this time—that is, in the late 1850's—was his stammer, and at some time between 1857 and 1859 he made an attempt to have this cured. Greville Macdonald tells us that his father, the Scottish novelist and poet, George Macdonald, met Dodgson through a certain Dr James Hunt, who had 'some distinction as a philologist, but more as a curer of stammering' and that Dodgson was one of his patients.[1] The attempt failed. To the end of his days Dodgson stammered, though he learned to make his impediment give point to an anecdote.

There were other reasons why he was unwilling to embark upon the career. His talents were at once more specialized and less scholarly than those of his father and at that time it probably seemed to him that his future must be bound up with his best subject, namely mathematics. Again, there was a reluctance to commit himself to the very strict rule imposed by custom on those who took priest's orders. He liked the theatre, saw nothing wrong in play-going and was determined not to give it up. It is also certain that his orthodoxy, derived from his father, was seriously undermined by doubts and speculations then very much in the minds of thinking people.

In 1857 he met Tennyson, and probably in the same year George Macdonald, each of whom, beginning from a different orthodoxy, had modified his religious views very considerably. Macdonald, starting from the plain Calvinism of the Congregational Church in Aberdeenshire, had freed himself from much

[1] Greville Macdonald: *George Macdonald and his Wife*, p. 301.

that was harsh and gloomy, and without losing his faith in God had won through to toleration and humour. When Dodgson met him he had published one long poem and a volume of short pieces. He was at work on *Phantastes*, the story of an allegorical and impossible quest, described in the sub-title as 'A Faerie Romance for Men and Women'. His later success came with his novels of Scottish life, beginning with *David Elginbrod* in 1862.

Tennyson, on the other hand, was like Dodgson himself the son of an English Church clergyman. As early as 1830 he had begun apologetically to express his doubts in the 'Supposed Confessions of a Second-Rate Sensitive Mind', in which he stated his life-long belief: 'It is man's privilege to doubt'. Twelve years later he developed his ideas more adequately in the 'Two Voices' which Dodgson parodied in his 'Three Voices'.[1]

The fullest expression which he gave to all the doubts and speculations of the age was in 'In Memoriam, A.H.H., 1850' which is in its very formlessness and incoherence the best reflection of a young man's mind in this period. It is clear that Tennyson was much impressed by what Newman had called 'the recent discoveries in geology', and also by the *Vestiges of Creation* published anonymously by Robert Chambers in 1844. Of this forthright attack on the Book of Genesis Tennyson wrote: 'It seems to contain many speculations with which I have been familiar for years, and on which I have written more than one poem'.[2]

Tennyson did not, however, abandon his Anglican beliefs. On the contrary, after trying himself with all the philosophies, religions and scepticisms, he found himself sadly but incurably optimistic:

> I can but trust that good will fall
> At last—far off—at last to all
> And every winter change to spring.

Man might be a fallen angel or an ascending brute but the way lay upward:

> Arise and fly
> The reeling Fawn, the sensual feast;
> Move upward, working out the beast,
> And let the ape and tiger die.

[1] *The Train*, Vol. II, pp. 278–84 (November, 1856).
[2] Amy Cruse: *The Victorians and their Books*, p. 87.

Dodgson first met Tennyson in September, 1857, at Tent Lodge, Coniston, where he called on the strength of having photographed the daughter of Tennyson's sister-in-law.[1] He readily obtained permission to photograph the children, and eventually took the Laureate himself, sitting bolt upright with a book on his knee. It is a sombre photograph. Nevertheless, Dodgson liked the 'strange, shaggy-looking man', finding him 'kind and friendly . . . a dry, lurking humour in his style of talking'.[2]

On one visit the conversation turned upon the Fall of Man and Tennyson remarked that the monkey's skull was not merely similar to the human, but showed a parallel development—downwards. A young monkey's skull, he said, is quite human in shape and gradually alters, while the human skull is at first more like the statues of the gods. Then, turning to Mrs Tennyson, he exclaimed: 'There, that's the second original remark I've made this evening'.[3]

Some time later Dodgson found himself at Freshwater in the Isle of Wight—it must have been in the Easter vacation of 1859—and called upon Tennyson whom he found 'mowing his lawn in a wideawake and spectacles'. In a letter to his cousin William he found it necessary to defend himself against a charge of running after the Laureate, and certainly Tennyson did not remember him. However, young Hallam Tennyson did, and there were the photographs, framed and hanging on the wall. Invitations to tea, dinner and lunch followed, and at one of these Dodgson heard the poet growl out to a shy, nervous clergyman that the clergy would do more good if they were less stuck-up. Dodgson writes: ' "What they want," he said, "is force and geniality—geniality without force will, of course, do no good, but force without geniality will do very little" '. This opinion, delivered in a little smoke-room after tea, Dodgson considered 'very sound theology'.

At dinner the following evening, Tennyson told them that he often dreamed long passages of poetry. 'You, I suppose,' he said, turning to Dodgson, 'dream photographs.'[4] To a mathematical don and literary aspirant the apparent rudeness of that

[1] Helmut Gernsheim, pp. 41–2.
[2] Coll., p. 69.
[3] Ib., p. 71.
[4] Handbook, p. 195.

remark is breath-taking. Dodgson saw no harm in it, and probably Tennyson meant none, for he sincerely admired Dodgson's photographs.

For Dodgson's part, he and his sisters knew 'In Memoriam' better than most people, for in 1862 they published an index to it. To conclude from this that Dodgson shared Tennyson's doubts may be unsafe, but the influence of the poet was in any case steadying rather than otherwise, for he admitted that his doubts were no more than doubts. Like George Macdonald he accepted the fact that the human reason is limited.

'Behold we know not anything.'

In view of Darwin's much more positive assertions, before whose impact the Church reeled, it was comforting to remember that. It might be true that there was nothing completely new in his *Origin of Species*, which was published in November, 1859, but unlike the *Vestiges of Creation* it could not be dismissed as unscientific, and it was horribly convincing.

'Therefore a man should examine for himself the great piles of superimposed strata and watch the rivulets bringing down mud and the waves wearing away the sea-cliffs in order to comprehend something about the duration of past time, the monuments of which we see all about us.'[1]

A monstrous vista of time opened up, time for all the varied species of earth to evolve, planlessly, it seemed, 'by natural selection' from a common ancestor of the simplest possible description. There was not even room for Lamarck's 'law of progressive development', nothing but blind chance and the struggle for survival.

'When we reflect on this struggle,' said Darwin, 'we may console ourselves with the full belief that the war of nature is not incessant, that no fear is felt, that death is generally prompt and that the vigorous, the healthy and the happy survive and multiply.'[2]

Among those who were not consoled by this reflection we must number Charles Lutwidge Dodgson and Samuel Wilberforce, Bishop of Oxford. Even thirty years later Dodgson could never refer to Darwin without bitterness, but, while he never accepted 'natural selection', there is good reason to believe that

[1] Darwin: *On the Origin of Species*, p. 266.
[2] Ib., p. 61.

he did cautiously adapt his attitude to the lower animals to suit
the probability that we and they have a common ancestry. So
far from accepting a universe without God or the soul, he came
to believe like Bishop Butler that animals have souls, and more,
that insects, even flowers, have souls and are quite literally
God's creatures.

The reactions of Bishop Wilberforce were quite different. He
began by reviewing Darwin's book in *The Quarterly*, picking out
with skill, as Darwin commented, all the most conjectural parts
and bringing forward all the difficulties. Darwin in the *Origin*
does no more than hint at the inclusion of man in his evolu-
tionary theory. 'Much light,' he said, 'will be thrown on the
origin of man and his history.'[1] The hint, however, was taken
and 'evolution' and 'natural selection' filled newspapers, political speeches, sermons and the conversation of all educated
people.

Was man an ape or an angel? The Church in 1860, like
Disraeli in 1864, was on the side of the angels, or, as Mitchell
puts it in his life of Thomas Henry Huxley, 'the accredited
defenders of religion gathered every force of argument, of mis-
representation, conscious and unconscious, of respectability and
of prejudice, to crush once for all the obnoxious doctrine and its
obnoxious supporters'.[2] Darwin himself was disinclined for
argument and Huxley undertook his defence. At the meeting
of the British Association in Oxford, 1860, there occurred the
memorable clash between Huxley and Wilberforce which
Dodgson may have witnessed and of which he certainly heard
much at the time.

The meeting was to have been held in a lecture-room but
the audience was so large that it had to be transferred to the
library of the Museum and this was crammed to the doors. The
Bishop was in good form. In his smooth but devastating manner
he held up Darwin to ridicule and Huxley to scorn, ending
with a jibe which brought Huxley to his feet. He asked Huxley
whether he was related to an ape on his grandfather's or his
grandmother's side. Huxley replied that a man had no reason
to be ashamed of having an ape for his grandfather. He would
feel more shame if he were descended from a man who tried to

[1] *Origin*, p. 428. *The Descent of Man* appeared in 1871.
[2] *Life of T. H. Huxley*, p. 120.

distort the truth by mere rhetoric and appeals to religious prejudice.

That evening the rooms of Dr Daubeny, Professor of Botany, were crowded with what Francis Darwin happily calls 'the black coats and white cravats of Oxford'. Long and late they fought the battle of the *Origin* over again, but ended by congratulating Darwin and Huxley as 'the winners in the combat'.[1]

The battle, however, was only beginning. In the same year as the meeting of the British Association at Oxford there was published a volume of 'Essays and Reviews' by seven distinguished men, including Jowett, Pattison and Baden-Powell, noted figures at Oxford, and Temple, the Rector of Dodgson's old school and later Archbishop of Canterbury.

Temple's essay on 'The Education of the World' was not controversial, merely suggesting that the classics, and in fact all knowledge, must be admitted to a place in forming our opinions and shaping our lives. He suffered, however, by his association with the other essayists, who were all in varying degrees further to the left.

Jowett began quietly, urging that the appeal should always be to the Bible itself and not to the commentators, but as he proceeded he ventured to question the Mosaic chronology and referred openly to the Darwinian theory: 'while it is possible, and may one day be known that mankind spread not from one but from many centres over the globe, or as others say, that the supply of links which are at present wanting in the chain of animal life may tend to new conclusions respecting the origin of man'.[2] That this contradicted the doctrine of the 'Verbal Inspiration' of the scriptures caused Jowett no alarm. The word was 'but of yesterday', nor was there any warrant for the doctrine in the Gospels or Epistles.

But even these were mild opinions compared to Baden-Powell's attack on the miracles or Goodwin's merciless exposure of the Mosaic cosmogony.

After referring to Darwin's *Origin* as 'a work which must soon bring about an entire revolution of opinion in favour of the grand principle of the self-evolving powers of nature', Baden-Powell

---

[1] Francis Darwin: *Life and Letters of Charles Darwin*, Vol. II, pp. 321–3.
[2] *Essays and Reviews*, p. 349.

demanded: 'If the most numerous ship's company were all to
asseverate that they had seen a mermaid, would any rational
persons at the present day believe them? That they saw something which they believed to be a mermaid would be easily
conceded.'[1] Miracles, he said, were once the mainstay of
Christianity; now they were an obstacle to its acceptance.

Goodwin compared the attitude of the Church to the recent
geological discoveries with that of the Church of Rome to the
opinions of Galileo. He quoted Galileo's recantation with eerie
effect.[2]

Mark Pattison called the movement 'Rationalism' and defined it as 'the growth and gradual diffusion through all
religious thinking of the supremacy of reason'.[3]

Strangely enough, or so it seems today, the essays which
caused most consternation were those by Henry Bristow Wilson,
Vicar of Great Staughton, and Roland Williams, Vice-Principal
of St. David's College, Lampeter. These challenged the doctrine of eternal punishment, which at that time was held to be
in store not merely for evil-doers but for the non-Christian and
pre-Christian races.

Dodgson himself did not accept the doctrine of eternal
punishment and was therefore against the authorities on this,
the greatest point at issue. He was, however, against the publication of *Essays and Reviews,* as can be seen in a pamphlet which
he published in 1865, *The New Method of Evaluation.*

In 1860 the controversy was too new and bitter for such a
balanced view as he then expressed, and in any case he had fish
of his own to fry. This year saw the publication of two mathematical works by Dodgson, *A Syllabus of Plane Algebraical
Geometry* and *Notes on the First Two Books of Euclid,* and the appearance of these in print was certainly important to him. He
also contributed a number of poems to *College Rhymes,* which he
edited for a time during the next three years. He published a
set of rules for a card game,'Court Circular', and was extremely
busy with his camera, though the Prince of Wales, who had
come to Christ Church in the previous year, would not sit for
him. A list of 159 photographs dates from about this time.

---

[1] *Essays and Reviews,* p. 141.
[2] Ib., p. 207.
[3] Ib., p. 259.

In 1860, too, he gave a lecture to the Ashmolean Society on the 'Hemispherical Problem' which had puzzled and amused the readers of *The Rectory Umbrella* ten years earlier. Unfortunately, the Ashmolean Society was at a very low ebb at this time and kept no records. On the other hand, if it had not been at a low ebb, Dodgson's lecture might not have been given. The Society had to compete with the more powerful Royal Society, whose origins are somehow mixed up with its own, and Professor Price seems to have taken his brilliant young protégé along to amuse rather than to enlighten a small and no doubt informal gathering. The lecture was never printed and probably never written down in the form in which it was then delivered, which is a pity, since it would scarcely be identical with the version in *The Rectory Umbrella*. The fact that he gave this lecture is, however, significant, as it proves that he had not forgotten the problem, which indeed, according to Collingwood, 'cast a gloom over many a pleasant party'.

Strangest of all products of this very important year in his life is the poem 'Faces in the Fire' which he copied into *Misch-Masch* in January, 1860; it was printed in *Phantasmagoria* and, after his death, reprinted in *Three Sunsets*. The faces that he saw in the fire were all of one person.

> 'Tis now a little childish form—
> Red lips for kisses pouted warm—
> And elf-locks tangled in the storm.
>
> 'Tis now a grave and gentle maid,
> At her own beauty half afraid,
> Shrinking and willing to be stayed.
>
> Oh, Time was young and Life was warm,
> When first I saw that fairy-form,
> Her dark hair tossing in the storm.
>
> And fast and free these pulses played
> When last I met that gentle maid—
> When last her hand in mine was laid.
>
> Those locks of jet are turned to grey,
> And she is strange and far away,
> That might have been mine own today.
>
> That might have been mine own, my dear,
> Through many and many a happy year—
> That might have sat beside me here.

> The race is o'er I might have run;
> The deeds are past I might have done;
> And seer the wreath I might have won.
>
> Sunk is the last faint flickering blaze:
> This vision of departed days
> Is vanished even as I gaze.
>
> The pictures with their ruddy light
> Are changed to dust and ashes white,
> And I am left alone with night.

It is to this poem that Collingwood refers when he says of *Three Sunsets*: 'One cannot read this little volume without feeling that the shadow of some disappointment lay over Lewis Carroll's life. Such I believe to have been the case, and it was this that gave him his wonderful sympathy with all who suffered. But those who loved him would not wish to lift the veil from those dead sanctities, nor could any purpose be served by doing so.'[1]

This extraordinary poem cannot be taken literally, for in 1860 Dodgson was only twenty-eight years of age and at the beginning, not the end, of a career. If it was a mere literary exercise, it was a very strange one, showing a young man already reconciled to loneliness and obscurity. If on the other hand it was a passing mood which he expressed, it was a mood which was to recur.

There is, according to Langford Reed, who had access to Dodgson's diaries and private papers, no evidence at all that he was ever in love with anybody and, says Mr Reed, 'the testimony of various friends with whom he occasionally discussed intimate and personal questions, and whom I have interviewed, is to the same effect'.[2] Miss F. Menella Dodgson, who now has the surviving diaries, agrees. And yet Collingwood knew something and could have told it if he had wished.

The lady, *la femme inconnue*, if she existed, cannot have been very old when Dodgson was twenty-eight. The poem was to some extent an anticipation. Then, he had known her as 'a little childish form'. She had been one of his child-friends. In 1860, there was only one, Alice Liddell, and the facts speak louder than any opinion that she and she alone was his lost love, the withered rose in his filing-cabinet, the little ghost that

---

[1] Coll., p. 355.
[2] Langford Reed: *Lewis Carroll*, p. 90.

was to come crying in the night to the windows of his bachelor rooms in Tom Quad.

Dean Liddell did not occupy the Deanery until extensive alterations had been completed, but at some time in 1856 Dodgson must have met Mrs Liddell and the children. There were four at that time, a son and three daughters, of whom Alice was the second daughter. Dodgson seems to have made friends with them at once, probably the more readily because the Dean was absent for health reasons in the island of Madeira during much of the winters of 1856–7 and 1857–8. In any case he was bound to see a good deal of them, since the Deanery is part of the great Christ Church group of buildings in which he himself lived.

From the first he 'fell in love' with Alice, who was born on 4 May, 1852, and was therefore four years of age in 1856 and about seven and a half in 1860.[1] Seven and a half is her age in *Through the Looking-glass* and the photograph which he mounted on the last page of the first draft of *Alice's Adventures*, the *Under Ground* version, was taken in 1859. In 1885 he wrote to Alice Liddell, by then Mrs Reginald Hargreaves: 'I have had scores of child-friends since your time, but they have been quite a different thing'. In 1891 he referred to her as 'one whom I can scarcely picture as more than seven years of age'. *The Theatre* of April 1887 contains an article by Lewis Carroll on '*Alice* on the Stage'. Here he says that he printed in manuscript and illustrated with his own crude designs the original story of *Alice's Adventures* to please a child he loved. She was indeed a beautiful child, dark, vivacious, 'loving as a dog', as he put it long afterwards. He photographed her in 1858 as a beggar-child, and Tennyson thought this the most beautiful photograph he had ever seen.

Yes, he loved her as a child, but in 1860 she was a child still. If the poem 'Faces in the Fire' is about Alice Liddell, and I have no doubt that it is, all the events are imaginary, but not imaginary in the sense that those of a purely literary exercise would be imaginary. He was looking forward in 1860 into his own life, and in a moment of clarity or despondency saw it exactly as it happened, perhaps as he made it happen, perhaps

---

[1] Private letter from Sir F. F. Liddell. See also *Cornhill Magazine*, July, 1932: 'Alice's Recollections', by Caryl Hargreaves.

as the Dean or Mrs Liddell or Alice herself made it happen.

The odds were against him in 1860. He was twenty years older than Alice, with no prospect whatever of being able to support as a wife the daughter of his aristocratic Dean. It seems fantastically unlikely that a man in his late twenties should renounce all intention of marrying because of a child not yet out of the nursery. That, however, is the conclusion forced upon us by the facts. 'Faces in the Fire' may not have been true when he wrote it, but it 'came true'.

Another problem began to worry him about this time. He knew that sooner or later, if he was to keep his Studentship, he must take orders, and actually he had postponed the step as long as he could without exciting remark. It was not that he had lost faith, but he had a very different conception of the Christian religion from those who were most vocal on the subject.

By this time Wilberforce was in full cry after the Essayists and Reviewers, first reviewing the book in *The Quarterly* and pooh-poohing it as all perfectly familiar and already discredited. That step accomplished, he arranged for the publication of *Replies to Essays and Reviews*, in the Preface to which he denounced the Rationalist Movement as 'a daring claim for the un-assisted human intellect to be able to measure and explain all things'.[1]

In both these respects Dodgson agreed with him, or at any rate came to agree with him. In *The New Method* he proved mathematically that there was no 'novelty' in *Essays and Reviews*. As to the human intellect, his religious training by his father had convinced him that it had its limits, and mathematics, the oldest of the sciences, has in this always added its voice.

Moreover, there were new and startling developments in mathematics during Dodgson's lifetime which, for those who knew of them, made the universe not more mechanical, as the geologists and botanists seemed to think it ought to be, but more mysterious. For example, in 1843 Arthur Cayley invented a geometry of any finite number of dimensions, and on the Continent there were coming into existence geometries in which parallel lines met; in which there were no parallel lines; in which there were straight lines that were really great circles; in

[1] Daniel, pp. 143–6.

which the sum of the angles in a triangle might be greater or smaller than two right-angles; and these new geometries were held to be as true as that of Euclid. The gap first detected by Berkeley in the old mathematical orthodoxy was being steadily widened. Again, Dodgson had come up to Christ Church under old Tractarian auspices and Newman had demonstrated to him mathematically how easy it was to believe in the supernatural. Miracles and apparitions presented no such difficulties to him as to Goodwin.

Yet he certainly did hesitate for nearly two years before he eventually compromised. Nor were his ostensible reasons for hesitation, his stammer and his visits to the theatre, entirely convincing. They were more of the nature of excuses. Wilberforce, whom he sounded through either Pusey or Liddon as to the obligations he would be incurring, told him that as a Deacon he could if he wished attend theatres and need not, unless he felt able to do so, undertake ministerial duties. On 22 December, 1861, he was ordained Deacon by the Bishop of Oxford, and he never proceeded to priest's orders though he did occasionally preach to the College servants.[1]

Two months previously he had, contrary to his later practice and convictions, 'taken sides' against one of the Essayists and Reviewers. This was in the strange case of Jowett's salary.

Benjamin Jowett had already been in hot water over his book on the Epistles of St Paul. Published in 1855, the year of his appointment as Regius Professor of Greek, this work raised the ire of the High Church party. When summoned before the Vice-Chancellor, however, Jowett simply demanded a pen.

'Mr Vice-Chancellor,' he interrupted a solemn preliminary harangue, 'I have come to sign the Articles.'[2]

That was effective at the time, but it did not help him financially. The conditions upon which he held his Chair were truly remarkable. A regius professor is appointed nominally by the Crown, but actually by the political party in power, and Jowett owed his appointment to Palmerston in recognition of his work in the matter of University reform and of his Liberal views in politics. His salary was £40 per annum, that being the stipend considered sufficient by Henry VIII, who founded the

[1] Coll., pp. 74–6.
[2] *Life of Jowett*, Vol. I, pp. 238–9.

Chair. It was paid by Christ Church, and the appointment had
formerly been held by Dean Gaisford. Liddell, who succeeded
him as Dean, declined to accept the Greek Chair also.[1]

Under Dean Gaisford the post has been a sinecure, for the
taciturn Dean 'never gave lectures', but Jowett's conception of
a professor's duties was quite different, and there was soon a
movement to have his salary raised. In October, 1861, Stanley
carried a proposal in the Hebdomadal Council to endow the
Greek Professorship from the University chest, but when submitted to Congregation it was defeated by three votes. Among
those who opposed it was Dodgson.

'Mr Dodgson,' says Collingwood, 'nothing if not a staunch
Conservative, sided with the majority against him.' In his
diary Dodgson recorded that 'the two points at issue, the en-
dowing a *Regius* Professorship and the countenancing Jowett's
theological opinions', becoming confused, he rose to separate
them, became heated and said more than he had intended.
They would never, he declared, 'tire the opposition by perpetually bringing the matter on'.[2] Collingwood, it will be
observed, alleges that Dodgson voted on political grounds, as a
Conservative against a Liberal or against a Professor appointed
by a Liberal government. Dodgson himself mentions Jowett's
theological opinions but underlines the word 'Regius', as if to
show that he had voted on academic grounds against any kind
of political interference in University affairs.

Whatever his motive, and all the logic in the world could not
prevent confusion of principle and prejudice, he helped to keep
Jowett's salary firmly pegged at £40 a year. There it remained
for another four years while Stanley 'perpetually brought the
matter on', *The Times* correspondence columns argued the rights
and wrongs of it, and even Pusey, feeling uncomfortable, introduced a statute to multiply the salary of the professorship by ten
while dissociating the University from Jowett's personal opinions
in religious matters. This proposal of Pusey's passed in Congregation, but Convocation, the large body of 'wild country
parsons' which had tried Newman and Ward, rejected it and
thereby renewed the heated correspondence in *The Times*.

In 1862 controversy was still further embittered by the trial

[1] *Life of Liddell*, Vol. I, p. 140.
[2] Coll., p. 91.

and condemnation in the Court of the Arches of Williams and Wilson, the two Essayists and Reviewers who disapproved of eternal damnation. This led to an attempt to try Jowett, but fortunately for him the prosecution haled him before the wrong body—the Chancellor's Court instead of the House of Congregation—and the case was dropped. Pressure was also brought to bear on Temple, the least controversial of the Essayists, to dissociate himself from the others, but while the issue was in doubt he very properly refused to do so.

Dodgson had voted against increasing Jowett's salary in 1861, and probably to some extent because of Jowett's theological opinions, though even then he tried not to allow these to influence his judgment. But he was really disgusted with controversy and more and more coming to the opinion that these trials were totally at variance with the spirit of Christianity and also that they were concerned with what seemed to him to be trivialities. His own conception of Christianity was, as he made abundantly plain later on, that it was a religion founded on love, not hate, love which resembled the love he felt for Alice Liddell and which she felt for him, 'the heart-love of a child', or the love between dog and man, rather than the passionate love of men and women, for of that it seems quite certain he never knew anything.

Again, though he did not believe in eternal punishment, nor in the popular idea of heaven for that matter, he did believe in the possibility of miracles and miraculous appearances, on grounds which were at least partly mathematical. For, if space has even one of the extra dimensions in which Arthur Cayley had made it possible to calculate, there is no reason why superior beings should not exist all about us and only be perceived by us accidentally or at moments of their own choosing. For this reason he always kept an open mind on the subject of spiritualism and later joined the Psychical Research Society. In 1862, however, no such society existed, for the technique of communicating with the spirits by means of rappings had only been discovered in 1848, and Dodgson's first contact with the spirit-world does not reveal him as a devotee, merely as not treating the matter as absurd.

'Mr Dodgson,' says Collingwood, 'took a great interest in occult phenomena and was for some time an enthusiastic

member of the "Psychical Society".[1] (Actually from its incep-
tion in 1882 until the year before his death.) Apparently he
called upon a certain Mr Heaphy, an artist who had painted a
ghost he had personally seen. Dodgson thought the tale
'curious and inexplicable' and the ghost herself (or possibly, he
suggests, *itself*) 'very lovely'.

Some of his serious poems of 1861 and 1862 have a curious
Pre-Raphaelite quality. 'After Three Days' was suggested by
Holman Hunt's 'The Finding of Christ in the Temple' and
others like 'Beatrice' and 'Stolen Waters' are reminiscent of
Christina Rossetti's hopeless (on religious grounds) passions,
though without the 'lunar rainbow coloration' which made her
succeed where he failed. He may have met the Rossettis by
this time, for George Macdonald knew them, but it is more
probable that he did not go to Tudor Lodge until the following
year. Their work he certainly knew.

'Stolen Waters' seems to record a renunciation of the world,
the flesh and the devil:

> 'Yea, take we pleasure while we may,'
>   I heard myself replying.
> In the red sunset, far away,
>   My happier life was dying:
> My heart was sad, my voice was gay.
>
> And unawares, I knew not how
>   I kissed her dainty finger-tips,
> I kissed her on the lily brow,
>   I kissed her on the false, false lips—
> That burning kiss, I feel it now!
>
> 'True love gives true love of the best;
>   Then take,' I cried, 'my heart to thee!'
> The very heart from out my breast
>   I plucked, I gave it willingly:
> Her very heart she gave to me—
>   Then died the glory from the west.

Now it is his voice that is sad, and his heart, or rather her heart
within his breast, that is gay. It is the voice of a child that
restores his own heart with the message:

> 'Be as a child—
> So shalt thou sing for very joy of breath—
>   So shalt thou wait thy dying,
>   In holy transport lying—

[1] P. 92.

So pass rejoicing through the gate of death,
    In garment undefiled.'

Then call me what they will, I know
    That now my soul is glad:
If this be madness, better so,
    Far better to be mad,
Weeping or smiling as I go.

For if I weep, it is that now
    I see how deep a loss is mine,
And feel how brightly round my brow
    The coronal might shine,
Had I but kept mine early vow:

And if I smile, it is that now
    I see the promise of the years—
The garland waiting for my brow,
    That must be won with tears,
With pain—with death—I care not how.

Into 'Only a Woman's Hair', also written in 1862, Alice Liddell pushed her way recognizably, in the lines,

Or fringing like a shadow, raven-black,
    The glory of a queen-like face.

Outwardly who so placid as the Rev. C. L. Dodgson, M.A., Mathematical Lecturer and Tutor in Christ Church, Oxford, in his clerical blacks and white or black bow-tie? Inwardly he was fermenting with ideas, ideas for mathematical works, prestige publications we may call them, ideas for games that would amuse the young Liddells or the young Macdonalds, and more serious ideas too, ideas about God and the nature of the universe. Deeper still, obscure impulses struggled for mastery; the old Adam grappled with the chimera of celibacy. And all about him raged the battle of the books, sermons, pamphlets and ecclesiastical courts of law.

There was also in 1862 a slight coolness between Dodgson and Mrs Liddell. Exactly what it was about it seems impossible now to discover, but in view of later developments, such facts as there are must be stated.

The first relevant entry in the diary is that of 25 May, 1862, when he has been talking 'about the difficulty the College are in about the ball; the two parties cannot agree on the rules and I am afraid much ill-feeling will result'. On 28 October, 1862, there is an entry to the effect that he has been out of Mrs

Liddell's 'good graces' since those difficulties arose. Nevertheless, he has been seeing the children in between, and on 21 November he received a message from Mrs Liddell asking whether he would go over to see them or whether they should come to him.[1]

The 'ball' does not seem to have taken place. Perhaps the Liddells dropped it in view of disagreement about the rules, in which disagreement Dodgson took a stand with others against the Dean or simply opposed the idea of having a ball. At all events, during the very significant period in which it has always been believed that his relations with the Liddells were idyllic, a little cloud passed over Christ Church, a cloud no bigger than a man's hand, lost among the thunderheads of politics and theology. And yet its shadow cast a chill.

[1] Private letters from Miss F. Menella Dodgson.

CHAPTER THREE

Mr Dodgson in Wonderland

IN the summer of 1862 occurred an apparently trivial incident which he later identified as the turning point of his life. Dodgson's diary for 4 July, 1862, bears the entry: 'I made an expedition *up* the river to Godstow with the three Liddells; we had tea on the bank there, and did not reach Christ Church till half past eight'. On the opposite page, says Collingwood, he added, 'somewhat later', the words, 'on which occasion I told them the fairy-tale of Alice's Adventures Underground, which I undertook to write out for Alice'.[1]

The myth that he composed the whole of *Alice's Adventures in Wonderland* on a single afternoon and wrote it down word for word afterwards is partly due to the poem which Dodgson himself prefixed to the published story and partly due to Collingwood's rather naïve statement: 'His memory was so good that I believe the story as he wrote it down was almost word for word the same that he had told in the boat. The whole idea came like an inspiration into his mind, and that sort of inspiration does not often come more than once in a lifetime.'[2]

Yet the poem was written as a prologue to the book and cannot be taken literally:

> Thus grew the tale of Wonderland:
> Thus slowly, one by one,
> Its quaint events were hammered out—
> And now the tale is done,
> And home we steer, a merry crew,
> Beneath the setting sun.

Certainly its quaint events were hammered out slowly, one by one, but not all on the same afternoon.

Alice Liddell, Mrs Reginald Hargreaves at the time when Collingwood wrote his biography, was under the impression that the story was first told down-river—one particularly hot afternoon when they sheltered from the sun under 'a new-made

[1] Coll., p. 93.
[2] Ib., p. 106.

hayrick', which suggests late June or early July. The day when
the story 'began in the boat' was 'another day' and it was on
this occasion that Dodgson feigned slumber.[1]

In April, 1887, Dodgson himself contributed an account of
the beginning to *The Theatre*:

Many a day had we rowed together on that quiet stream—the
three little maidens and I—and many a fairy tale had been extem-
porized for their benefit—whether it were at times when the narrator
was 'i' the vein', and fancies unsought came crowding thick upon
him, or at times when the jaded Muse was goaded into action, and
plodded meekly on, more because she had to say something than
that she had something to say—yet none of these many tales got
written down: they lived and died, like summer midges, each in its
own golden afternoon, until there came a day when, as it chanced,
one of my little listeners petitioned that the tale might be written out
for her. That was many a year ago, but I distinctly remember now,
as I write, how in a desperate attempt to strike out some new line of
fairy-lore, I had sent my heroine straight down a rabbit-hole, to
begin with, without the least idea what was to happen afterwards.[2]

It is clear then that the trip to Godstow was not the first time
he had taken the three young Liddells on the river. Alice tells
us that they usually went out four or five times during the
summer term for afternoons, on which occasions they took a
kettle and a basket of cakes. They made tea, which was a special
treat for them, as 'five o'clock tea' was not in those days a
regular meal in households like the Deanery. (The Liddells had
luncheon at one o'clock, dinner at seven and, as a general rule,
nothing in between.)

On rarer occasions they made a whole day of it and took a
more substantial meal with them. Sometimes they went down
to Nuneham and picnicked in one of the huts available to
boating parties, borrowing crockery and cutlery from riverside
cottages. Sometimes Dodgson's younger brother Skeffington,
who had evidently given up roaring and not been abolished—
he had instead followed Charles to Christ Church—completed
the party. Generally the fifth member was Mr Duckworth,
later Canon in Westminster Abbey. Once two of Dodgson's
sisters, rather stout and formidable, made it a party of seven
and threatened to sink the boat. There were no songs or stories
that day and the rain came on. The party had to go ashore at

---

[1] Coll., p. 96.
[2] *The Lewis Carroll Picture Book*, p. 165.

Iffley and, after an attempt to dry out the two stolid Miss Dodgsons at a cottage fire, return to Christ Church by road. This incident, transformed to fantasy, appeared in the *Under Ground* version but was 'improved' out of existence in the published story.

Nor were all his stories told on the river or during the summer. Alice in her 'Recollections' remarks: 'As it is, I think, many of my earlier adventures must be irretrievably lost to posterity, because Mr Dodgson told us many, many stories before the famous trip up-river to Godstow'. She explains that when they went to be photographed in his rooms he used to put them in a good mood by telling them stories, illustrating them as he spoke on odd pieces of paper and holding up the crisis by means of his stammer. Afterwards he let them go into the dark room.[1]

The importance of the Godstow trip was that on it he told a particularly good story and Alice asked him to write it out for her. This is confirmed by Canon Duckworth, who says: 'I also well remember how, when we had conducted the three children back to the Deanery, Alice said, as she bade us goodnight, "Oh, Mr Dodgson, I wish you would write out Alice's Adventures for me". He said he should try, and he afterwards told me that he sat up nearly the whole night, committing to a MS. book his recollections of the drolleries with which he had enlivened the afternoon. He added illustrations of his own and presented the volume, which used often to be seen on the drawing-room table at the Deanery.'[2]

The myth, you see, refuses to be explained away. Like the snake in Macbeth, she'll close and be herself in spite of us. However, there is the evidence of Dodgson's diary that he did not start the MS. book until 13 November, 1862, though the headings were written out in the train on his way to London on the day following the boating expedition.[3] No doubt he did write out that night the story he had told in the boat, but only in rough, so that he might not forget. Duckworth's account was written more than thirty years after the event.

Bearing all this in mind then, let us reconstruct the boating-trip to Godstow on which the White Rabbit made his first

---

[1] *Cornhill Magazine*, July, 1932.
[2] *L. C. Picture Book*, p. 359.
[3] Private letter: Miss F. Menella Dodgson.

appearance in this world and immediately ducked out of it into a very different one.

It began with the three young Liddells, Lorina, Alice and Edith, dressed in white cotton frocks, white socks, black shoes and shady hats, emerging from the Deanery into Tom Quad. With them was their governess, Miss Prickett, known as 'Pricks', who conducted them along the gravel path, now replaced by a stone pavement, to the Old Library, now replaced by the Meadow Buildings. Here Mr Dodgson had his rooms at this time, and here the children were left in his charge, for Miss Prickett was not to accompany them on the river.

He was waiting for them, dressed in white flannel trousers, black coat, black boots and white straw hat. With him, similarly attired, was Mr Duckworth. Picnic baskets, filled with cold chicken, salad and other delicacies, were already packed. Presently the five water-wayfarers walked along the banks of the unsavoury Till Mill stream to Salter's, where they chose a large boat with plenty of cushions.[1]

The three children were seated in the stern, where they made a charming nosegay. Lorina, aged twelve or thirteen, had brown hair, Alice, who had secured the tiller ropes, almost black hair cut in a fringe across her forehead, while Edith, the youngest, had auburn curls.[1] Mr Dodgson rowed bow and Duckworth stroke, so that Dodgson was looking over Duckworth's shoulder at the three little girls.[2]

As they moved upstream between the great meadow and the trees Dodgson began to tell them a story. It was, he remembered in 1887, a 'golden afternoon'. 'I can call it up almost as clearly as if it were yesterday—the cloudless blue above, the watery mirror below, the boat drifting idly on its way, the tinkle of the drops that fell from the oars, as they waved so sleepily to and fro, and (the one bright gleam of life in all the slumbrous scene) the three eager faces, hungry for news of fairy-land, and who would not be said "Nay" to: from whose lips "Tell us a story, please," had all the stern immutability of Fate!'[3]

Duckworth informs us that he figured as the 'duck', Lorina as the 'lory', and Edith as the 'eaglet', so that the story was by

---

[1] *Cornhill Magazine*, July, 1932.
[2] *L. C. Picture Book*, p. 358.
[3] Ib., p. 165.

no means a monologue. The persons in the boat had parts, or at least their names suggested characters in the adventures, and their frequent interruptions, Alice says in her 'Recollections', 'opened up fresh and undreamed of possibilities'.

Nor should it be forgotten that there was an adult in the boat, Duckworth, in whose presence the story would not be quite as it would have been had the audience consisted only of children. At one point Duckworth suddenly realized that something very unusual was happening and interjected a query: 'Dodgson, is this an extempore romance of yours?' to which Dodgson replied in the affirmative.

Sometimes he lapsed into silence, or pretended to fall asleep, 'whereas, of course,' says Mr Walter de la Mare, 'he had actually come wide-awake'. But they kept him at it.

'That's all till next time,' he would say.

'Ah, but it *is* next time.'

The story began with a White Rabbit going down a burrow and Alice following it down into a long low hall with many doors and one very small curtained door, the little gold key to which lay on a glass table. Beyond the little door lay an enchanted garden, but when Alice was tall enough to reach the gold key on the glass table she was too big to squeeze through the little door.

'Size and Tears' he called a poem on the disadvantages of stoutness which he contributed to *College Rhymes* in the following year. The poem was no doubt suggested by Alice's variations in size, which led to her swimming about in a pool of her own tears.

Eventually she found her way out into the garden, met the card-characters, played croquet with the duchess and was a witness in the trial of the Knave of Hearts.

Meanwhile, the chicken and salad went the way of chicken and salad, the boat's head pointed downstream and as the children's bedtime approached songs took the place of stories. They sang the popular songs and hymns of the day, 'Star of the evening', 'Twinkle, twinkle little star', 'Will you walk into my parlour', and these Dodgson later parodied.

The boat was tied up, the empty baskets and the tired children returned to Christ Church. And then, according to Duckworth, Alice asked Mr Dodgson to write out her Adventures for her. She had rather a habit of getting her own way, this darkly beautiful child. Dinah, the cat in the Adventures, was really Lorina's but Alice somehow managed to appropriate her. Miss Prickett did not like Alice.[1]

Dodgson went back to his rooms in the Old Library and, fired by this at once cool and gratifying request, began to write. 'In writing it out,' he said in his *Theatre* article of 1887, 'I added many fresh ideas, which seemed to grow of themselves upon the original stock; and many more added themselves when, years afterwards, I wrote it all over again for publication.' The first version of the story which has been preserved is that called *Alice's Adventures Under Ground* and this he made available to the public in 1886 when he published it in facsimile.

It will be noted that even in the boat Dodgson was not creating the story out of nothing. The white rabbit, for instance, and his watch, gloves and fan, are all conjuror's properties and Dodgson had been an amateur conjuror. The Lory had already amused the readers of *The Rectory Umbrella* and was recalled to him by Lorina's name. In 1860 he had published rules for a card game 'Court Circular', and the year after the Godstow trip was to publish rules for 'Croquet Castle', an elaborate form of croquet which he worked out with the Liddell children. Both these games supplied him with ideas and characters.

In writing out the story he discovered other fruitful sources of 'nonsense', and some of these are of great interest. One was the Fall of Alice to the centre of the earth, which may well have been told to some children on the beach at Whitby in 1854 and was certainly based on the dynamics of a particle. This he inserted immediately after Alice had followed the White Rabbit 'under ground'. Another was the beautiful little mathematical puzzle which apparently he tried out on Greville Macdonald, who says that 'he loved to question the very multiplication-table's veracity'. This is what he was doing when he made Alice say, 'Let me see: four times five is twelve, and four times six is thirteen, and four times seven is—oh dear! I shall never get to twenty at that rate.'

Mathematicians will have no difficulty in recognizing this as a problem based on scales of notation, but even the non-mathematical should make an effort to follow the explanation I

---

[1] *Cornhill Magazine*, July, 1932.

propose to give, since this is proof positive that Dodgson was, in some cases at least, doing something quite different from what he was pretending to do in this apparently guileless story for children.

$$4 \times 5 = 12 \text{ (on the scale 18).}$$

On the scale 18, the numbers go 1, 2, 3, 4, 5, 6, 7, 8, 9, (10) (11) (12) (13) (14) (15) (16) (17) 10, 11, 12 (12 being really one-two and equivalent to 20 on the scale 10, which is the one we normally use).

$$4 \times 6 = 13 \text{ (on the scale 21).}$$

On this scale, the numbers go 1, 2, 3 . . . 9, (10) (11) (12) . . . (20) 10, 11, 12, 13 (13 being really one-three and equivalent to 24 on the scale 10).

So it goes on:

$$4 \times 7 = 14 \text{ (on the scale 24)}$$
$$4 \times 8 = 15 \text{ (on the scale 27)}$$

till we reach

$$4 \times 12 = 19 \text{ (on the scale 39),}$$

but 4×13 does not equal 20 on the scale 42, because on the scale 42 the numbers go 1, 2, 3 . . . 9 (10) (11) (12) . . . (41) 10, 11, 12 . . . 19, 1(10). On this scale the number which follows 19 (really one-nine) is not twenty (two-nothing) but 1(10) (one-ten, equivalent to 52 or 4×13 on the scale 10).

' "Oh dear!" said Alice, "I shall never get to twenty at that rate." ' And at that rate she never would, that is, if the scale of notation was increasing by three at each step and the product by only one. At that rate she could never get to 20 at all.

This was exactly the kind of problem to interest Dodgson. He could not use it as a problem to interest Alice Liddell, aged ten, but he could and did use it to amuse and bewilder her—to give the effect of nonsense. So far as I am aware he has remained undetected; he never told anybody what he had done and he did not refer to it in his diary. Nevertheless, it can hardly be a coincidence; nor could he invent such a problem in a kind of day-dream, without knowing what he was doing. And it is not the only case of the kind, though for those who can follow a mathematical explanation it is probably the most convincing.

Satire, and allegory too, crept into the story. Even when telling it in the boat he must have been conscious that the little gold key, the little low door into the bright garden, the bottle and the little cake were all potential symbols, and as he wrote the story 'many new ideas added themselves'. It is, I think, a mistake to look, as Shane Leslie does, for a consistent allegory in *Alice's Adventures*. The story grew out of separate bits and pieces linked together more by the association of ideas than by cause and effect.

In 'Lewis Carroll and the Oxford Movement', Shane Leslie[1] treats both the Alice books as a 'secret history of the Oxford Movement'. 'Alice,' he says, 'may be regarded as the simple freshman or Everyman, who wanders like a sweet and innocent undergraduate into the wonderland of a Victorian Oxford, where everybody was religious in some way or other.' That is profoundly true but not in the sense that Dodgson wrote, or even rewrote, the book with that intention uppermost in his mind. Rather did he accept gratefully all and any suggestions that came to him from the life of Oxford around him, from his mathematics or elsewhere, and these he transformed with the object of amusing and bewildering. His gift was the opposite of the poet's. He could abstract airy nothings from their local habitations and dissociate them from their names. He could also render them pictorial and then use them as symbols.

Sometimes we can catch him in the act, but we cannot hope to identify all the originals of his caricatures, nor must we expect the same symbol always to have the same meaning. Meaning comes and goes like the colours in shot silk. When Alice first 'looked along the passage into the loveliest garden you ever saw', no doubt the garden was a symbol of happiness or fulfilment. It was only later that he began to identify himself with Alice and turn it (as Shane Leslie suggests) into the Garden of Preferment, with the gardeners hard at work painting the roses red instead of white to please a queen who preferred red roses. No doubt the garden was also the Deanery garden at Christ Church into which Dodgson could see from the windows of the library as he catalogued the books. No doubt, beyond that, it was the garden of his boyhood at Croft, the garden of his childhood at Daresbury, the golden age of the poet, the maternal womb of psychoanalysis. All these explanations have been offered. But only the Garden of Preferment theory satisfactorily accounts for the painting of the white roses red.

[1] *The London Mercury*, 1933, p. 233.

A moment later, however, we find the card-gardeners being used to illustrate another sort of truth. When they are lying face-downwards it is impossible to tell if they are crowned heads or plain numbers.

> Sceptre and crown
> Shall tumble down
> And in the dust be equal made
> With the poor crooked scythe and spade.

The bottle of medicine which tasted so pleasantly of all Alice's favourite dishes but which made her wonder if she would go out like a candle is like the apparently innocuous doctrine of the Rationalists which led in the direction of pure materialism. It will be remembered that Alice, after drinking, was small enough to pass through the little low door but had forgotten the gold key, though she could still see it through the glass of the table. The cake had to be swallowed in its entirety before it produced any effect, but then Alice opened out like a telescope and her head was out of touch with her feet. Dogma would produce the same effect in the theological world: all or nothing; and if all, then up in the clouds or very High Church.

The Caterpillar, seated on a mushroom and smoking a hookah, superior, intolerable, but not unkindly, is identified by Shane Leslie as Oxford Philosophy.

'One side will make you grow taller, and the other will make you grow shorter.'

'One *side* of *what*? The other side of *what*?' thought Alice to herself.

'Of the mushroom,' said the Caterpillar, just as if she had asked it aloud; and in another moment it was out of sight.

Alice remained looking thoughtfully at the mushroom for a minute, trying to make out which were the two sides of it; and as it was perfectly round, she found this a very difficult question. However, at last she stretched her arms round it as far as they would go, and broke off a bit of the edge with each hand.

By nibbling these bits alternately she could make herself any size she pleased, thus illustrating most exquisitely the process, essential to all who were to succeed in the Oxford of those days, of acquiring a 'balanced outlook'.

> Our little systems have their day:
> They have their day and cease to be:
> They are but broken lights of thee,
> And thou, O Lord, art more than they.

E

In her left hand, no doubt, Alice held the 'system' or attitude called Rationalism, in her right the extreme High Church form of dogmatism. A discreet mixture of the two had led Dodgson himself to take Deacon's orders but not priest's orders, and he always held to the middle way. In his church attendance he was perhaps a little to the right of centre; in his secret speculations perhaps a shade to the left; in no case far from the middle way.

In this, however, he was in advance of his time. Oxford, the English Church and the country as a whole were fiercely divided on the question of dogma and reason. The Cheshire Cat puts the case for one side; which side is unimportant, but let us take it, as Shane Leslie does, that Cat is a symbol for Catholic and Dog for Protestant or Dissenter.

'To begin with,' said the Cat, 'a dog's not mad. You grant that?'
'I suppose so,' said Alice.
'Well then,' the Cat went on, 'you see a dog growls when it's angry and wags its tail when it's pleased. Now I growl when I'm pleased, and wag my tail when I'm angry. Therefore I'm mad.'

Those who claim that there is no moral in Lewis Carroll's stories might spend a moment here. To a dog, a cat is wrong or mad; to a cat, the opposite is the case. An impartial observer, however, will admit that both the cat's and the dog's method of expressing pleasure or anger may be right. Neither need be considered mad. It is a plea for toleration. The Cheshire Cat's 'Therefore I'm mad' is irony. The moral is Tennyson's 'Force without geniality will do very little', but small heed is paid to that moral in Wonderland. Perhaps, after all, Alice was nearer the truth than she supposed when she thought she might land at the 'antipathies'. Dodgson himself had landed there when he arrived at Oxford.

The Cheshire Cat, strange as it seems, was not one of the original characters. Not even its grin appeared in the *Under Ground* version, though the threat of Dinah hung over the little creatures from time to time as later the moon-like Cat's Head in Wonderland. All the changes of size were there, the White Rabbit and Bill the Lizard, the Pool of Tears, Terrier, Caterpillar and Father William, Pigeon, Procession and Croquet Match, Mock Turtle and Gryphon; but no Cheshire Cat, no Pig and Pepper, no Mad Tea Party and a very short trial of the Knave of Hearts.

'Now for the evidence,' said the King, 'and then the sentence!'
'No!' said the Queen, 'first the sentence and then the evidence!'
In the early 1860's that was happening above as well as under
ground.

Such was the first version of the story which he wrote between
5 July, when he noted the chapter headings, and 10 February,
when the text was finished. The actual words of the diary are
'Text finished before Feb. 10, 1863', as if he had presented it to
Alice on that day. If he did, he had not finished the illustrations,
for the pictures in the MS. were not finished until 13 September,
1864.[1] Yet Henry Kingsley saw the MS. at the Deanery and,
according to Duckworth, it was at his suggestion that Dodgson
published it.

It seems then that Alice was first given the text to read in
February, 1863. Henry Kingsley, whose brother Charles had
just published his *Water Babies*, saw Dodgson's MS. and recognized its merit. He urged Mrs Liddell to persuade Dodgson to
publish it. She made the suggestion to Dodgson, who wrote to
Duckworth asking him to come and read the MS. and give a
candid opinion as to the advisability of publishing, 'as he himself
felt very doubtful and could not afford to lose money over it'.[2]

Not content with Duckworth's opinion, Dodgson approached
his old friend George Macdonald, now established as a successful novelist. 'It was about this time, but at Tudor Lodge,' says
Greville Macdonald, 'that he asked my father's opinion upon a
story he had written and named "Alice's Adventures Underground", illustrated with pen-and-ink sketches by himself and
minutely penned in printing characters.'[3] George Macdonald
having suggested that the story be tried on the family, Mrs
Macdonald read it aloud and the response was enthusiastic.

Accordingly, Dodgson retained the MS. and during the next
year and a half completed the illustrations in it while re-writing
the story for publication. He finished the illustrations in the MS.
on 13 September (on which day he noted the important dates in
connection with the book), but did not present it to Alice until
26 November, more than two months later.[4] By that time, no
doubt, the re-writing was complete.

---

[1] Private letter: Miss F. Menella Dodgson.
[2] *L. C. Picture Book,* p. 359.
[3] Greville Macdonald: *George Macdonald and his Wife,* p. 342.
[4] Private letter: Miss F. Menella Dodgson.

Meanwhile, the *Essays and Reviews* controversy had not been forgotten. Early in 1863 Jowett was prosecuted but, fortunately for him, in the wrong court, the Vice-Chancellor's instead of the House of Congregation. This brought from Dodgson's pen a College Rhyme or Oxford Idyll, 'The Majesty of Justice'. After describing the Vice-Chancellor's Court as 'A Court obscure' existing to punish undergraduates who do not pay their bills, he proceeds:

> A case I'm told was lately brought
>   Into that tiniest of places,
> And justice in that case was sought—
>   As in most other cases.

> 'Well! Justice as I hold, dear friend,
>   Is Justice, neither more than less:
> I never dreamed it could depend
>   On ceremonial or dress.
> I thought that the imperial sway
>   In Oxford surely would appear,
> But all the papers seem to say
>   She's not majestic *here*.'

> The portly Don he made reply
>   With the most roguish of his glances,
> 'Perhaps she drops her Majesty
>   Under peculiar circumstances.'
> 'But that's the point!' the young man cried,
>   'The puzzle that I wish to pen you in—
> How are the public to decide
>   *Which* article is genuine?

> 'Is't only when the Court is large
>   That we for "Majesty" need hunt?
> Would what is Justice in a barge
>   Be something different in a punt?'
> 'Nay, nay!' the Don replied, amused,
>   'You're talking nonsense, sir! You know it!
> Such arguments were never used
>   By any friend of Jowett.'

Eventually he reaches the conclusion:

> 'The Majesty of Justice, then,
>   Is seated in the Wig.'

On 8 February, 1864, Williams and Wilson, who had appealed against their condemnation in the Court of the Arches, were acquitted by the Privy Council. Stanley, the recently appointed Dean of Westminster, who was present in court, declared that the Church of England had made its position clear and that it no longer upheld the 'Verbal Inspiration' of the Scriptures, nor the doctrine of 'Eternity of Torment'.[1] The Bishop of Oxford, however, did not agree with the findings of the Privy Council and used his carefully-nursed Convocation of the Clergy to promulgate his views. This Convocation must not be confused with the Oxford body of the same name. It was the Lower House he had revived, in an attempt to take Church affairs out of Parliament, without, however, bringing about the disestablishment of the Church of England.

When this antique body met in June, 1864, Wilberforce asked its members to put on record their disagreement with the findings of the Privy Council in the form of a 'synodical condemnation' of *Essays and Reviews*. This they did, though Stanley, once more on the spot, raged at them that they were flouting the authority of the supreme court of appeal.[2] The matter was raised in the House of Lords on 15 July, when Lord Westbury described the 'synodical judgement' as 'a well-lubricated set of words—a sentence so oily and saponaceous that no one can grasp it'. With one exception, the Lords were convulsed, the exception being Soapy Sam himself. 'Ribaldry,' he said.

The Oxford Convocation also met about this time to consider the latest proposal to raise Jowett's salary and, as a reprisal for the Privy Council's action, once more turned it down. The correspondence columns of *The Times* waxed bitter on the subject.

It was while these things were happening that Dodgson was re-writing *Alice* for publication. He had also read Charles Kingsley's *Water Babies* by this time and found there all the questions of the day 'wrapped up', as Kingsley said in a letter to Maurice, 'in seeming Tom-Fooleries'.[3]

So far as it is intelligible, the story of *The Water Babies* concerns a little chimney-sweeper who comes down the wrong chimney into the bedroom of the Squire's daughter. A hue and cry is raised, but, eluding pursuit, he finds his way over the moors to a dame school in a valley, where he is treated kindly and given a bed in the hay-shed. Distressed at his dirtiness, he

[1] *Life of Stanley*, Vol. II, p. 43.
[2] Ib., p. 183.
[3] Guy Kendall: *Charles Kingsley and his Ideas* (1947), pp. 117–18.

gets up to wash and is drowned in the brook. Then, transformed into a sucking eft or naughty water-baby, 3·87902 inches long, he has to learn by living among the water-creatures. He swims down to the sea and saves a lobster from a pot, after which he is admitted to the society of middling-good water-babies, where Discipline (Mrs Be done by as you did) and Morality (Mrs Do as you would be done by), both of whom are Mother Carey, who is Dame Nature, who is God, take him in hand.

To be worthy of Ellie, the Squire's daughter, a lady born and a good water-baby from the moment she dies (as she does from a fall among the rocks on the beach), he must go on a long adventurous journey and do the thing he does not like; in his case, undertake the reclamation of Mr Grimes, his cruel master. He too is dead, having been drowned on a poaching expedition.

In Kingsley's after-life, the punishment fits the crime and Mr Grimes is stuck in a chimney. Tom, accompanied by a little water-dog, succeeds in reaching him and in earning for him the dubious promotion to a job on the cleaning of Mount Etna from the inside. Tom is then considered to have won his spurs. Magically transported to St Brandan's Isle, he joins Ellie and apparently becomes the power responsible for social-amelioration-through-science on earth, while his faithful little sea-hound is translated to the stars.

The story floats along on a stream of genial sermonizing. Evolution, spiritualism, materialism and other vexed questions of the day are faithfully dealt with and the whole is enlivened by eulogies of the landed gentry from whom Kingsley sprang and of the joys of hunting, shooting and fishing. It is a mystery how children pick out the story, but they do, and love it.

A copy of *The Water Babies* was in Dodgson's library, and he had certainly read it before *Alice* was ready for publication. It probably encouraged him to introduce more allegory and satire, but he wisely refrained from appearing in the story in person as Kingsley does in *The Water Babies*.

One valuable suggestion was the caucus of hoodie crows by means of which Kingsley satirized the republicans or extreme radicals. Dodgson used this in his caucus-race, perhaps the most striking change, as opposed to addition, that he made. In the *Under Ground* story, the Dodo, the Lory, the Eaglet and the other characters did not dry themselves by running a caucus-race. They followed the water, 'for the pool had by this time begun to flow out of the hall and the edge of it was fringed with rushes and forget-me-nots', till they came to a little cottage: 'And there they sat snugly by the fire, wrapped up in blankets, until the rest of the party had arrived and they were all dry again'.

This was roughly what his sisters had done in the cottage at Iffley, but while the general public could not have enjoyed the private joke, there was no reason to change the story if he was interested only in pleasing children. It was simple, quaint and charming as it was.

A caucus-race is a much more sophisticated method of inducing dryness.

There was no 'One, two, three and away', but they began running when they liked and left off when they liked, so that it was not easy to know when the race was over.

Nor was it easy to see who had won, but all demanded and received prizes.

Alice thought the whole thing very absurd, but they all looked so grave that she did not dare to laugh.

In a caucus—a meeting of wire-pullers, generally for the purpose of influencing an election—arguments run just that kind of race and those who compose a caucus usually want prizes. As Alice had to provide all the prizes, including her own, Dodgson probably meant her to represent the public in this particular little cartoon. To prove that Dodgson had this view of 'caucuses' or 'cauci', whichever is the plural of that etymologically obscure word, it is necessary to go forward two years and glance at his pamphlet of 1866, *The Elections to the Hebdomadal Council*. In this fable, the cats are Conservatives and the rats and mice Radicals.

> The Cats, it seems, were masters of the house
> And held their own against the rat and mouse.
> Of course, the others couldn't stand it long,
> So held a caucus.

He was not, however, content to alter the *Under Ground* version as it stood. He added whole chapters, and of these by far the most original and striking was 'The Mad Tea Party'. *Alice* without the Mad Hatter seems almost impossible, yet he, the

March Hare and the Dormouse were afterthoughts, since they
do not appear in the *Under Ground* version.

In *The Water Babies* Kingsley sent Tom swimming 'to the
centre of Creation (the hub, they call it there) which lies in
latitude 42.21 south and longitude 108.56 east'. Dodgson had
independently sent Alice to the hub or centre of the earth, or at
least made her wonder during her fall if she would arrive there,
and if so what latitude and longitude she would then be in.
This is really a very remarkable coincidence and could not fail
to strike him as he read *The Water Babies*. Kingsley gave fanci-
ful co-ordinates for his hub, but Dodgson's hub has no co-
ordinates, since the centre of the earth is in no latitude and no
longitude. It is much further off the map than even a spot in
the Indian Ocean, and nobody knows what it is really like four
thousand miles down.

Time, for example, would have quite a different meaning in
no longitude. Our time, clock time, depends entirely on longitude. Eastern American time is 'five hours back' because
Washington is so many degrees of longitude west of Greenwich.
When it is midday in Greenwich it is breakfast-time in Boston,
Mass., and tea-time in mid-Europe. But what time is it at the
centre of the earth? By the sun, it is all times or no time.

Consider the Mad Hatter's watch:

Alice had been looking over his shoulder with some curiosity.
'What a funny watch!' she remarked. 'It tells the day of the month,
and doesn't tell what o'clock it is!'

'Why should it?' muttered the Hatter. 'Does *your* watch tell you
what year it is?'

'Of course not,' Alice replied very readily: 'but that's because it
stays the same year for such a long time together.'

'Which is just the case with *mine*!' said the Hatter.

Alice felt dreadfully puzzled. The Hatter's remark seemed to
have no meaning in it, and yet it was certainly English. 'I don't
quite understand,' she said, as politely as she could.

'The Dormouse is asleep again,' said the Hatter, and he poured
a little hot tea upon its nose.

The Hatter's remark has a great deal of meaning in it, including a characteristic Dodgson pun. The watch does not tell
the time in hours because it stays the same hour for so long at
the bottom of this very deep *mine*. It does, however, tell the days
of the month; of the month, be it noted. Even if it were possible

to see the sun from the centre of the earth, it would be impossible
to tell the time by it. It would always look the same, neither
rise nor set, be neither higher nor lower in the sky. It would,
however, be possible to measure time by the phases of the moon,
and this is the principle of the Mad Hatter's watch. It goes by
the moon.

'What day of the month is it?' he said, turning to Alice: he had
taken his watch out of his pocket, and was looking at it uneasily,
shaking it every now and then, and holding it to his ear.
Alice considered a little and then said, 'The fourth.'
'Two days wrong!' sighed the Hatter. 'I told you butter wouldn't
suit the works.'

The bread-knife successfully draws our attention away from the
fact that there is about two days' difference between the lunar
and calendar months.

The 'Fourth' was the 'Fourth of May' (Alice's birthday), as
we learn from the previous chapter: 'the March Hare will be
much the most interesting, and perhaps, as this is May, it won't
be raving mad—at least not so mad as it was in March'. On
that memorable date, the Mad Hatter's watch would read 'the
Sixth'!

Professor L. J. Russell of Birmingham University on reading
this took the trouble to consult an almanac and found that on
that day, 4 May, 1862, there was exactly two days' difference between the two ways of reckoning the date. As the amount varies
with every month and year, there can be no doubt that Dodgson
too consulted an almanac and based his calculations upon it.

In the Hemispherical Problem, it will be remembered, it was
the day which disappeared. It was always 'today', and the
Battle of Waterloo happened so many hours ago. In the case of
the Mad Hatter's watch it is the hour which has disappeared as
a unit of time, and the day which is retained, but it is the lunar,
not the solar, day. In the Hemispherical Problem, there was a
suggestion, finally rejected as impracticable, that people might
be allowed to choose what day it was for themselves. The Mad
Hatter and the March Hare had to choose what hour it was and
they chose tea-time: 'It's always six o'clock now'. That was the
hour the Deanery children would have chosen.

'That last game I had with my sweet cousin,' says Lamb in
'Mrs Battle on Whist', '—(dare I tell thee how foolish I am?)—I

wished it might have lasted for ever, though we gained nothing and lost nothing, though it was a mere shade of play: I would be content to go on in that idle folly forever.' There are such occasions, when 'time seems to stand still', to use the familiar phrase, and one of them certainly occurred on another Fourth, 4 July, 1862, perhaps throughout that delightful boating expedition.

A bright idea came into Alice's head. 'Is that the reason so many tea-things are put out here?' she asked.

'Yes, that's it,' said the Hatter with a sigh: 'It's always tea-time, and we've no time to wash the things between whiles.'

'Then you keep moving round, I suppose?' said Alice.

'Exactly so,' said the Hatter: 'as the things get used up.'

'But what happens when you come to the beginning again?' Alice ventured to ask.

'Suppose we change the subject,' the March Hare interrupted, yawning. 'I'm getting tired of this.'

This is the reductio ad absurdum. The eternal Now dissolves in laughter and the clatter of picnic crockery. Time in our world does not stand still. Nevertheless, there is in this maddest of mad tea-parties the delicious thrill of something imminent, something great and solemn, which does not after all make its appearance.

Alice in her 'Recollections' suggested that Dodgson added some of the other stories he had told them 'to make the difference between *Alice in Wonderland* and *Alice's Adventures Under Ground*'. One such fragment which was left out of the *Under Ground* version was the 'Three Little Sisters' story which is told by the Dormouse. This was originally told in the boat on 4 July, 1862, when it was woven round the names of the three Liddell children, Elsie being invoked out of Lorina Charlotte's initials (L.C.), while Lacie was an anagram for Alice, and Tilly short for Matilda, Edith's pet name.

'Treacle' is significant; it expressed his opinion of the popular songs and hymns of the day, for example,

> Twinkle, twinkle little star
> How I wonder what you are:
> Up above the world so high,
> Like a diamond in the sky.

Why 'like a diamond'? Simply because it is bright and sparkling? Or does the value of a diamond in money enter into the comparison? In *Sylvie and Bruno* he aired his views on this subject (as on many others) quite openly: 'Look at the literature of Hymns, now. How cankered it is, through and through with selfishness! There are few human compositions more utterly degraded than some modern Hymns!' and he quotes the stanza:

> Whatever, Lord, we lend to Thee,
> Repaid a thousandfold shall be,
> Then gladly will we give to Thee,
> Giver of all.

In his parody of 'Twinkle, twinkle' he substituted 'bat' for star no doubt because a 'bat' would be a natural inhabitant of a deep 'mine', and 'tea-tray' for diamond—a 'tea-tray' being an appropriate simile for those whose whole world consists of table and chairs, cups and saucers, milk, tea-pot, bread and butter; the world of tea. Such creatures might be expected to interpret the universe in terms of tea, as Swift's Houyhnhnms interpreted it in terms of the stable. 'An effect,' said Sir John Herschel in one of his *Popular Lectures on Scientific Subjects*, published about this time, 'the precise parallel to the scintillation of the stars, might be produced, affecting the ear instead of the eye, by sounding together two strings, at first exactly in unison and then very slightly increasing and diminishing alternately the tension of one of them.'[1] The squeak of a bat could perhaps be taken as an approximate twinkle.

Sometimes Dodgson seems to be thinking of the Mad Hatter and his friends as living at the bottom of a very deep mine or well, sometimes as inhabiting a transparent globe like goldfish. It will be remembered that in the trial scene the jurymen fell out of their box:

And there they lay sprawling about, reminding her very much of a globe of goldfish she had accidentally upset the week before.
'Oh, I *beg* your pardon,' she exclaimed in a tone of great dismay, and began picking them up again as quickly as she could, for the accident of the goldfish kept running in her head and she had a vague sort of idea that they must be collected at once and be put back into the jury-box, or they would die.

Many of the characters were playing-cards, 'oblong and flat, with their hands and feet at the corners', and Dodgson's own illustrations, though technically far inferior to Tenniel's, do

---

[1] Sir John Herschel: *Popular Lectures on Scientific Subjects*, p. 339.

insist on this flatness. His Queen of Hearts has a nightmarish quality no solid figure could ever have. 'Off with his head!' she keeps shouting, though nothing but a passing unpleasantness and anxiety ever comes of it. This was the attitude of the orthodox High Church party to all who dared to express views contravening the Thirty-nine Articles—for example, Jowett, of whom Dodgson wrote a year later: 'In an earlier age of mathematics, J. (Jowett) would probably have been referred to rectangular axes, and divided into two unequal parts—a process of arbitrary elimination which is now considered not strictly legitimate'.[1] How clever that is! And how much more vital and effective is the card queen with her four monosyllables! Dodgson in his *Theatre* article of 1887 says he intended her as 'a sort of embodiment of ungovernable passion—a blind and aimless fury', such, we may add, as animated the English Church at that time. I do not think any more particular identification is possible.

What he meant by 'pepper' in 'Pig and Pepper' Dodgson for once actually does explain, at the beginning of the Mock Turtle's Story:

'When I'm a Duchess,' she said to herself (not in a very hopeful tone though), 'I won't have any pepper in my kitchen *at all*. Soup does very well without—Maybe it's always pepper that makes people hot-tempered,' she went on, very much pleased at having found out a new kind of rule, 'and vinegar that makes them sour— and camomile that makes them bitter—and—and barley-sugar and such things that make children sweet-tempered.'

The Duchess, the Cook and the Baby are certainly another of Dodgson's cartoons. Shane Leslie suggests Wilberforce as the Duchess who is calling the Baby (the Faithful) a pig—it turns into one—while the Cook who has made the soup too peppery and is throwing things at her mistress he identifies as Stanley. The latter put plenty of pepper in his sermons and threw many a verbal missile at the Bishop of Oxford, whose plans he opposed at every turn.

The Cat, grinning at this smoky, peppery scene of discord, might well be Cardinal Wiseman amused at Anglican squabbles. The Archdeacon had put it in 1852, 'When Rome, insidiously watching us, saw in our diversities of practice as well as of faith,

---

[1] *The New Method of Evaluation, as applied to* π.

a real point of weakness and taunted us with our want of unity what should have been our course?'[1] Not throwing pepper or calling names. Yet here they were, more than ten years later, still at it.

It is tempting to accept the Wilberforce-Stanley situation as the original of the new chapter 'Pig and Pepper'. On the other hand, the Cook might be any Servant of the Church who threw things at her mistress, and the soup *Essays and Reviews* or Colenso on the Pentateuch or any 'peppery' concoction of the kind. The general resemblance to the situation at Oxford and in the English Church is far too close to argue about.

'There's no sort of use in knocking,' said the Footman, 'and that for two reasons. First because I'm on the same side of the door as you are; secondly because they're making such a noise inside, no one could possibly hear you.'

This caricatures the indifference of the Churchmen as to the effect their disputes were having on the people.

He was looking up into the sky all the time he was speaking, and Alice thought this decidedly uncivil.

Was he looking perhaps for a reappearance of the Cheshire Cat's head there? If so, its smiling presence inside becomes almost sinister. Nevertheless, I cannot agree with Shane Leslie that the Knave of Hearts is Newman, whose trial had taken place nearly twenty years earlier. It is much more likely that Dodgson was burlesquing all the trials from that of Newman to that of Wilson and Williams; but if he was thinking of one in particular it would be the most recent.

'What trial is it?' Alice panted as she ran; but the Gryphon only answered 'Come on!' and ran the faster, while more and more faintly came, carried on the breeze that followed them, the melancholy words:

> 'Soo-oop of the e-e-vening,
> Beautiful, beautiful Soup!'

The trial was greatly extended in the published story and works up to a climax in two chapters of the most exquisite dialogue ever written.

The judge, by the way, was the King; and as he wore his crown over the wig (look at the frontispiece if you want to see how he did it), he did not look at all comfortable, and it was certainly not becoming.

[1] *Ritual Worship*, p. 23.

Dodgson could not write these words in 1864 without thinking of the Erastian principle and the intervention of the Crown in the case of Wilson and Williams, where Lord Westbury represented Queen Victoria as Head of the English Church. Jowett, the Majesty of Justice, and the Wig, all made their contribution.

The King's question: 'What are tarts made of?' has two different answers:

'Pepper, mostly,' said the cook.
'Treacle,' said a sleepy voice behind her.

Shane Leslie's view that the pepper was put into the Thirty-nine Articles to please Protestants and the treacle to please Catholics is convincing. Certainly people of all shades of opinion tended to see in the Articles just what pleased themselves. Those who liked protesting, arguing and theorizing thought the tarts were composed of pepper. Those who wanted a more soothing type of religion thought they were made of treacle.

What did Dodgson think?

'Who cares for you?' said Alice (she had grown to her full size by this time). 'You're nothing but a pack of cards!'
At this the whole pack rose up into the air and came flying down upon her: she gave a little scream, half of fright and half of anger, and tried to beat them off and found herself lying on the bank, with her head in the lap of her sister, who was gently brushing away some dead leaves that had fluttered down from the trees upon her face.

It would, in my opinion, be quite wrong to regard *Alice's Adventures in Wonderland* as an allegory or a satire. It is equally wrong to insist, as so many children of uncertain age have insisted, that it is a story for children of all ages. Certainly it began as a story for children, the three Liddell children, though even then two out of the five persons in the boat were adults. Next it became a private and personal matter between Dodgson and Alice Liddell, and for inspiration he drew on his mathematics and anything else that would yield this fascinating new amalgam or distillation which he called nonsense. Lastly he rewrote the story for a public which was to consist, like Kingsley's, of 'children and grown folks'. The mathematician and the statesman quote from Alice every time they open their mouths in public or try to explain to us the latest theory of space and time. In the dug-outs of the First World War ('How doth the little crocodile' in *Journey's End*) or the Anderson shelters of the

Second ('remembering her own child-life, and the happy summer days' in *Mrs Miniver*) it became the symbol of normality and sanity, good days gone by and better days, we hoped, ahead.

To call it a minor triumph or a 'tiny little masterpiece' is intolerable condescension. It will be read, and not by children only, when all its critics and commentators, their comments and criticisms, are dust.

CHAPTER FOUR

Alice Waves her Handkerchief

AS early as 25 January, 1864, Dodgson had called on Tenniel to ask him to do the illustrations, but the final agreement was not reached until 5 April. One difficulty was to decide on Alice's appearance in these pictures, and it may be that Dean Liddell helped to settle this point, for in January, 1864, Dodgson was engaged in a rather disagreeable correspondence with the Dean over a point of business.[1] The Dean might well regard the publication of the *Adventures* with mixed feelings and insist that there be no obvious resemblance between the heroine of the book and his daughter. On the other hand, the 'business' may have been University business.

In any case, the Alice of the book had changed almost unnoticed from Alice Liddell to just Alice. No longer could she look like Alice Liddell. Something more piquant and less appealing was required, and one day in 1864 Dodgson saw in the rooms of a Mr Gray a photograph of Canon Badcock's daughter, Miss Mary Hilton Badcock, who had a snub nose, long, thick fair hair and a determined little mouth. This he recommended to Tenniel, who eventually called on the Canon at Ripon and sketched Mary from life.[2] 'As a rule,' says Alice in her 'Recollections', 'Tenniel used Mr Dodgson's drawings as the basis for his own illustrations and they held frequent consultations about them.'

The first batch of proofs reached Dodgson on 16 December,[3] when he and Duckworth dined over them. On 10 June he had written to Tom Taylor about the title, declaring that 'Alice's Adventures Under Ground' had been thought (by whom he does not tell us) 'too like a lesson-book about mines'. In a way and in part that is what is it. Incidentally, Dodgson himself is the only person who troubles to separate 'Under' from 'Ground', but he does so invariably. He offered Tom Taylor a wide

---

[1] Private letter: Miss F. Menella Dodgson.
[2] Falconer Madan in the *Handbook*, p. 22.
[3] Private letter: Miss F. Menella Dodgson.

choice of names, but added: 'Of all these I prefer "Alice's Adventures in Wonderland" '.[1] He had a habit of making up his own mind and then asking for the advice he wanted to be given.

The story of Dodgson's visit to Penmorfa in Llandudno during the summer of 1864—his readings from *Alice's Adventures* while Sir William Richmond painted 'The Three Graces' (Lorina, Alice and Edith) and the Dean sneezed over his lexicon—is almost too good to spoil. Mrs Lennon's evidence, however, is ultimately based on hearsay.[2] Nor did the Liddells occupy Penmorfa until 1865,[3] while the diary which Mrs Lennon thought had disappeared actually survives, covers both summers fully and does not mention the visit to Llandudno.[4] Dodgson spent both summers taking photographs, in London, Freshwater Croft and other places, but not in Llandudno.[5]

Before *Alice* was published two other little works of Dodgson's appeared in print. Early in 1865 the matter of Jowett's salary was at last settled, E. A. Freeman and Charles Elton having proved that Christ Church actually held lands granted by the founder for just the purpose which was now being systematically thwarted. Christ Church then behaved very handsomely. After establishing that no legal obligation existed, the Dean and Chapter nevertheless raised Jowett's salary to £500. Dodgson was moved to mirth and astonishment and in March, 1865, published a pamphlet on the subject entitled *The New Method of Evaluation, as applied to* π which ran through several editions.

It began with a verbal cartoon:

> Little Jack Horner
> Sat in his corner
> Eating his Christmas pie.

The problem, Dodgson proceeds, hitherto regarded as arithmetical, is really a problem in dynamics.

The following are the main data of the problem: Let U=the University, G=Greek, and P=Professor. Then G.P.=Greek Professor; let this be reduced to its lowest terms, and call the result J. (Jowett).

[1] F. M. in *Handbook*, p. 18.
[2] See Florence Becker Newman: *Lewis Carroll*, pp. 130–2.
[3] Thompson: *Life of Liddell*, p. 252.
[4] Private letter: Miss F. Menella Dodgson.
[5] Helmut Gernsheim, pp. 54–60 (extracts from diary).

Also let W=the work done, T=*The Times*, p=the given payment, π the payment according to T and S=the sum required; so that π=S.

The problem is, to obtain a value for π which shall be commensurable with W.

In the early treatises on this subject, the mean value assigned to π will be found to be 40·000,000. Later writers suspected that the decimal point had been accidentally shifted, and that the proper value was 400·00000.

He considers various methods of obtaining this result:

I. Rationalization.

The peculiarity of this process consists in its affecting all quantities alike with a negative sign.

To apply it, let H=High Church, and L=Low Church, then the geometric mean=$\sqrt{HL}$: call this 'B' (Broad Church)

$$\therefore HL=B^2$$

Also let x and y represent unknown quantities.

The process now requires the breaking up of U (the University) into its partial factions; of the two principal factions thus formed, that corresponding with P presented no further difficulty

(being that of the Rationalists, to which Jowett belonged by virtue of his essay in *Essays and Reviews*)

but it appeared hopeless to rationalize the other.

(This was the extreme High Church party known as the Puseyites, though Pusey himself said they had gone far beyond old Tractarians like himself.)

A reductio ad absurdum was therefore attempted, and it was asked 'why should π *not* be evaluated?' The great difficulty now was to discover y . . .

II. The Method of Indifferences.

Let E=Essays, and R=Reviews; then the Locus of (E+R), referred to multilinear co-ordinates, will be found to be a superficies (i.e. a locus possessing length and breadth, but no depth).

In other words, the writers of *Essays and Reviews* were superficial. They lived in a world of only two dimensions, a superficies, or surface. This is a more mathematical form of the same idea which he expressed in the trial of the Knave of Hearts, who, it will be remembered, could not swim, 'being made entirely of cardboard'.

Let V= novelty, and assume (E+R) as a function of V,[1]

[1] This is the Greek v (nu).

and he proceeds to prove Bishop Wilberforce's contention that there was no novelty in *Essays and Reviews*.

It was now necessary to investigate the locus of E B P [Essays—Broad Church—Professor, but these were also Dr Pusey's initials]: this was found to be a species of Catenary, called a Patristic Catenary, which is usually defined as passing through Origen

(a pun on the Saint whom the Tractarians and their successors, the Ritualists were in the habit of quoting on points of doctrine)

and containing many multiple points.

The puns here crowd so thick upon us that we had better cut the Gordian knot. He means that those who were concerned with ancient Church history and mere ceremony were as 'superficial' as the Rationalists. They were concerned only with the surface of things.

Section IV was the 'Elimination of J.' The suggestion that he should be referred to rectangular axes and divided into two unequal parts ('Off with his head!') being ruled out of court, Dodgson proceeds:

It was proposed, therefore, to eliminate J. by an appeal to the principle known as '*the permanence of equivalent formularies*': this, however, failed on application, as J. became indeterminate.

The reference here is no doubt to the abortive proceedings against Jowett in the Vice-Chancellor's Court.

Some advocates of the process would have preferred that J. should be eliminated *in toto*. The classical scholar need hardly be reminded that *toto* is the ablative of *tum tum*, and that this beautiful and expressive phrase embodied the wish that J. should be eliminated by the compulsory religious examination.

J. was to be eliminated 'in toto', that is to say, by making him subscribe to the Thirty-nine Articles *in toto*. And he did subscribe to the Articles *in toto* ('Mr Vice-Chancellor, I have come to sign the Articles'), according to Dodgson, for the sake of his tum-tum. It would be quite wrong to identify the little monster-slayer in Jabberwocky as Jowett, but the tum-tum tree by which he rested is certainly derived from its ablative *toto*.

> So rested he by the tum-tum tree
> And stood awhile in thought.

The ideas which underlie *Through the Looking-glass* were already whirling nebulously in Dodgson's mind.

Meantime, the conclusion of the pamphlet:

V. Evaluation Under Pressure.

Of this last method it need only be noted that

by continually increasing E A F

(E = Enlightened, A = Able, and F = a force acting equally in all directions, and varying inversely as T, *The Times*; also the initials of E. A. Freeman who proved the case for increasing Jowett's salary)

the result was at last obtained.

$\pi = S$ (the sum required) $= 500\cdot00000$.

The result differs considerably from the anticipated value, namely $400\cdot00000$: still there can be no doubt that the process has been correctly performed, and that the learned world may be congratulated on the final settlement of this most difficult problem.

In June, 1865, appeared another pamphlet, *The Dynamics of a Parti-cle*, in which the skit on Jowett's salary was reprinted as Chapter III. Chapter I consists of definitions, postulates and axioms, which parody those of Euclid. 'Let it be granted that a controversy may be raised about any question, and at any distance from that question.'

Chapter II is on the Dynamics of a Parti-cle and is a political squib. The occasion was the Gladstone-Gathorne-Hardy election at Oxford in 1865, when Gladstone, who had been Tory member for Oxford since 1847, lost his seat.

From the Tory point of view, and it must be remembered that throughout his life Dodgson was 'nothing if not a staunch Conservative', Gladstone had been behaving very oddly. His career had begun most promisingly with a speech directed against the Reform Bill and another claiming that there was scriptural sanction for slavery. He had married the daughter of a baronet, published a sound book on Church Principles, and in 1843, as President of the Board of Trade, declared himself in favour of withdrawing the bill which provided education for children employed in factories. Alas for misplaced confidence! In 1859 he had voted with the Government in support of a mild Reform Bill. On the Government's defeat, Gladstone, again returned by the University, accepted office in Palmerston's Whig administration. In 1864 he spoke of enfranchising the working-class, and in 1865 of disestablishing the Irish

Church. He was also known to have agreed with Lord West-bury's findings in the Wilson and Williams case.

It was too much. The man was a radical. In July, 1865, Parliament was dissolved and in the subsequent election Gladstone was defeated.

'At last,' he told South Lancashire, which returned him immediately afterwards, 'I can speak freely.'

There was therefore some justification for Dodgson's witticisms such as: 'A surd is a radical, whose meaning cannot be exactly ascertained. This class comprises a very large number of particles.'

More important than these wonderful puns and subtle innuendoes which lose all point when explained ('Particles are logically divided according to GENIUS and SPEECHES') is the little mathematical fantasy which serves as prologue:

It was a lovely Autumn evening, and the glorious effects of chromatic aberration were beginning to show themselves in the atmosphere as the earth revolved away from the great western luminary, when two lines might have been observed, wending their way across a plane superficies.

Here is a 'flatland' twenty years earlier than Edwin Abbott's.

The elder of the two had by long practice acquired the art, so painful to young and impulsive loci, of lying evenly between his extreme points; but the younger, in her girlish impetuosity, was ever longing to diverge and become an hyperbola or some such romantic and boundless curve.

The staid, respectable, masculine line and the young, romantic, feminine line suggest irresistibly himself and Alice Liddell. It would have been strange had all the excitement of the book in progress not made some impression on a girl of thirteen.

They had lived and loved: fate and the intervening superficies had hitherto kept them asunder, but this was no longer to be: a line had intersected them, making the two interior angles together less than two right angles. It was a moment never to be forgotten, and as they journeyed on, a whisper thrilled along the superficies in isochronous waves of sound. 'Yes! We shall at length meet, if continually produced!'

The line which intersected them was the story *Alice's Adventures*, but they were not after all destined to meet. The superficies continued to intervene.

On 4 July, 1865, the third anniversary of the boating trip to
Godstow, Alice received the first presentation copy of her
Adventures. Princess Beatrice received the second.[1] That was
the right order, one feels, but none-the-less, a tremendous, a
most flattering compliment. Moreover, the book was dedicated
to Alice:

> Alice! a childish story take,
>   And with a gentle hand
> Lay it where Childhood's dreams are twined
>   In Memory's mystic band,
> Like pilgrim's wither'd wreath of flowers
>   Pluck'd in a far-off land.

The book was full of memories for her, private jokes and local
associations, not all of which had been polished out, and though
Dodgson himself always regarded as holy and apart the original
MS. book with his own quaint pictures, there is something
magical and heart-warming about print. The despised public
was about to be interested in this, her book, written for her
by special appointment, featuring her as heroine.

The public, however, was not after all given much chance to
acquire copies of this new book for children. A fortnight after
its appearance Dodgson had heard from Tenniel, who was
dissatisfied with the reproduction of the illustrations, and on
2 August Dodgson decided on a reprint, even though he calculated his probable loss on the first edition at £100. A second
edition would wipe this out and any further editions show a
profit, but that he thought extremely unlikely.[2]

About 48 copies of the 'first issue of the first edition' had been
given away before 2 August, and Dodgson called in as many of
these as he could. The remainder of the edition was sold by
Macmillan to Messrs Appleton of New York and appeared there
about the same time as the second edition ordered by Dodgson.
On both sides of the Atlantic these editions were quickly sold
out, as were the two larger editions of 1867. Thereafter Alice
sold steadily, though not, as is the general impression, pheno-
menally, for the rest of his life. In 1881, for example, fifteen
years after its first appearance, the book was in its 83rd thousand,
and it is calculated that 110,000 copies were sold in his lifetime.[3]

---

[1] Coll., p. 104.
[2] Facsimile page of Dodgson's diary, *Handbook*, opp. p. 25.
[3] S. H. Williams in the *Handbook* is the authority for book-collectors.

It was not, by modern standards, a best-seller. Still, with his income from Christ Church, it put him far above mere independence and established him as a writer. Hitherto he had published mathematical works and contributed to periodicals. There was a quality about *Alice* which must have shaken up the Pre-Raphaelites, who had welcomed him more for his rosewood camera than because they took him seriously. There is nothing like financial success to make people see merit in a work of art, and whereas in 1862 Dodgson was ineffectually imitating Christina Rossetti, by 1874 she was avowedly imitating him (in 'Speaking Likenesses') and to no better purpose.

In the year 1866 he enhanced his reputation as a mathematician by having a paper accepted by the Royal Society. George Macdonald, in *Orts*, throws a curious sidelight on the subject. 'The imagination of man,' he writes, 'is made in the image of the imagination of God . . . our consciousness, in the resembling conditions, must afar off resemble his.'[1] Macdonald admits that 'the facts of Nature are to be discovered only by observation and experiment. True. But how does the man of science come to think of his experiments? Does observation reach to the non-present, the possible, the yet unconceived? . . . It is the far-seeing imagination which beholds what might be a form of things and says to the intellect "try whether that may not be the form of these things" . . . and the construction of any hypothesis whatever is the work of the imagination.'

In a footnote to the above he adds:

This paper was already written, when, happening to mention the present subject to a mathematical friend, a lecturer at one of the universities, he gave us a corroborative instance. He had lately *guessed* that a certain algebraic process could be shortened exceedingly if the method which his imagination suggested should prove to be a true one—that is, an algebraic law. He put it to the test of experiment—committed the verification, that is, into the hands of his intellect—and found the method true. It has since been accepted by the Royal Society.[2]

The friend was the Rev. C. L. Dodgson, M.A., Student of Christ Church, Oxford, whose 'Condensation of Determinants', being a new and brief method for computing their arithmetical values, was published by the Royal Society in its *Proceedings*,

[1] *Orts*, p. 3.
[2] Ib., p. 13.

17 May, 1866. Dodgson was of course, unable to send this paper
to the Royal Society himself. It was sent by his former tutor,
Professor Price. Dodgson also published it separately and in the
following year an expanded version called *An Elementary Treatise
on Determinants*.

Indeed, in the year 1866 things were going almost suspiciously
well. His mathematical work, though not really advanced, had
achieved the distinction of being published by the Royal Society.
In the University he was noted as a wit and he probably added to
that reputation by publishing 'The Elections to the Hebdomadal
Council', though there is more wit than humour in its eighteenth
century couplets. And by the end of the year he had already
decided upon a sequel to *Alice's Adventures*, since he had applied
unsuccessfully to Tenniel and to Sir Noel Paton to do the illustrations for it, before writing on 22 January, 1867, to Richard Doyle.[1]

Referring to the 'lost' stories—those never written down—
Alice says: 'Much of *Through the Looking-glass* is made up of
them too, particularly the ones to do with chessmen, which are
dated by the period when we were excitedly learning chess'.
This period is fixed, though not exactly, by her remark: 'About
the time when the *Alice* was told, we used to spend a good many
happy hours in the Deanery garden trying to play croquet.
Chess came later.'[2]

In casting about for successors to his playing-card characters,
Dodgson was bound to hit on chess, that most mathematical and
picturesque of games. In his library were *Walker on Chess*,
Staunton's *Chess Player's Companion* and Staunton's *Chess Tourna-
ment*,[3] and it is on record that he once mated Lionel Tennyson
in six moves—not a difficult feat against a beginner, but one
that showed he knew something about the game.

One game they certainly played was the queening of a pawn,
Alice taking the pawn and he the rest of the pieces. He showed
her the powers of the knight and the queen and began to think
about those powers in relation to the powers of a pawn. It was
fascinating. Here was another undiscovered country, a little,
strange world, with its own laws. No doubt Alice's reactions
helped to provide the new world with a flora and fauna.

[1] S.H.W. in the *Handbook*, p. 238.
[2] *Cornhill Magazine*, July, 1932.
[3] *Catalogue*, Bodleian.

It was fortunate that he had lost no time in acquiring this new set of Alice's reactions, for the delightful relationship could not last. Exactly what happened is not clear, but the evidence is very strong that something did happen, as a result of which there was estrangement and emotional tension.

In the first place, Mrs Skene (Lorina Liddell, Alice's elder sister, known as Ina) told Mrs Florence Becker Lennon in the course of a brief conversation that there was a breach between Dodgson and the Liddell family while Alice was growing up. This she said was due to Dodgson's extreme sensitiveness.[1] Then Alice herself, in her 'Recollections', says, 'Unfortunately my mother tore up all the letters Mr Dodgson wrote to me when I was a small girl. I cannot remember what any of them were like, but it is an awful thought to contemplate what may have perished in the Deanery wastepaper basket.'

Again, there was Alice's fall from her pony and Dodgson's strange neglect of her during her long confinement to bed with a broken thigh. Unfortunately no exact date can be given even for this memorable incident, for Caryl Hargreaves does not know when it occurred[2] and it is not mentioned in Dodgson's diary.[3] It was almost certainly after the publication of the first *Alice* and before the publication of the second. This is confirmed by the age of the pony 'Tommy', which was given to Alice's brother Harry soon after the Liddell family moved to Oxford, that is, about 1856. 'When Tommy got too old,' says Alice, 'my father bought a bigger pony for us.' That would happen about the critical period now being considered.

'One Boxing Day' (she remembered the day, but not the year) 'this pony crossed its legs and came down with me on the Abingdon road.' Alice's thigh was broken and her father went to get help. Some strangers came along in a wagonette and proceeded to borrow from a nearby farm a feather-bed on which they conveyed Alice back to the Deanery. When shut, the door of the wagonette crushed her a little, causing her great pain, so that she was tearful and almost delirious by the time old Bultitude, the Deanery coachman, who had taught her to ride, carried her indoors.

'You won't let them hurt me any more, will you?' said Alice.

[1] Florence Becker Lennon: *Lewis Carroll*, p. 182.
[2] Private letter: Wing-Commander Caryl Hargreaves.
[3] Private letter: Miss F. Menella Dodgson.

In telling the story afterwards, Bultitude used to say that he 'nearly let Miss Alice drop'.

Alice continues: 'As it was, I was on my back for six weeks with a broken thigh. During all these weeks Mr Dodgson never came to see me. If he had, perhaps the world might have known some more of Alice's adventures.' Had the 'breach' been a mere quarrel between Dodgson and his 'child-friend' who was no longer a child, he must surely have gone to see her. A broken thigh wipes off all scores of that nature. Something more fundamental is implied in his failure to condole.

Lastly there is the evidence of the diary,[1] which, however, was not of the modern uninhibited type. It was intended to help him remember what had happened and not to enable us to see into his life.

It appears that after each long vacation he found some difficulty in resuming friendly relations with the children. On 29 April, 1863, he writes: 'There is no variety in my life to record just now *except* meetings with the Liddells, the record of which has become almost continuous'. Then came the long vacation. It was the following December before Dodgson spent an evening at the Deanery. He says: 'Mrs Liddell was with us part of the time. It is nearly 6 months since I have seen any-thing of them to speak of.' In January, 1864, came that 'rather disagreeable correspondence' with the Dean, and then nothing about the Liddells for more than a year.

The next scrap of evidence is on 16 March, 1865: 'Coming down Oriel Lane, I met Ina and Miss Prickett and had a short talk with them. It is long since we interchanged a word, but we met as if it had been yesterday.' On 11 May there is the inter-esting entry: 'Met Alice and Miss Prickett in the quadrangle. Alice seems changed a good deal'. She would be changing. It was just a week after her thirteenth birthday.

Then, on 30 November, 1866, he had two invitations for the evening, one being to the Deanery. He chose the other one, giving no reason. Yet five days later he dined with the Liddells and had 'one of the pleasantest evenings I have had there for a very long time'. Ina sat beside him and he 'had a good deal of talk with Mrs Liddell'.

---

[1] What follows is based on a summary of Lewis Carroll's relations with the Liddells between 1862 and 1873 sent me by Miss F. Menella Dodgson.

In 1867 there is no mention of Alice, but two references to her parents. One day in April he had a 'little talk' with the Dean and Mrs Liddell at the Museum and on 18 May he paid 'a visit to Mrs Liddell and had a long chat with her, walking about the Deanery Garden, a thing I have not done for years'. In the diaries for 1868 and 1869 there are large gaps, those from 24 January to 2 April, 1868, from 28 January to 6 April, 1869, and from 14 June to 3 August, 1869, being the longest. There is no mention of the Liddell family at all for more than three years after his long chat with Mrs Liddell in the Deanery garden.

Suddenly, on 25 June, 1870, the silence is broken. It appears that the Liddells have not vanished from the earth. Mrs Liddell brought Ina and Alice to be photographed, which was, he says, 'a wonderful thing to have happened—(the last occasion was
                                        ¹)'. The next reference to the family is on
16 November, 1871. He was at a reception and 'met the Deanery party—I took in Edith Liddell and found her (when the ice was broken) a v. pleasant neighbour'. When the ice was broken—with the Eaglet! In the following year there is again no mention of the Liddells.

It was indeed a delicate situation, especially after the publication and resounding success of *Alice's Adventures*, and there is every sign that it was handled with true Victorian firmness and discretion.

1867 was rather a bleak year for Dodgson, or at any rate for Lewis Carroll. In May appeared 'The Deserted Parks', a skilful parody of Goldsmith's 'Deserted Village', in which he once more hunted his bête noir, Jowett:

> A man he was to undergraduates dear,
> And passing rich with forty pounds a year.

Probably Jowett had to pay for the suffering inflicted on Dodgson himself by time and the Liddells.

That summer he spent two months travelling on the Continent with Henry Parry Liddon, later Dean of St Paul's. They went to Moscow, a considerable journey for those days, by Brussels, Cologne, Berlin, Königsberg and St Petersburg, returning by Warsaw, Breslau, Dresden and Paris.

Liddon was acting as unofficial ambassador from Wilberforce

---

¹ Space left blank.

to the Greek Orthodox Church and had conversations with Bishop Leonide and with Philaret, the Metropolitan. He was relieved to find that the English Church was recognized in Russia as a separate and 'valid' branch of the original Church. They agreed that the Pope had no historical warrant for his claim to supremacy. Liddon approved in general of the 'supernatural' aspects of Russian religion but had to refrain from joining in certain responses concerning the Virgin Mary.[1]

Dodgson spoke German and French, though with difficulty, could follow the Greek service from the book and took the trouble to learn the Russian alphabet. He enjoyed the journey, but found the Continental church services too gorgeous and the hotel cutlery none too clean. He and Liddon had long conversations on religious and other matters. Liddon thought the clergy should voluntarily accept celibacy and said that though he had formerly enjoyed the theatre he had not been in one since 1852. On this last point Dodgson disagreed with him, and in Paris visited the Théâtre Vaudeville and the Opéra Comique (without Liddon).

He was susceptible to beauty, and his *Russian Journal* contains many descriptions of religious paintings. He could have spent hours gazing at the Sistine Madonna and he wept in Cologne Cathedral. 'Dodgson,' says Liddon in his diary for 15 July, 'was overcome by the beauty of Cologne Cathedral. I found him leaning against the rails of the choir and sobbing like a child. When the verger came to show us over the chapels, he got out of the way. He said that he could not bear the harsh voice of the man in the presence of so much beauty.'

He was also moved by the return across the channel from Calais. He stood in the bow all the way, chatting to the sailor on the lookout and watching the lights until the white cliffs came out of the morning twilight.[2]

Behind those cliffs the English Church continued to explode at intervals and the latest development was called 'Ritualism'. In 1865 Jowett is described as being greatly concerned about it and its spread 'amongst the weaker undergraduates, some of whom got up the semblance of a chapel in their rooms, with vestments and incense'. Nor was it confined to undergraduates.

---

[1] *Life and Letters of Henry Parry Liddon*, by J. O. Johnson.
[2] *Russian Journal*, by Lewis Carroll.

'If you were to walk abroad,' said Jowett in a letter of 26 December, 1865, 'you would be very much surprised to see the changes in our London churches. There is a sort of aesthetico-catholic revival among them. I wonder how many more spurious forms of Christianity are to appear in these latter days.'[1]

In this Dodgson would for once have agreed with him, though he would probably have felt indignant at having to do so. 'My dear father,' he wrote a good deal later, 'was what is called a "High Churchman" and I naturally adopted those views, but have always felt repelled by the yet higher development called "Ritualism".'[2]

Later still, in *Sylvie and Bruno*, 1889, he explains his attitude more fully. The Narrator and his friends have been to the village church, where:

The service would have been pronounced by any modern asthetic religionist—or religious aesthete, which is it?—to be crude and cold: to me, coming fresh from the ever advancing developments of a London Church under a soi-disant 'Catholic' Rector, it was unspeakably refreshing.

There was no theatrical procession of demure little choristers, trying their best not to simper under the admiring gaze of the congregation: the people's share in the service was taken by the people themselves, unaided, except that a few good voices, judiciously posted here and there among them, kept the singing from going too far astray.

There was no murdering of the noble music contained in the Bible and the Liturgy, by its recital in a dead monotone, with no more expression than a mechanical talking-doll.

No, the prayers were *prayed*, the lessons were *read* and—best of all—the sermons were *talked*.

'Yes,' said Arthur as if in answer to my thoughts, 'those "high" services are fast becoming pure formalism. And it's specially bad for the little boys.'

In the Preface to *Sylvie and Bruno Concluded* Dodgson mentions that objections have been made to the severe language he has put into the mouth of Arthur on the subjects of sermons, church services and choristers. While protesting against the assumption that he, the author, is ready to endorse the opinions of characters in his story, he says, 'But in these two instances, I admit that I am much in sympathy with Arthur . . .'. Then, as to choristers, 'and all other accessories of music, vestments, processions, etc.—

[1] *Life of Jowett*, Vol. I, p. 381.
[2] Coll., p. 340.

which have come, along with them, into fashion—while freely
admitting that the "Ritual" movement was sorely needed, and
that it has effected a vast improvement in our Church Services,
which had become dead and dry to the last degree, I hold that,
like many other desirable movements, it has gone too far in the
opposite direction and has introduced many new dangers'.

This was the movement which in 1867 Parliament attempted
to curb by legislation. Against this Wilberforce set his face,
though his own Lower House of Convocation had in the previous year passed a resolution asking the upper House to take
steps for 'clearing the doubts and allaying the anxieties that
existed on the subject of Ritualism'.[1] On this occasion Stanley
had also declared for toleration 'on the general principle by
which the Church of England tolerates all that it can include
within the pale'.[2]

Lord Shaftesbury, however, had a bill ready, which if carried
would make 'the 58th Canon the absolute and sole rule of the
Church of England as to ornaments, dresses, etc.'. He was
known to have the backing of the Archbishop of Canterbury
and most of the bishops. Wilberforce got Gladstone to intervene
with the suggestion of a Royal Commission, and when Shaftesbury moved the second reading in May, 1867, it was the Archbishop of Canterbury himself who proposed the amendment.
The bill was not brought on again, and when the Royal Commission was set up Wilberforce was on it.

Shaftesbury protested in the House of Lords that, as he
himself had refused to serve on it 'as an extreme man', Wilberforce ought also to keep off it.

'It is very easy,' said Wilberforce in reply, 'for the Noble Lord
to attack me, though he knows I have no extreme views, and
though he confesses that he is himself an extreme man. I am
not an extreme man. I am one who holds that middle position
as to doctrine in the Church that Richard Hooker held.'

The fate of the commission was sealed. Wilberforce dictated
its policy and its recommendations were phrased in words vague
enough to tolerate anything.[3] At the present day 'ritual' still
causes occasional breaches of the peace in London and elsewhere.

---

[1] Daniel, pp. 178–9.
[2] *Life of Stanley*, Vol. II, p. 210.
[3] Daniel, pp. 180–5.

There seemed no end to these controversies. First there was the Oxford Movement, which led to numerous secessions to the Church of Rome. Next came the intrusion of science in the form of *Essays and Reviews*, and no sooner was that settled—if it ever was settled—than another drift to the right had begun, with more impassioned speeches and futile argument.

Perhaps most ridiculous of all was the case of John William Colenso, Bishop of Natal, who five years previously had published a 'Rationalist' work on the Pentateuch. His case was still dragging on. Now he was deposed, now he was invited to retract. The Privy Council supported him against the Bishop of Capetown. He returned to Natal only to be excommunicated 'to be taken of the whole multitude of the faithful as a heathen man and a publican'. Stanley's impassioned speech on Colenso's behalf, in which he called upon Convocation to deal out to himself the same measure as was dealt to the Bishop of Natal, was published in September, 1867, during the Pan-Anglican Conference in Lambeth. Stanley also refused the Abbey to the Conference for its final service, because he feared that Wilberforce had swayed the delegates against Colenso and the Privy Council.

Such controversies were entirely alien to Dodgson's conception of religion.

'Jabberwocky', which might be called the theme-song of *Through the Looking-glass*, was probably complete by this time. Collingwood tells us that the poem was composed as Dodgson's contribution to a game of verse-making at the home of his cousins, the Misses Wilcox. Collingwood gives no date for this game of verse-making nor does he say whether he is referring to the first stanza only or the rest of the poem. The first stanza, as we know, appeared in *Misch-Masch*, dated Croft, 1855, with the title 'A Stanza of Anglo-Saxon Poetry'. This looks more like the result of a game than the rest of the poem, which cannot have been written before 1862, since only the first stanza appears in *Misch-Masch* and he was still keeping up that private anthology till then.

The first verse of 'Jabberwocky' is, let us freely admit, pure nonsense. It has the sound without the sense of the first verse of any poem. Like the mournful features of Charles Lamb's Dream Children, without speech it strangely impresses upon us the effects of speech. He invented pictures for it and explanations for the words, but it is better entirely unexplained. Then it does powerfully affect some region of the mind akin to that which appreciates music.

The remainder of the poem was written to conform. In 1850 he had invented a monster with 'face of grimliest green' for the readers of *The Rectory Umbrella*, with no other purpose than to make their flesh creep. He called it 'Horrors'. On this preliminary sketch, and all monsters whatever, he based his Jabberwock, which, its title shows, also acquired an allegorical significance. About 1884, the Fourth class of the Girls' Latin School in Boston, U.S., started a magazine and asked his permission to call it *The Jabberwock*. He replied that he had much pleasure in granting this request and added a derivation. 'Jabberwocky', it seems, is derived from the Anglo-Saxon 'wocer' or 'wocor' (offspring or fruit). 'Jabber' is the ordinary word 'jabber' meaning 'excited and voluble discussion' and the whole word thus means 'the result of much excited discussion'.[1]

That was very gracefully done. But the hideous monster which he must have encouraged Tenniel to draw for him suggests a different kind of excited discussion. It is, in fact, an embodiment of Controversy. The little St. George with his vorpal sword is made very attractive in Tenniel's drawing and could not possibly galumph. In the poem the monster-slayer is burlesqued as well as the monster. The Tum-tum tree is certainly the Thirty-nine Articles which people like Jowett signed, according to Dodgson, for the sake of their bread-and-butter (another of his recurrent symbols). It will be remembered that tum-tum is derived from its ablative *toto* or *in toto*, the manner in which the Thirty-nine Articles had to be accepted.

He may have written the poem without any precise meaning in mind, but the disgust he felt at the religious controversies around him and the apparent hopelessness of ending them by force ('Force without geniality,' said Tennyson, 'will do very little') found their way into the poem.

So far with confidence. It seems to me, also, that the Jubjub bird has some affinity with the 'treacle' of *Alice's Adventures* and the Bandersnatch with pepper. A jubjub, then as now, was sweet and soothing. Bandersnatch has a harsher sound. They

[1] Coll., p. 274.

might be the two opposite sides again, the Catholic and Protestant aspects of the English Church. Vorpal seems to be
concocted out of Verbal and Gospel by taking alternate letters
from each, and the poem vaguely burlesques the dragon-slayer
of *The Faerie Queen*, whose sword was the word of God.

The last verse is a repetition of the first. Nothing has really
changed. One Controversy has been slain (by the Church or
the University or the country), but the outgribing of the mome
raths is as strident as ever.

' "Somehow," said Alice, "it seems to fill my head with ideas
—only I don't exactly know what they are!" ' That was the
effect he intended to achieve. It seems incredible that the same
pen, and at about the same time, could have produced 'Bruno's
Revenge' for *Aunt Judy's Magazine*, edited by Mrs Alfred Gatty.
Sylvie and Bruno (1889) and *Sylvie and Bruno Concluded* (1893) had
cast their shadow before.

The little sermon on revenge is not without interest. Bruno is
a naughty little fairy who is spoiling Sylvie's garden because she
makes him do his lessons. The Narrator teaches him a better
kind of revenge—to make the garden beautiful. There are side-
glances at 'honours' (the various queer things we call 'an
honour' in this world) and fox-hunting (Bruno liked snail-
hunting). Bruno also gave an interesting account of the phases
of the moon:

'The moon's face gets dirtier and dirtier every night, till it's black
all across. And then, when it's dirty all over—so—' (he passed his
hand across his own rosy cheeks as he spoke) 'then she washes it.'

'Then it's all clean again, isn't it?'

'Not all in a moment,' said Bruno. 'What a deal of teaching oo
wants! She washes it little by little—only she begins at the other
edge, oo know.'

A most observant little fellow!

The Narrator too has some curious notions—'for instance, I
never could quite settle, supposing I were a moth, whether I
would rather be kept out of the candle, or be allowed to fly
straight in and get burnt'. Compare 'Looking-glass Insects':
'I wonder if that's the reason insects are so fond of flying into
candles—because they want to turn into Snap-dragon-flies!'
Lastly, there is the rule about finding fairies: 'that it must be a
very hot day—that we may consider as settled: and you must be
just a *little* sleepy—but not too sleepy to keep your eyes open,

G

mind. Well, and you ought to feel a little—what one may call "fairyish"—the Scotch call it "eerie", and perhaps that's a prettier word.' This is the state, a moment of trance, a falling from her, vanishing, which comes upon Alice as she stands musing before the looking-glass with the black kitten in her arms. But that was not written for *Aunt Judy*.

In 1866 Dodgson had printed an enigma by Bishop Wilber-force and his own 'explication' thereof. The answer was Man. In 1868 he produced two ciphers, a Telegraph-cipher and an Alphabet-cipher. To 1868 also belongs 'The Offer of the Clarendon Trustees', with its priceless suggestion that the University should provide 'a narrow strip of ground, railed off and carefully levelled, for investigating whether parallel lines meet or not: for this purpose, it should stretch, to use the expressive language of Euclid, "ever so far". This last process of "con-tinually producing the lines" may require centuries or more; but such a period, though long in the life of an individual, is as nothing in the life of the University.' A more serious mathe-matical work appeared about the same time, *The Fifth Book of Euclid, treated algebraically, so far as it relates to commensurable magnitudes*.

On 21 June, 1868, his father died, and this, he said, was the greatest blow that had ever befallen him.[1] There is no record of the conversations those two enjoyed at Croft or Ripon when Charles went home on vacation, but his father probably under-stood him better than anybody. First his mother, then Alice, now his father. There were still his brothers and sisters, but the family was scattered, and Croft Rectory with all its memories went with the living and like dreamy old Daresbury was trodden by the foot of the stranger. As if to emphasize the break with the past, he moved in November into his new and spacious rooms in Tom Quad.

By now *Through the Looking-glass* was beginning to take shape and we find its ideas spilling over into his correspondence. In three letters to the children of Arthur Hughes he produced a delightful little fantasy out of the *Looking-glass* symbols.

It seems from these letters that three cats came to his door at half-past four one afternoon. Enraged at their 'cross and dis-agreeable' appearance he seized a rolling pin and knocked them

[1] Coll., p. 131.

down, 'as flat as pan-cakes'. In the next letter he makes it clear
what he means by 'flat'. They lay there 'like dried flowers' till he
lifted them up and put them to bed in the portfolio with pen-
wipers for pillows and blotting paper for sheets. In the third
letter he describes how he gave them each a spoonful of ink as a
treat, as a result of which they 'made dreadful faces', and one
that had been white turned black.[1] Here are the cats, the
blotting-paper out of which the White Knight was trying to
cook his pudding, the idea of flatness again and the bottle of ink
which was the only liquid Alice could find in Looking-glass
House.

He was also preparing his poems for publication and presumably writing 'Phantasmagoria', the piece of pure levity on
the subject of ghosts which gave its title to the volume. He
chose thirteen of his lighter poems and thirteen serious ones. All
but seven had appeared in various periodicals.

'The Valley of the Shadow of Death' was written two months
before the death of his father and has therefore no reference to it.
Rather is it a confession of world-weariness in which the idea of
suicide is allowed to appear.

> I heard a whisper, cold and clear,
>   That is the gate of Death.
>
> O bitter is it to abide
>   In weariness alway:
> At dawn to sigh for eventide,
>   At eventide for day.
> Thy noon hath fled: thy sun hath shone:
> The brightness of thy day is gone:
> What need to lag and linger on
>   Till life be cold and gray?
>
> 'O well,' it said, 'beneath yon pool
>   In some still cavern deep,
> The fevered brain might slumber cool,
>   The eyes forget to weep:
> Within that goblet's mystic rim
> Are draughts of healing, stored for him
> Whose heart is sick, whose sight is dim,
>   Who prayeth but to sleep!'

He flees temptation, of course, and is restored to happiness by
the sight of two children in a cottage reading the Bible. One
he eventually marries, but she dies and leaves him alone again

[1] Coll., pp. 420–3.

with his only son, to whom on his death-bed he is confiding this long-kept secret.

> But if there be—O if there be
> A truth in what they say,
> That angel-forms we cannot see
> Go with us on our way,
> Then surely she is with me here,
> I dimly feel her spirit near—
> The morning-mists grow thin and clear,
> And Death brings in the day.

The mood is significant.

More important, perhaps, were some of the poems he left out of this selection, for these were the ones he intended to use in *Through the Looking-glass*. One was the White Knight's ballad, which, as 'Upon the Lonely Moor' had appeared in *The Train* in 1856. It was then offered as the original of Wordsworth's 'Resolution and Independence', 'painful as its appearance must be . . . '. Like almost all Dodgson's parodies, however, it had a dual purpose—to imitate a well-known original and to express some definite idea of his own. Here are two voices both apparently talking nonsense. They are, however, clearly distinguishable; it is impossible to mistake one for the other.

> He said, 'I look for soap-bubbles
> That lie among the wheat
> And bake them into mutton-pies
> And sell them in the street . . .'
>
> His accents mild took up the tale:
> He said, 'I go my ways,
> And when I find a mountain-rill
> I set it in a blaze,
> And thence they make a stuff they call
> Rowland's Macassar Oil;
> But fourpence-halfpenny is all
> They give me for my toil.'
>
> He said, 'I hunt for haddock's eyes
> Among the heather bright,
> And work them into waistcoat buttons,
> In the silent night.
> And these I do not sell for gold,
> Or coin of silver shine,
> But for a copper halfpenny,
> And that will purchase nine.'

It is a humble, yet practical voice, the voice of commerce or applied science. The aged, aged man takes the wonders of nature, subjects them to some ridiculous process or other and gains some insignificant reward.

The other is an irritable but preoccupied voice, the voice of one who has suddenly noticed something inexplicable and is attempting to force an explanation from it while attending to more important matters.

> But I was thinking of a way
>   To multiply by ten,
> And always in the answer get
>   The question back again.
> I did not hear a word he said
>   But kicked that old man calm,
> And said, 'Come tell me how you live!'
>   And pinched him in the arm.

> But I was thinking of a plan
>   To paint one's gaiters green
> So much the colour of the grass
>   That they could ne'er be seen.
> I heard him then, for I had just
>   Completed my design
> To keep the Menai bridge from rust
>   By boiling it in wine.

Here we have mathematics, philosophy, pure science as opposed to their mercenary derivative with his low cunning and ingratiating manner.

> 'And that's the way' (he gave a wink)
>   'I get my living here,
> And very gladly will I drink
>   Your honour's health in beer.'

The last verse has something more profound to yield, a really startling idea from the borderland of mathematics and metaphysics:

> 'And now,' says the voice of theory,
> 'And now if e'er by chance I put
>   My fingers into glue
> Or madly squeeze a right-hand foot
>   Into a left-hand shoe,
> Or if a statement I aver,
>   Of which I am not sure,
> I think of that strange wanderer
>   Upon the lonely moor.'

In the *Looking-glass* version, the last verse is altered significantly.

In place of:

> Or if a statement I aver,
> Of which I am not sure.

he introduced an illustration of the law of gravity:

> Or if I drop upon my toe
> A very heavy weight,

and his aged, aged man was no longer 'upon a lonely moor', but 'a-sitting on a gate'. But he retained:

> And now, if e'er by chance I put
> My fingers into glue
> Or madly squeeze a right-hand foot
> Into a left-hand shoe.

These lines contain two illustrations of a strange phenomenon, so obvious that we never notice it. It might be called 'oppositeness', the difference and the resemblance between our right and left hands, or feet or ears. They seem to be identical in all respects, these pairs of opposites, and yet they cannot be proved identical. They are known as 'mirror-images': Kant called them 'incongruent counterparts'. The ancient world failed to notice the principle altogether.

Take a pair of triangles, oppositely situated one to another. It is easy to prove them congruent.

Apply the triangle ABC to the triangle DEF—lift it up, that is, take it out of its plane surface, in which it has lived all its life, turn it over in our space, of which it knows nothing, and lay it down so that it coincides with its counterparts or mirror-image.

Unfortunately we cannot use this method to prove the congruence of the spaces occupied by our hands—spaces such as might be left if we put them into glue and took them out again, or such as we leave when we take our feet out of our shoes.

Kant thought the fact that we cannot use 'superposition' with such bodies as screws with left and right threads, pairs of hands and feet, and (simplest possible case) spherical triangles, was due to the nature of our space, which lacked an additional dimension where the 'turning over' of a left hand into a right hand could be performed.

I think it extremely probable that Dodgson had read, or at least heard discussed in some detail, Kant's little pre-critical work *On the First Ground for the Distinctions of Regions in Space* (1768). In trying to make clear the nature of an asymmetrical

body, Kant uses a written page: 'In a written page, for instance
. . . the very same writing becomes unrecognizable when seen
in such a way that everything which formerly was from left to
right is reversed and is viewed from right to left'.[1] This, of
course, is how all Looking-glass books appear to Alice. She has
to hold them up to a looking-glass to read them. Dodgson had
a special block made, with reversed type, to illustrate this.

Again, he must have known about Pasteur's work on crystals
which began in 1846 when he was studying tartaric and paratartaric acids. Pasteur knew that natural tartaric acid, as found in
wine, polarized light to the right, whereas paratartaric acid
made in the laboratory had no polarizing effect on light whatever. He examined the crystals of paratartaric acid and saw
that they were of two kinds, identical except that they were
what Kant would have called 'incongruent counterparts'. These
he separated by hand, with the result that he could now make
two substances, one polarizing light to the left and the other to
the right.

'His delight,' says his son-in-law, 'was so great that he quitted
the laboratory abruptly.' Hardly had he gone outside when he
met the assistant of the physical professor. He embraced him,
told him that he had just made an exciting discovery and haled
him off to the Luxembourg to explain it in detail. The Academy
of Sciences was excited but sceptical. M. Biot insisted on having
the experiment repeated. Pasteur was asked to prepare the
crystals, whereupon M. Biot performed the rest of the experiment himself. Its success was complete. Visibly moved, the old
man seized Pasteur by the arm and said, 'My dear child, I have
loved science so well throughout my life that this makes my
heart beat'.[2]

Pasteur on various occasions philosophized on his discovery.
He noted that the universe as a whole is dissymmetric, and
thought that symmetry and dissymmetry might provide the
long-sought distinction between animate and inanimate matter.
His arguments were seized on by people who, as Professor
Tyndall said, 'dreading materialism were ready to welcome any
generalization which seemed to differentiate the living world
from the dead'.

[1] Translation by John Handyside, pp. 21–2.
[2] Lady Claud Hamilton: *Life of Pasteur*, pp. 18–20.

Pasteur also thought that it might be possible to produce not only new substances, but new vegetable and animal species by replacing in the living cells cellulose, albumen and so on by synthetic substances with an opposite polarizing effect on light. Microscopic plants, he noticed, preferred one form of tartaric acid to the other.[1] 'Perhaps,' Alice mused, holding the kitten up to the looking-glass, 'perhaps Looking-glass milk isn't good to drink—'

On 1 December, 1856 (the year of the White Knight's ballad), at the Anniversary Meeting of the Royal Society, the Rumford Medal was awarded to M. Pasteur 'for his discovery of the nature of racemic acid and its relations to polarized light'. In the absence of the Foreign Secretary, Dr Sharpey was asked to transmit the medal to M. Pasteur 'in testimony of the value which we attach to his brilliant discovery'.

A clear account of Pasteur's work in this field (not that for which he is now so universally known) was given by the President: 'The acid,' said Lord Wrottesley, 'obtained from the right-handed crystals proved to be absolutely identical with tartaric acid in all its properties; that obtained from the left-handed crystals proved to be identical, so to speak, with the image of tartaric acid in a mirror.'[2]

No doubt the Rev. Bartholomew Price, F.R.S., knew about Pasteur's discoveries long before 1856, and it was the kind of subject in which his young friend Dodgson could hardly fail to be interested.

It was a different Alice who first went through the looking-glass, Alice Raikes, a distant relative of Dodgson's, afterwards Mrs Wilson Fox. He was staying with his uncle in Onslow Square, South Kensington, when he overheard some children who were playing in the gardens address one of their number as Alice.

Dodgson introduced himself to the party. 'So you are another Alice,' he said to the little girl. 'I am very fond of Alices. Will you come with me and see something which is rather puzzling?'

He took the whole party into his uncle's house and putting an orange into Alice's hand, said: 'Which hand is that orange in?'

[1] Lady Claud Hamilton: *Life of Pasteur*, pp. 29–38.
[2] *Proceedings of the Royal Society*, Vol. VIII, pp. 254–6.

'My right hand,' said the child.

'Now,' he said, 'go and look at the little girl in the glass over there and tell me which hand *she* is holding the orange in.'

Alice surveyed her reflection gravely. 'She is holding it in her left hand,' she said.

'How do you explain that?'

The reply, when it came, he regarded as a good one.

'Supposing I was on the *other* side of the glass,' she said, 'wouldn't the orange still be in my right hand?'

'Well done, little Alice,' he exclaimed. 'It's the best answer I've had yet.'[1]

Apparently he told friends afterwards that this incident suggested Looking-glass Land to him; but the anecdote itself proves that he was already thinking about the matter.

Another source of *Looking-glass* ideas was a scientific fantasy or paradox propounded by Gustav Theodor Fechner. Fechner was Dodgson's counterpart at the University of Leipzig. In 1839 he had resigned his professorship of physics owing to an injury to his eyes, but continued to give public lectures; he published serious books under his own name and lighter work under a pseudonym, 'Dr Mises'. It was in any case probable that Dodgson-Carroll would hear of Fechner-Mises, but the presence of Max Müller at Christ Church made this inevitable. Professor Müller had been at school (1836–41) and University (1841–4) in Leipzig before coming to Oxford by way of Berlin, Paris and London. He probably corresponded with Fechner and there were books by Fechner in his library.

'Space Has Four Dimensions' was one of the *Vier Paradoxe* (Four Paradoxes) published by Fechner, as Dr Mises, in 1846. It is a delightful mixture of science and satire, with asides very much after Dodgson's own manner. Fechner proves that time is really a fourth dimension by the process, now quite familiar, of removing one of the other three. He imagines a small coloured manikin running round on the paper in a camera obscura (a character in one of Walt Disney's animated cartoons would be a modern equivalent) and points out that such a being would know as little of the third as we of a fourth dimension. Yet the third exists for us.

---

[1] *A Selection from the Letters of Lewis Carroll to his Child Friends,* ed. E. M. Hatch, pp. 8–9. See also Mrs Wilson Fox's letter in *The Times,* 15 January, 1932.

What is this fourth dimension? Pass the silhouette or manikin of the surface through the third dimension along the beam of light. 'As it comes into other areas of light, it will itself be altered thereby and perhaps at the end of the way it will appear pale and wrinkled, whereas at the beginning it was smooth and round.' It cannot understand this, of course, but remarks rather pathetically: 'There is something which I call time and in time everything changes, even I', which is exactly what we say ourselves.

This, says Fechner, is due to the movement of our space of three dimensions through the fourth, of which movement we perceive only the passage of time and the consequent change. At each moment we have a cross-section of this larger reality, of which as a whole we know nothing, any more than, shall we say, Donald Duck, were he conscious, would know of the world beyond his screen.

There is no reason, says Fechner, in this following Plato, why time should not run back instead of forward, and he imagines, as Plato does, the graves opening, and the whole history of the world in reverse. There is no golden age in Fechner's vision. All humanity returns to Adam, while Adam himself is crushed into clay and taken up with the earth, sea, sun and stars into the original Oneness of God.

Another weird idea of Fechner's was that motion is an illusion. This he illustrated by means of beams of light. Here is his diagram:

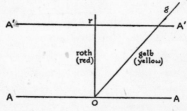

A beam of red light and a beam of yellow light are focused on one spot on a sheet of paper, producing an orange patch. If the paper is now passed along the red beam, the red spot will remain where it is in the centre of the paper, but the yellow spot will appear to travel across the sheet towards the edge and the more oblique the beam the more rapid will be the 'movement' of the spot.

Movement in our world of three dimensions, therefore, is due merely to the movement of our universe along the fourth dimension. Mathematicians, he says, will have to face a new geometry of four dimensions (Arthur Cayley had already done so) but will no longer have to worry about the subject of dynamics. The variable 't' will appear as the fourth co-ordinate of space.

As will be shown, Dodgson used ideas identical to these in his White Queen who 'lived backwards' and his Red Queen who made Alice run 'faster, faster' in order to remain in the same place.

From the satirical asides, too, he derived some valuable hints. Fechner distinguishes two classes of people who will be particularly difficult to convince of the existence of the Fourth Dimension: 'naturalists, who believe only what they see, and philosophers, who see only what they believe'. They have in fact very little notion of the third dimension:

Naturalists know only length and breadth—except, that is, for astronomers who spend all their time looking up, only to see everything the wrong way round in their telescopes. The fall of bodies forces them to recognize the third dimension at least as a hypothesis. But where, they ask, is the fourth dimension?

From this Dodgson got further hints for his White Queen and White Knight, while his Red Queen has affinities with Fechner's philosophers:

Philosophers try to get as far as possible from reality so that it will not confuse them. They sit in an armchair until the pure concept of space comes to them. It comes, but it has four dimensions, and the door-keeper will admit only three. Space leaves a dimension outside and the philosophers are satisfied.

Fechner was not proving a scientific theory. He was exploring possibilities of humour as well as of metaphysics and one of his humorous ideas was that of a world of one dimension—that along which people make progress. 'All friends of progress, freedom and equality will recognize their ideal in this world of One Dimension.' He wishes them joy of it: 'How thin must be the sausage if the whole world is only as thick as a mathematical line'.[1]

When Dodgson became acquainted with Fechner's profound flippancies or frivolous profundities it is impossible to say. He

[1] Condensed from an oral translation by Mr David Penman, M.A.

had had some fleeting glimpses of flatland before the *Looking-glass* period, but these he could easily have obtained for himself direct from mathematics.

The same applies to the looking-glass idea, which is strikingly illustrated in the subject of algebra:

$$a^2 + 1 = 0$$
$$a^2 = -1$$

'One' seems to have gone through the looking-glass into a mysterious country where everything is the wrong way round.

Again, if a^2 equals minus one then a must equal the square root of minus one ($a = \sqrt{-1}$) and that as a quantity is meaningless or, as mathematicians say, 'imaginary'.

The great adventurer in this imaginary world was Sir William Rowan Hamilton, born in Dublin in 1805, whose *Elements of Quaternions* was published in 1866 and attracted the attention of mathematicians everywhere. I think it quite certain, however, that Dodgson had read his earlier work on the subject, the *Lectures on Quaternions* of 1852, where the words of the introduction chime in so remarkably with Dr Mises, his notion of time as a dimension and even his world of one dimension, progress.

Hamilton thought that expressions which had hitherto been regarded as 'merely symbolical' might acquire reality and significance if Algebra were regarded not as a science of quantity but as the Science of Order in Progression.

It was, however, a part of this conception that the progression here spoken of was understood to be *continuous* and *undimensional*, extending indefinitely *forward* and *backward* but not in any *lateral* direction. And although the successive *states* of such progression might (no doubt) be represented by *points upon a line*, yet I thought that their simple successiveness was better conceived by comparing them with *moments of time*, divested, however, of all reference to *cause* and *effect*; so that the 'time' here considered might be said to be abstract, ideal or *pure*, like that 'space' which is the object of geometry. In this manner I was led, many years ago, to regard algebra as the Science of Pure Time.

A chess-board is a squared surface, like a piece of graph-paper. Its two dimensions need not be length and breadth. One of them, the length of the board, might be time. In that case the other could represent any or all of the dimensions of our space. But mathematicians know of a time of two dimensions, to which they are led by the elliptic functions discovered by Abel in 1825 and made known to the mathematical world by Jacobi four years later.[1] At the end of his charming little 'quotation' about the lines that wended their way across the plane superficies, Dodgson wrote: 'Jacobi's *Course of Mathematics*, Chap. I'. Now, Jacobi never published a Course of Mathematics, nor was Dodgson's fantasy a quotation from any of Jacobi's works. He was simply 'showing off'. He was the kind of mathematician to whom Jacobi meant something. We may take it that he knew about the elliptic functions.

In *Alice* he had had some fun with scales of notation and the dynamics of a particle. In *Through the Looking-glass* he needed quaternions, elliptic functions and multi-dimensional geometry! Fortunately, however, the use he made of them was purely imaginative, when it was not purely mischievous. He used them, or the ideas they suggested, to make a non-Euclidean world, peopled it with chess-men and nursery-rhyme grotesques, and into it sent his lost Alice, wool-gathering.

> Still she haunts me, phantomwise,
> Alice moving under skies,
> Never seen by waking eyes.

He met her there—there the two lines could meet, though not for long.

'I'll see you safe to the end of the wood—and then I must go back, you know. That's the end of my move.'

Then they parted, and as Alice 'turned away with an eager look' on the last stage of her pawn's progress to Queendom, he had to say—'But you'll stay and see me off first? I shan't be long. You'll wait and wave your handkerchief when I get to that turn in the road? I think it'll encourage me, you see.'

So they shook hands and then the Knight rode slowly away into the forest . . . and then she waved her handkerchief to him, and waited till he was out of sight.

[1] E. T. Bell: *History of Mathematics*, pp. 365 and 370.

CHAPTER FIVE

Through the Looking-glass

THE first chapter of *Through the Looking-glass* was sent to the press 'a few days after the publication of *Phantasmagoria*', which appeared in January, 1869.[1] Dodgson must therefore have been writing, as opposed to jotting down ideas, at least since his removal to Tom Quad. On 19 April, 1870, he wrote to Miss Mary Marshal, 'I don't know when it will be finished'.[2] It was published in December, 1871. Fortunately Tenniel had relented and did supply the illustrations.

In *Alice's Adventures* Dodgson had ingeniously concealed certain amusing little problems and 'leg-pulls'. He deliberately cast *Through the Looking-glass* in the form of an enigma, a form which appealed to his love of innocent deception and which Kingsley had suggested in *The Water Babies*:

> Come read me a riddle
> Each good little man:
> If you cannot read it
> No grown-up folks can.

And if you will read this story nine times over, and then think for yourself, you will find out why. It is not good for little boys to be told everything, and never to be forced to use their wits.

Compare with this the old sheep's remark: 'I never put things into people's hands; that would never do. They must get them for themselves.'

In 1888 he wrote to Nellie Knight from Eastbourne: 'I'm rather puzzled which book to send to Sydney. He looks so young for *Through the Looking-glass*. However, he found out one puzzle . . . that I don't remember anyone of his age ever guessing before, so I think it won't be too old a book for him.' What Sydney made of it as a puzzle is not recorded. No doubt he enjoyed it as a story.

It is not my intention to go through the book squeezing the last drop of meaning from every word. That would take a very long time—supposing it to be possible, which is by no means

---

[1] Coll., p. 138; *Handbook*, p. 236.
[2] *Letters of Lewis Carroll*, ed. E. M. Hatch, p. 79.

certain. As Dodgson said in a letter to a friend in America, 'words mean more than we mean to express when we use them; so a whole book ought to mean a great deal more than the writer means'.[1] Let us, however, examine some of the ideas on which the book is based.

In the first place he used the time-honoured dream-machinery, that mediaeval framework for allegory and satire, but he used it with a difference. How long does a dream last? By the clock, Alice's dream lasts hardly any time at all. When it begins Dinah is washing her white kitten and she is still washing it when Alice awakes—if she has ever been asleep. She has been in some kind of trance, like 'the vision of the prophet Mahommed, in which he saw the whole wonders of heaven and hell, though the jar of water which fell when his ecstasy commenced had not spilled its contents when he returned to ordinary existence'.

In *Bruno's Revenge* (1867) Dodgson had explained what he meant by the 'eerie' state. Twenty-six years later, in the Preface to *Sylvie and Bruno Concluded*, he elaborated his views:

It may interest some of my Readers to know the *theory* on which this story is constructed. It is an attempt to show what might *possibly* happen, supposing that Fairies really existed; and that they were sometimes visible to us and we to them; and supposing also, that human beings might sometimes become conscious of what goes on in the Fairy-world—by actual transference of their immaterial essence, such as we meet with in 'Esoteric Buddhism'.

I have supposed a Human Being to be capable of various psychic states, with varying degrees of consciousness, as follows:

(*a*) The ordinary state, with no consciousness of the presence of Fairies;

(*b*) The 'eerie' state, in which, while conscious of actual surroundings, he is *also* conscious of the presence of Fairies;

(*c*) A form of trance, in which, while *un*conscious of actual surroundings and apparently asleep, he (i.e. his immaterial essence) migrates to other scenes, in the actual world, or in Fairyland, and is conscious of the presence of Fairies.

I have also supposed a Fairy to be capable of migrating from Fairyland into the actual world, and of assuming at pleasure a Human form; and also to be capable of various psychical states, viz.:

(*a*) The ordinary state, with no consciousness of the presence of Human Beings.

(*b*) A sort of 'eerie' state, in which he is conscious, if in the actual

[1] Coll., p. 173.

world, of the presence of actual Human Beings, if in Fairy-
land, of the presence of the immaterial essences of Human
Beings.

I will here tabulate the passages in both Volumes, where abnormal
states occur.

And he does.

In *Through the Looking-glass* Alice is in the normal state at the
beginning and the end of the story. She is 'eerie' in Looking-
glass House and when she has 'entered the palace', just before
she awakes. In the garden and on the chess-board she is in the
trance state.

The chess-pieces, too, have their various states. In Looking-
glass House they are unconscious of Alice's presence; that is,
they are in 'the ordinary state, with no consciousness of the
presence of Human Beings'. But in the game they are conscious
of the presence of Alice's immaterial essence. Near the end of
the game the Queens fall asleep and dream of Alice's world.
They are presumably in the trance state then. The Red King is
in the trance state throughout and the White Knight might be
said to be permanently 'eerie'.

The rather irritating question 'Which dreamed it?' with its
Kantian or Berkeleyan overtones derives from Dodgson's
original ending to *Alice's Adventures Under Ground*:

But her sister sat there some while longer, watching the setting
sun, and thinking of little Alice and her adventures, till she, too,
began dreaming after a fashion, and this was her dream.

She saw an ancient city, and a quiet river winding near it along
the plain, and up the stream went slowly gliding a boat with a merry
party of children on board—she could hear the voices and laughter
like music over the water—and among them was another little
Alice, who sat listening with bright, eager eyes, to a tale that was
being told, and she listened for the words of the tale, and lo, it was
the dream of her own little sister.

Less original was the looking-glass idea. It cannot be a
coincidence that within a year of each other appeared *Through
the Looking-glass* (1872) and *Erewhon* (1871), both about worlds
where everything is the mirror-image of what we regard as
normal. Yet it is as certain as anything can be that the books
were written independently. Kingsley had used a similar idea
in *The Water Babies*, where Tom found the Other-End-of
Nowhere much more like This-End-of-Somewhere than he had
been in the habit of expecting. And before that there was the

THROUGH THE LOOKING-GLASS

Taylor sisters' *Signor Topsy Turvey's Wonderful Magic Lantern; or The World Turned Upside Down* (1810). Yet Dodgson's use of the looking-glass idea was all his own.

The difference between *Erewhon* and *Through the Looking-glass* is profound. Butler begins realistically, as Swift did in *Gulliver's Travels*, but soon throws aside all pretence and reveals his purpose as satirical. Dodgson pretends throughout to be writing 'nonsense'. He acknowledges no obligation to stick to one subject but slides from topic to topic by subtle associations of ideas. Nevertheless, meaning is always there, flowing along like a deep, dark river, with the puns and patter as the play of light on the surface.

Again, Butler used his reversals to cast doubts on the moral and ethical standards of Victorian England. His looking-glass was the circle of stone figures at the head of the pass, six or seven times larger than life, of great antiquity and ten in number, our tribal taboos, the Ten Commandments. Dodgson's satire was directed, as on previous occasions, against controversy in religious matters, while his explorations were mainly in that no-man's-land between mathematics and theology into which he had already made some short expeditions.

Another basic idea was that of sending his heroine into a game of chess, and for this he had made, as we have seen, some preliminary sketches from life. Drawing from life was a matter of principle with him and he recommended it in the most explicit manner to all his illustrators, even over-ruling Tenniel, who said he no more needed a model in front of him than Dodgson needed a multiplication table.

Chess to Dodgson was something far more than a game. As a mathematician he saw the board like a sheet of graph-paper on which it is possible to represent almost anything, and as a theologian he saw in the two sides a far more powerful means of expressing the opposing factions in Church and University than any he had previously hit upon.

Let us begin by examining the most striking and original episode in the whole book, the Red Queen running. Alice, it will be remembered, had met her—by walking away from her —in the garden of live flowers. With her she went to the top of the Principal Mountain and saw all the world she was to enter spread out beneath her in the form of a large chess-board.

H

'It's a great game of chess that's being played—all over the world—if this *is* the world at all you know.'

Alice longed to join in and would have preferred to be a Queen, but at first she could only be the White Queen's Pawn, though the post held good prospects of eventual Queendom.

Just at this moment, somehow or other they began to run.

Alice never could quite make out, in thinking it over afterwards, how it was that they began: all she remembers is, that they were running hand in hand, and the Queen went so fast that it was all she could do to keep up with her: and still the Queen kept crying 'Faster!'

Stranger still was the fact that 'the trees and the other things round them never changed their places at all: however fast they went, they never seemed to pass anything'.

No doubt many of the clever and profound things said of this running are perfectly true. It may anticipate Einstein. It may be a spiritual journey which leaves her where she started. But the basis of the running is a mathematical trick. In our world speed is the ratio of distance to time: $s = d \div t$. For a high speed, the distance is great and the time small; so many miles per hour. Through the Looking-glass, however, speed is the ratio of time to distance: $s = t \div d$. For a high speed the time is great and the distance small. The higher the speed, the smaller the distance covered. The faster Alice went in time, the more she stayed where she was in space.

'Now *here*, you see, it takes all the running *you* can do to keep in the same place.'

This is Fechner's variable 't' which became the fourth co-ordinate of space.

'Are we nearly there?'

'Nearly there?' the Queen repeated. 'Why, we passed it ten minutes ago! Faster!'

They had left our space behind and were running in time.

The Queen propped her against a tree, and said kindly, 'You may rest a little now.'

Alice looked round her in great surprise. 'Why I do believe we've been under this tree all the time! Everything's just as it was.'

Note 'all the time'. No wonder the clock on the chimney-piece had the face of a little old man and grinned at her!

The White Queen, too, was at home in this unfamiliar

element, as her 'living backwards' shows. In this, Dodgson was using an idea developed by Plato in the *Statesman* and by Fechner in his 'Space Has Four Dimensions'. Plato's reversal of time involves an earth-shaking convulsion, after which the dead rise from the earth and 'live in the opposite order'. This, he says, was the fabled golden age. Fechner's is set in the future but is upon the same cosmic scale. 'Growing old will cease,' he says, 'but all life will consist of rejuvenation.' He goes further than Plato and returns us all to our grand ancestor Adam in the Garden of Eden, and Adam, with the whole earth and sea and the sun and the stars, into the Oneness of God.

Dodgson's treatment of the idea is quite different, but certainly not less effective. In the simplest possible terms, he states and then illustrates the principle:

'It's a poor sort of memory that only works backwards,' the Queen remarked.

'What sort of things do *you* remember best?' Alice ventured to ask.

'Oh, things that happened the week after next,' the Queen replied in a careless tone.

This, of course, follows from the game of chess, as well as the looking-glass oppositeness. If the length of the board is time, then one direction must be forwards and the other backwards. The King's Messenger, for instance, Hatta (the Mad Hatter) is 'in prison now, being punished: and the trial doesn't even begin till next Wednesday: and of course the crime comes last of all'.

All through this particular *reductio ad absurdum* the White Queen is plastering her finger. Then she screams that it is bleeding, though she has not pricked it yet. She will—and does —when she fastens her shawl again.

'That accounts for the bleeding, you see,' she said to Alice with a smile. 'Now you understand the way things happen here.'

'But why don't you scream now?' Alice asked, holding her hands ready to put over her ears again.

'Why, I've done all the screaming already,' said the Queen. 'What would be the good of having it all over again?'

Alice was a pawn. 'Let's pretend we're kings and queens,' she had said to her sister, but a pawn she had to be. In time, we human beings are the merest pawns. We move in one direction, forward from one moment to the next, as a pawn moves forward from one square to the next. A pawn's world is Fechner's world of one dimension, pure progress, or Hamilton's abstract, ideal or pure time, like that space which is the object of geometry. Nevertheless, the pawn's world is not a knife edge, a time-line. Alice does not appear to be able to see even the whole of one square all at once, yet she has some knowledge of the square on either side of her. Dodgson is no doubt conventionalizing the taking move, which does affect the square on either side one ahead. Alice is not interested in 'taking' anything, unless we count 'taking notice'. Or he may be thinking of the fact that pieces are not always set exactly in the centre of the square they occupy, but jostle each other a little and overlap into adjoining squares. 'J'adoube.'

At all events, Alice when she is a pawn is continually meeting chess-men, red and white, and according to the key, they are always on the square next to her on one side or the other. To the right, she meets the Red Queen, the Red King, the Red Knight, the White Knight and, at the end of the board, the Red Queen again. To the left, she meets the White Queen, the White King and, at the end of the board, the White Queen again. Of what is happening in the other parts of the board she has no knowledge. She sweeps a narrow track, and events more than one square distant to either side, or behind, or ahead of her, are out of her world. A certain lack of coherence in her picture of the game is understandable, particularly as it is in an advanced stage when she begins to move.

In the *Lewis Carroll Handbook*, Falconer Madan regrets that 'the chess framework is full of absurdities and impossibilities' and considers it a pity that Dodgson did not bring the game, as a game, up to chess standard, as, says Mr Madan, he could easily have done. He points out that among other absurdities the white side is allowed to make nine consecutive moves, the White King to be checked unnoticed; Queens castle, and the White Queen flies from the Red Knight when she could take it. 'Hardly a move,' he says, 'has a sane purpose, from the point of view of chess.'[1] There is also a mate for White at the fourth move (Dodgson's reckoning): W.Q. to K.'s 3rd instead of Q.B.'s 4th. Alice and the Red Queen are both out of the way and the Red King could not move out of check.

Dodgson's own words, in a preface written in 1887, in reply to criticism of this kind, are as follows:

[1] *Handbook*, pp. 48–9.

As the chess problem given on a previous page has puzzled some of my readers, it may be well to explain that it is correctly worked out so far as the *moves* are concerned. The alternation of Red and White is perhaps not so strictly observed as it might be, and the 'castling' of the three Queens is merely a way of saying that they entered the palace; but the 'check' of the White King at move 6, the capture of the Red Knight at move 7, and the final 'checkmate' of the Red King, will be found, by any one who will take the trouble to set the pieces and play the moves as directed, to be strictly in accordance with the laws of the game.

He was not interested in the game as a game, but in the implications of the moves. Dodgson could easily have 'worked out a problem'. He spent a considerable part of his life doing that kind of thing. But in *Through the Looking-glass* he was otherwise engaged. In the first place it would be illogical to expect logic in a game of chess dreamed by a child. It would be still more illogical to expect a pawn which can see only a small patch of board to understand the meaning of its experiences. And there is a moral in that. This is a pawn's impression of chess, which is like a human being's impression of life.

Alice never grasps the purpose of the game at all and when she reaches the Eighth Square tries to find out from the two Queens if it is over. None of the pieces has the least idea what it is all about. The Red King is asleep. The White King has long ago abandoned any attempt to intervene. 'You might as well try to catch a Bandersnatch.' The Red Knight is quite justified in his battle-cry of 'Ahoy! Ahoy! Check!' but the White Knight, too, leaps out of the wood, shouting 'Ahoy! Ahoy! Check!' and he is not giving check at all but capturing the Red Knight. Neither of them has any control over the square on which Alice is situated, yet the Red Knight thinks he has captured her and the White Knight that he has rescued her. Alice cannot argue with either of them but is simply relieved to have the matter settled in a manner favourable to herself.

As for the Queens, they 'see' so much of the board that they might be expected to know what is happening fairly well. But, as will appear, their manner of 'seeing' is so peculiar that they know less about it than anybody. To understand one's part in a game of chess, one would have to be aware of the room and the unseen intelligence which is combining the pieces. Deprived of any such knowledge, the chess-men have to explain things as best they can. Nor is this a game between two players. To have made it that would have been tantamount to a confession that he believed in two separate and opposite Powers above us. Dodgson deliberately avoided any such implication.

He based his story, not on a game of chess, but on a chess lesson or demonstration of the moves such as he gave to Alice Liddell, a carefully worked-out sequence of moves designed to illustrate the queening of a pawn, the relative powers of the pieces—the feeble king, the eccentric knight and the formidable queen whose powers include those of rook and bishop—and finally a checkmate. That is to say, he abstracted from the game exactly what he wanted for his design, and expressed that as a game between a child of seven-and-a-half who was to 'be' a White Pawn and an older player (himself) who was to manipulate the other pieces.

Only the other day, it will be remembered, Alice had had a long argument with her sister about playing kings and queens. Alice had been reduced at last to saying, 'Well, *you* can be one of them, then, and *I'll* be all the rest.' Through the Looking-glass she was 'one of them' and the Other Player 'all the rest'. Perhaps that is how things are. Dodgson certainly hoped so.

Observe the Red Queen about to do her disappearing-trick:

'At the end of two yards,' she said, putting in a peg to mark the distance, 'I shall give you your directions—have another biscuit?' The biscuit is deliberately used to distract our attention from the fact that these pegs mark out the stages of Alice's pawn-life.

'At the end of *three* yards I shall repeat them—for fear of your forgetting them. At the end of *four*, I shall say good-bye. And at the end of *five*, I shall go!'

She had got all the pegs put in by this time, and Alice looked on with great interest as she returned to the tree, and then began slowly walking down the row.

At the two-yard peg she faced round, and said, 'A pawn goes two squares in its first move.'

To demonstrate that, she had walked two yards. As a pawn starts from the second square, that takes us to the fourth square on the board. The third peg marks the fifth square, the fourth the sixth and the fifth the seventh. There is still another square, the eighth, but on that Alice will no longer be a pawn. ' "In the Eighth Square we shall be Queens together, and it's all feasting and fun!" '

The Red Queen had begun 'slowly walking down the row'. At the two-yard peg she paused to give Alice her instructions. Alice got up and curtseyed, and sat down again. At the next peg the Queen jerked out some staccato remarks. She did not wait for Alice to curtsey this time, but 'walked on quickly' to the next peg, where she turned to say goodbye and then 'hurried' on to the last. She was getting up speed. 'How it happened, Alice never knew, but exactly as she came to the last peg, she was gone.'

What happened we can represent but not really imagine. According to the key, the Red Queen moved away from Alice at an angle across the board (R.Q. to K.R.'s 4th).

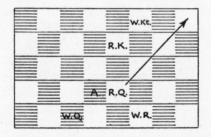

So long as the Red Queen was in the square next to her, Alice could see her and hear her, but when she steamed off in a direction which did not as yet exist for Alice, she simply vanished.

Whether she vanished into the air, or ran quickly into the wood ('and she *can* run very fast!' thought Alice), there was no way of guessing, but she was gone, and Alice began to remember that she was a pawn, and that it would soon be time to move.

The moves of the two Queens are inexplicable to Alice because of a limitation in her powers. She is unable to conceive of such moves as R.Q. to K.R.'s 4th or W.Q. to Q.B.'s 4th. They can zig-zag about the board, sweep from end to end of it if they like, or from side to side. She must laboriously crawl from square to square, always in one direction, with a half-remembered promise to spur her on: ' "In the Eighth Square we shall be Queens together, and it's all feasting and fun!" '

But if the length of the board is time, the breadth of the board must be time also, a kind of time known only to mathematicians and mystics: the kind of time we call eternity.

For was and is, and will be are but is;
And all creation is one act at once,
The birth of light: but we that are not all
As parts, can see but parts, now this now that,
And live, perforce from thought to thought and make
One act a phantom of succession; thus
Our weakness somehow shapes the Shadow, Time.

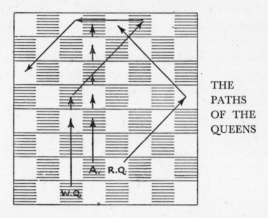

THE
PATHS
OF THE
QUEENS

What Tennyson put in poetry, Dodgson represented on his chess-board. Alice as she trotted along could see but parts, now the Red King to her right, now the White Queen to her left, but once she became a Queen there was a change:

Everything was happening so oddly that she didn't feel a bit surprised at finding the Red Queen and the White Queen sitting close to her, one on each side: she would have liked very much to ask them how they came there,

(we can follow their moves by the key)

but she feared it would not be quite civil.

She could see them both at once; in the language of psychology, she could attend to a plurality of impressions to which formerly she would have attended in succession.

However, she was by no means sure of herself or her crown as yet, and the Queens put her through her paces:

'In *our* country,' Alice remarked, 'there's only one day at a time.'
The Red Queen said, 'That's a poor thin way of doing things. Now *here*, we mostly have days and nights two or three at a time, and sometimes in the winter we take as many as five nights together —for warmth, you know.'

'Are five nights warmer than one night, then?' Alice ventured to ask.

'Five times as warm, of course.'

'But they should be five times as *cold*, by the same rule—'

'Just so!' said the Red Queen. 'Five times as warm, *and* five times as cold—just as I'm five times as rich as you are, *and* five times as clever!'

(Note clever and rich as opposites here.)

Alice sighed and gave it up. 'It's exactly like a riddle with no answer!' she thought.

It is, however, the answer to the 'chess-problem', or at any rate, one part of it, the checkmate which, Dodgson said in the 1887 Preface, was strictly in accordance with the laws of the game, while Mr Madan in the *Handbook* gives him the lie direct: 'whereas there is no attempt at one'.

According to the key, the position would appear to be:

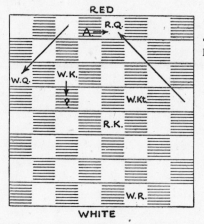

'All sorts of things happened in a moment.'

There is therefore something very like a checkmate and a fairly complicated one. The only objection is that the White King must have been in check while the White Queen moved to Q.R. 6th (soup) at Move 10. On the other hand, when Alice was on the Seventh Square she was still a pawn. The White King was behind her and if he had moved to Q.B. 5th she would not have known and he would not have been in check.

As to the succession of the moves, Dodgson admitted that was 'perhaps not so strictly observed as it might be'. When Alice reached the Eighth Square and became a Queen she naturally acquired new powers, but not all at once. She could now see from end to end of the board, but her sweep of vision from side to side was limited by the presence of the White Queen on one side and the Red Queen on the other. Whenever the White Queen moved to Q.R. 6th Alice had to wake up. ' "I can't stand this any longer!" she cried', and as the chess world collapsed in ruins she seized the Red Queen and accomplished the checkmate.

Dr Bell in a footnote to his *History of Mathematics* makes a two-fisted attack upon Priestley and Dunne for the use they have made of 'mathematical' ideas; Mr Priestley in his time-plays, Mr Dunne in his dream-philosophy. It is a good thing, Dr Bell thinks, that the literary world has still not discovered the elliptic functions 'whose double periodicity leads at once to a two-dimensional time', expressed, says Dr Bell, 'in the lozenges of a skewed chess-board'. On the other hand, he thinks there might be dollars in it.[1] Too late, Dr Bell! It has been done.

But Dodgson had other reasons for departing from the rules of chess and for avoiding a normal checkmate. These Queens, whose powers in time are far more remarkable than those of the Time Traveller in the 'scientific' romance by H. G. Wells, are none the less flatlanders. They live—or think they live—on a surface, a time-surface. But the cream of the jest is that their world is no more flat than ours. Like the people of the Middle Ages, they are on a globe and do not know it.

When Alice went Through the Looking-glass, she went into the room she had just left, the other way round. It was the drawing room and the door was open. She went along the passage, downstairs, and out by the 'front door' into the front garden, reversed. In the game of chess she went down the length of the board and at the end came to a door. By this time she was a Queen and could look both ways, forward and back (in time). Which door had she come to, the front door or the back door?

She was standing before an arched doorway, over which were the words QUEEN ALICE in large letters, and on each side of it there was a bell-handle; one marked 'Visitors' Bell', and the other 'Servants' Bell'.

Visitors' Bell: the Front Door. Servants' Bell: the Back Door. Time had gone full circle, or rather, Alice had gone full circle on

[1] E. T. Bell: *History of Mathematics*, p. 555, Note 15.

time, which unknown to her was a little planet like that in *Sylvie and Bruno Concluded*, on which 'the vanquished army ran away at full speed, and in a very few minutes found themselves face-to-face with the victorious army, who were marching home again, and who were so frightened at finding themselves between two armies that they surrendered at once'. Her front and back doors—the two ends of the board—were one and the same; in the words of Donne,

> As east and west
> In all flat maps (and I am one) are one.

In the *New Method of Evaluation* Dodgson had shown that the University, like the Church of England and, in a still wider sense, the whole country, was broken up into two 'partial factions'. One of these, the Rationalist faction, had as its locus a superficies, and the other, the extreme High Church party, had as its locus a catenary 'known as the Patristic Catenary', which he defined as 'passing through Origen and containing many multiple points'. A Catenary is a curve formed by a cord or chain suspended at each end and acted upon only by gravity.

No doubt these notions, working in his mind, helped him towards the idea of the two Queens, those mighty opposites in chess, living on a surface which was actually curved and representing once more two partial factions in the University, the Church or the human mind.

'The Red Queen,' said Dodgson, in his *Theatre* article of 1887, 'I pictured as a Fury, but of another type: her passion must be cold and calm; she must be formal and strict, yet not unkindly; pedantic to the tenth degree' (I suspect that he wrote n-th here), 'the concentrated essence of all governesses!' Clearly, she is on the Dogmatic side. She lays down the law to Alice, stresses her title (Apostolic Succession), claims that all the walks belong to her, demands the use of French (Latin services?) and curtseying (genuflection). She is condescending, pats Alice on the head, and has 'heard nonsense, compared with which that would be as sensible as a dictionary'.

The biscuit which the Red Queen offered Alice as a thirst-quencher might be dry on the Looking-glass principle, simply as the opposite of a refreshing drink, or it might partake of the woody nature of visible, tangible chess-pieces and be made of sawdust; but over and above these meanings, its dryness must be

similar to that of the passage read by the mouse in *Alice*. ('This
is the driest thing I know. Silence all round, if you please!')
Shane Leslie suggests that the biscuits were sermons and it is true
that the High Church sermons, regarded as of less importance
than sacrament, were often perfunctory.

In his general view of the allegory, Shane Leslie is wide of the
mark. He identifies the Red Queen as Archbishop Manning
and the White Queen as Dr Newman, who were on the same
side in everything of any significance. It is true that they had
their disagreements, but to regard the Queens as both representing Catholics reduces the allegory to triviality. The grand
opposites of Dodgson's day were Reason and Dogma, and to
regard the two sides as anything less fundamental is to under-
estimate him. Besides, he had already represented these great
principles as they worked themselves out in Oxford over the
serio-comic business of Jowett's salary, and represented them as
superficial in mathematical terms.

'Lastly,' said Dodgson in *The Theatre* of 1887, 'the White Queen
seemed to my dreaming fancy, gentle, stupid, fat and pale;
helpless as an infant; and with a slow maundering, bewildered
air about her just suggesting imbecility, but never quite passing
into it; that would be, I think, fatal to any comic effect she
might otherwise produce.'

Dodgson repeatedly asserted that he was 'no conscious imi-
tator' in the Alice books, and so far as the general design is
concerned, his claim was just. But certain resemblances to
passages in Swift's *Tale of a Tub*, *Battle of the Books* and *Gulliver's
Travels* are too close to be mere coincidence.

'Once upon a time,' says Swift in *A Tale of a Tub*, 'there was a
Man who had Three sons by one Wife, and all at a Birth,
neither could the Mid-wife tell certainly which was the Eldest.'
Wotton's footnote reads: 'By these three sons, Peter, Martyn and
Jack, Popery, the Church of England, and our Protestant
Dissenters are designed' (Martyn: Martin Luther, Jack: John
Calvin). Each was left a new coat and a copy of the Will,
containing instructions for wearing it. In *Through the Looking-
glass* the coats become shawls; otherwise the White Queen is
Jack, the Red Queen Peter.

The White Queen has trouble with her shawl, and Alice has
to help her to put it on again while the White Queen looks at

her in a helpless, frightened sort of way and whispers something that sounds like 'Bread-and-butter, bread-and-butter'. Compare this with Jowett signing the Articles for the sake of his tum-tum.

Again, she has been 'a-dressing' herself. 'Every single thing's crooked,' Alice thought to herself, 'and she's all over pins!' These pins are no doubt the counterpart of the Red Queen's thorns. The latter was wearing a crown of thorns when Alice met her, only the thorns were turned outward. ' "She's one of the thorny kind," said the Rose.' Because she was a-dressing herself, because every single thing was crooked and she was all over pins, the White Queen must represent the side of the Church which argued, protested and tried to re-interpret religious ideas by the light of reason—the Protestant side of the Church of England and in particular the Rationalist 'mode of thinking'.

Alice herself does duty in the allegory for Martin or the Church of England, though she certainly does not represent the Church of England as it was in Dodgson's day. Rather she is the essential quality of the Christian religion—the one all the sects seemed to have forgotten—love.

She took the place of Lily, the White Queen's Imperial Kitten—no doubt the Imperial Church of England which might be expected to result from the first 'Pan-Anglican' Conference at Lambeth in 1867. That was why Lily was too young to play and also why she was the child of the King and Queen of Controversy. Alice was the True Church, hoping all things, believing all things, suffering long. In the *Theatre* article, she was to be 'loving as a dog' and 'gentle as a fawn', courteous

even as though she were herself a King's daughter and her clothing of wrought gold: then trustful, ready to accept the wildest impossibilities with all that utter trust that only dreamers know; and lastly curious—and with the eager enjoyment of Life that comes only in the happy hours of childhood.

Compare with Dodgson's 'even as though she were herself a King's daughter and her clothing of wrought gold' his father's words about his ideal Church:

so did He prepare for His Church a covering, hidden within these ordinances for her spiritual nakedness, 'a clothing of wrought gold'

(Ps. xix, 13) rendering her meet to be brought into the Palace of the Heavenly King.[1]

To have used a real chess-problem would have been fatal to the allegory, for it was by no means Dodgson's view that the opposition of the two sides Red and White, two aspects of the same Church, sprang from the operations of two Hostile Players. On the contrary, the two Queens are really two kittens who come from one cat, Dinah, and Dinah in Tenniel's final illustration is both black and white.

The Queens and Alice were used as mathematical symbols to illustrate certain ideas about time and space. They were also used satirically and allegorically, as described above. In addition there are signs that he borrowed ideas for the appearance and nature of each character from real persons, and in Alice's case we know the original. It is true that the process of remaking her in accordance with his own ideas and attitude to life has gone far, but we can still recognize the first Alice in the last.

It has been suggested that Dodgson's own parents sat for the portraits of the chess Queens,[2] but I think the Dean and Mrs Liddell are much more likely models. Dodgson's relations with his father and mother were never anything but happy and normal, whereas a state of emotional tension, in which there was jealousy on both sides, the insolence of office on theirs and the pangs of despised love on his, existed between him and Alice's parents.

The Red Queen was tall, half a head taller than Alice, which was about the Dean's superiority in height to Dodgson. She had heard nonsense, compared to which 'that would be as sensible as a dictionary' and it would be difficult for Dodgson or anybody at Christ Church to use the word 'dictionary' without thinking of Liddell and Scott. Her coldness, too, her pride and pedantry, suggest the Dean.

There was emphatically no outward resemblance between the White Queen and Mrs Liddell, who, according to Sir William Richmond, was dark and beautiful.[3] But she was once pinning a dress on Alice when the Prince of Wales burst in unexpectedly and Alice fled. Mrs Liddell hid her agitation and

---

[1] *Ritual Worship*, p. 13.
[2] F. B. Lennon: *Lewis Carroll*, pp. 174–5.
[3] Ib., p. 131.

the Prince did not add to it until about to depart, when he remarked, 'Tell Alice I saw her.'[1] If Dodgson knew the story it was the kind of thing to worry him, and may have suggested the situation Through the Looking-glass, with the figures transposed and Alice pinning on the White Queen's shawl. The allegorical and mathematical ideas would coat the rather dangerous and embarrassing idea of Alice incompletely dressed, as mother-of-pearl coats an irritant within the oyster-shell.

Working as he did by associations of ideas, there was no limit to the variety of topics he could introduce. His art was to keep variety from becoming chaotic, to make some unexpected departure lead back to the last remark but one. Why some topics appealed to him and others did not is an enquiry which would take us over the threshold of consciousness and into that dark region where ambiguous forms and uncouth hybrids loom and dwindle. Psycho-analysis, however, is no technique for amateurs. We must be content to follow those trains of thought in which we can perceive intention, and we shall lose little by this, for the intention is fundamental.

There is in existence a photograph just published (1949)[2] but taken by Dodgson in 1858. It shows two of his aunts, the Misses Lutwidge, playing chess. One wears a dark dress and plays black against a dark background; the other, in a chequered or tartan dress, much lighter in tone, plays white against a pale background. The effect is of a battle of light and shade. The disposition of the pieces bears no relation to that in the *Looking-glass* chess problem, but the germ of the idea is there in the opposed forces. In the course of his chess lessons to Alice, Dodgson transferred the conflict from the players and setting to the chess pieces, in particular to the two Queens. Their powers of movement brought in his mathematics; their opposition suggested the theological controversies of his time, and because he disliked controversy, the Queens also acquired some characteristics from his more personal antipathies.

In Fechner's 'Space Has Four Dimensions' the opposites are the Naturalists, who believe only what they see, and the Philosophers, who see only what they believe. The Naturalists, like Dodgson's White Queen, 'know only length and breadth

[1] *Cornhill Magazine*, July, 1932.
[2] Helmut Gernsheim: *Lewis Carroll, Photographer.*

—except that is for the astronomers who are forced by the fall of
bodies to recognize the third dimension, at least as a hypothesis'.
In this respect Fechner's astronomers resemble Dodgson's
White Knight, whose ballad he re-wrote for *Through the Looking-
glass*, adding the lines:

> Or if I drop upon my toe
> A very heavy weight,

as an illustration of the fall of bodies.

Of all the chess-men, the Knight alone has the power of
leaping. This is the symbolism of chess, the horseman's leap
expressed by allowing the Knight to move two squares in any
direction and one at right angles to that direction—a cross-
section of a leap. Nevertheless, it makes no difference to the
Knight if the intervening squares are packed with friends or
foes. He can leap to a vacant square, take an enemy piece or
deliver check over their heads. It is this third dimension which
enables him to perform his little miracles, his sudden, unlooked-
for interventions in the game.

> 'And really,' said Alice,

referring to the game she had played the previous day, on our
side of the Looking-glass,

> 'I might have won, if it hadn't been for that nasty Knight that
> came wriggling down among my pieces.'

In Looking-glass House he was sliding down the poker and
balancing very badly. He represents a stage half-way between
the Queens, who are flatlanders pure and simple, and Alice,
who is a child or Human Being.

It is not necessary to relate the Knight's powers to time-length
and time-breadth as in the case of the Queens. Probably
Dodgson developed the ideas about the Knight quite separately
and fitted them into the general pattern later. However, if it is
desired to do so, then his third dimension was the whole of our
space.

Of our world he has had only the most tantalizing glimpses,
enough to unfit him for his own but not enough to enable him to
understand. Yet he is by no means contemptible, this knight in
tin armour. He has seen wonders, has even brought back with
him odd bits and pieces from *his* Wonderland, which is our common workaday world—beehives and mousetraps, carrots and

fire-irons, outlandish bric-à-brac, whose true nature and purpose are externally beyond him but which he collects hopefully and about which he theorizes happily.

He is Science.

By constantly falling on his head, he has grasped that things never fall upwards, you know, and his experience of rain has confirmed this. Accordingly he turns his box upside down, so that the rain will not wet his things, but alas! his theory is incomplete. He has overlooked the possibility that his things might fall downwards and he has lost them.

Then he has thought of a brilliant scheme for turning himself over in our space—a thing, it is safe to say, no other chess-man but a knight could think of doing:

'Now first I put my head on the top of the gate—then the head's high enough—then I stand on my head—then the feet are high enough, you see—then I'm over, you see.'

'Yes, I suppose you'd be over when that was done,' Alice said thoughtfully: 'but don't you think it would be rather hard?'

She means the ground.

'I haven't tried it yet,' the Knight said gravely: 'so I can't tell for certain—but I'm afraid it *would* be a little hard.'

The charming simpleton is thinking only of the difficulty (for him) of the operation. The consequences to himself have never occurred to him.

Compared to the other inhabitants of the chess-world he is a genius, like Newton, voyaging through strange seas of thought alone. His scheme for training hair upwards, like fruit trees, might be impracticable, or it might not. Experiment would have settled the matter, and he was a little dashed by Alice's lack of enthusiasm—but then so few of his schemes had ever met with an enthusiastic reception. In the kingdom of the blind the one-eyed man is thought to suffer from hallucinations.

The principle which eluded the White Knight was, of course, gravity. The word gravity is carefully avoided during the whole of this chapter, but he looked a little grave, and more than once he remarked gravely. The pun had no existence for himself or Alice. His elevated and vertical position on horseback was extremely precarious. Even when sliding down the poker he balanced very badly. As a planesman or inhabitant of the surface 'balance' was an idea he had failed to grasp. He was

I

unbalanced. But his difficulties were due to no lack of practice. He had had *plenty* of practice—both in mounting and in dismounting.

There is something sublime in his persistence and in his ability to rise above circumstance, to theorize from a head-downward position. Moreover, he had realized that he would probably never be able to stay on horseback without some sort of support and so had invented a helmet in the form of a sugar-loaf. This was a conical mass of sugar displayed in confectioners' windows in our grandfathers' day. The White Knight's sugar-loaf helmet was like a large fool's cap and touched the ground all round him. True he lost himself in it (as one is apt to do in a theory) and the other knight put it on, thinking that it was *his* helmet.

But his cleverest invention was a pudding—during the meat course. It was not cooked in time for the next course, or the next day:

'In fact,' he went on, holding his head down, and his voice getting lower and lower, 'I don't believe that pudding ever *was* cooked! In fact, I don't believe that pudding ever will be cooked! And yet it was a very clever pudding to invent.'

After the cone, the sphere. He was trying to frame the notion of a solid sphere but his world was flatland. It contained blotting-paper, which could be bent round into a cylinder, or twisted into a cone, but no matter how he stuck it together with sealing-wax, he could not make even a hollow sphere out of it, much less a solid one. He even thought of blowing it to pieces with gunpowder and then re-assembling the minute fragments. Theoretically, if the fragments were small enough, the feat should be possible. Practically, he had almost abandoned hope of that pudding.

'It began with blotting-paper,' the Knight answered with a groan. 'That wouldn't be very nice, I'm afraid—'

'Not very nice *alone*,' he interrupted, quite eagerly: 'but you've no idea what a difference it would make, mixing it with other things —such as gunpowder and sealing-wax. And here I must leave you.'

The White Knight's appearance without his helmet is worth noting:

'Now one can breathe more easily,' said the Knight, putting back his shaggy hair with both hands, and turning his gentle face and large mild eyes to Alice.

Does not this suggest a dog or a horse, rather than a man? The Knight is being compared to one of the higher animals which has some rudimentary intelligence; an animal which is gentle, unselfish and uncomplaining. The equation may be stated: man attempting to reason about the universe is like one of the higher animals attempting to understand our world. Both collect data and frame theories. Neither has any chance of understanding the reality. And the symbol by means of which Dodgson demonstrated this profound truth was the knight in chess with his leap over the intervening squares, in the course of which he lost contact with the surface and, however briefly, glimpsed our world.

Of all the strange things that Alice saw in her journey Through the Looking-glass, this was the one that she always remembered most clearly. Years afterwards she could bring the whole scene back again, as if it had been only yesterday—the mild blue eyes and kindly smile of the Knight—the setting sun gleaming through his hair and shining on his armour in a blaze of light that quite dazzled her—the horse quietly moving about, cropping the grass at her feet—and the black shadows of the forest behind—all this she took in like a picture, as, with one hand shading her eyes, she leant against a tree, watching the strange pair, and listening in a half-dream to the melancholy music of the song.

The song was 'Upon the Lonely Moor', the parody of Wordsworth's 'Resolution and Independence' which Dodgson had sent to *The Train* in 1856, but had partly rewritten and garnished with four new titles. Some of the changes are mere improvements in the verse; for example:

> He said 'I look for butterflies
> That sleep among the wheat'

is much better than

> He said 'I look for soap-bubbles
> That lie among the wheat.'

Others seem, if anything, more nonsensical than what he had written at first:

> But I was thinking of a plan
> To dye one's whiskers green,
> And always use so large a fan
> That they could not be seen.

However, 'a-sitting on a gate' is a significant attitude for his aged, aged man. If the White Knight's plan of standing on his head

on the top bar was likely to prove 'hard', it was at least original
and showed a desire to go somewhere. Again, the new lines,

> But I was thinking of a plan
> To feed oneself on batter
> And so go on from day to day
> Getting a little fatter,

suggest the White Knight trying another method of inventing,
or, at all events, producing the sphere, and Dodgson returned to
this in his Spherical Professor (*Sylvie and Bruno Concluded*) who
finally succeeded in making himself into a perfect sphere and in
acquiring sufficient momentum to fly off the Earth at a tangent.
But the main lines were already laid down in the 1856 version
and it seems quite clear to me through all the nonsense that the
White Knight is Pure Science and the Aged, Aged Man is
Applied Science.

The book, so far from having no moral, is thus a new kind of
Morality. The characters are all abstractions and we are prevented from realizing this only by sheer verbal sleight-of-hand.
The symbols are deceptively simple—but so are the properties
of a great conjuror. It is the second-rate magician who requires
elaborate scaffoldings of chromium-plated tubes and other
complicated apparatus. Give Dodgson a ball of wool, a kitten,
some chess-men, a looking-glass and a little girl out of the
audience—and watch carefully.

CHAPTER SIX

—And What Alice Found There

WITH our suspicions aroused, let us go back Through the Looking-glass into the room, or, as the chess-men would say, 'The Room', for our world is as mysterious to them as theirs to us. Indeed, if the Queens with their astonishing powers of appearing and disappearing seemed Superior Beings to Alice as a pawn, she herself as a Human Child was a Superior Being to them.

Right from the beginning Dodgson develops this system of analogies. The black kitten had been playing with a ball of wool—a reasonable approximation to a solid sphere— and had been 'rolling it up and down till it had all come undone again, and there it was, spread over the hearth-rug'—or surface—'all knots and tangles, with the kitten running after its own tail in the middle'.

Alice demonstrated the vast superiority of her human intelligence by rolling up the ball, while 'Kitty sat very demurely on her knee, pretending to watch the progress of the winding, and now and then putting out one paw and gently touching the ball as if it would be glad to help if it might'. It could not, however, grasp the nature or purpose of a ball of wool. Alice presently snatched the kitten up out of its own familiar world of hearth-rug and firelight, showed it its reflection in the looking-glass and tried to interest it in thoughts beyond the reaches of its soul. Through the Looking-glass it had its revenge, since the kittens became chess Queens and Alice only a pawn.

In Looking-glass House, however, Alice was still a Human Being, something large and strange beyond the wildest dreams or speculations of the chess-men whom she found walking about down in the hearth among the cinders.

'I don't think they can hear me,' she went on, as she put her head closer down, 'and I'm nearly sure they can't see me. I feel as if I were invisible.'

One of the chess-men had been overlooked and left on the table. It was Lily, the White Pawn Alice was to replace, infant daughter of the White King and Queen, and hailed by the latter as 'My precious Lily! My Imperial Kitten!' Alice with the best intentions lifted the White Queen up to the table, forgetting that to the White Queen, who had no knowledge of her existence, this experience would be very alarming and quite inexplicable. The White Queen in fact thought she had been blown up by a volcano and warned her consort to come up the regular way.

The regular way was to struggle up from bar to bar of the fender, and then, no doubt, down to the hearth-rug and up the leg of a chair, keeping to the surface all the way. Alice lifted him too, dusted him carefully, and when the shock was too much for him, 'went round the room to see if she could find any water to throw over him. However, she could find nothing but a bottle of ink and when she got back with it, she found he had recovered.'

That was fortunate for him. But ink belongs to the allegory and we are at present studying the demonstration of, shall we say, Superiority.

'The horror of that moment,' the King went on, 'I shall never, never forget!'

'You will, though,' the Queen said, 'if you don't make a memorandum of it.'

Accordingly, Alice is able to demonstrate her superiority still further by taking hold of the end of the pencil and forcing the little King to write thoughts other than his own. The resemblance here to the automatic writing which had been in the news since 1850 is too close to be accidental. Alice is a Superior Being to the little White King; not God, but a powerful and invisible force clearly possessing intelligence.

In the game she is the humble, creeping pawn and even the Kings are superior beings to her; not very formidable superior beings certainly, but confined neither to one square nor to one direction. The Queens are great, mysterious creatures who appear and vanish at will and take their Tuesdays in sets. However, as Alice frees herself from the trammels of sleep and the Queens succumb to its influence, the position is once more reversed. Now it is their turn to dream of Alice's world and even the inanimate objects of our world are worthy of all reverence to mere creatures of the surface.

The leg of mutton is therefore introduced to Alice and she to it and, despite her protests, the pudding also. Tenniel's leg of mutton is an approximation to a cone, or sugar-loaf, while the pudding was of the boiled-in-a-cloth variety—the solid sphere which the White Knight tried so hard to invent. Only in dreams and speculations could such wonders appear to the chess-men.

But the demonstration cannot really be separated from the allegory in this way. The two are indissolubly blended. The tangled wool on the hearth-rug, for example, shows what could happen to religious ideas when irresponsible little minds got at them. And the White Queen's shawl would no doubt be made of wool, as would the Old Sheep's fleece in the chapter 'Wool and Water'.

'Do you know what to-morrow is, Kitty?' Alice began. 'You'd have guessed if you'd been up in the window with me—only Dinah was making you tidy, so you couldn't. I was watching the boys getting in sticks for the bonfire—and it wants plenty of sticks, Kitty! Only it got so cold, and it snowed so, they had to leave off.'

The very idea of the bonfire causes yards and yards of wool to get unwound again. What day was 'tomorrow'? Was it Guy Fawkes' Day? Alice, according to herself in conversation with Humpty Dumpty, was exactly seven-and-a-half. The exactitude is insisted upon. Alice's birthday being 4 May, and the first adventure happening on that day, we may conclude that the voyage of discovery Through the Looking-glass occurred on 4 November. The year is less important, but he was writing the story in 1869 and 'Alice', as distinct from Alice Liddell, might be said to be seven-and-a-half then. At all events it seems that the sticks were for a bonfire on Guy Fawkes' Day. The snow, on the other hand, kissing the window all over outside and covering up the trees and fields with a white quilt, suggests Christmas. Perhaps he meant that to some people it is always Christmas, always peace and goodwill; to others it is always Guy Fawkes' Day, with its old hatreds, its 'No Popery!' and 'Off with his head!'

Saving up the kitten's punishments for Wednesday week is eternal damnation, the rock on which the Essayists and Reviewers came near to perishing, with Alice for the moment as God and the kitten as erring humanity. Going without fifty dinners at once provides the *reductio ad absurdum*.

It is for such ideas that we must look in Looking-glass House and beyond, and we have already noticed one rather obvious symbol—ink. 'Ink,' says Swift in *The Battle of the Books*, 'is the great missive weapon, in all the battles of the learned, which convey'd thro' a sort of engine, called a quill, infinite numbers of these are darted at the enemy, by the valiant on each side, as if it were an engagement of porcupines. This malignant liquor was compounded by the engineer who invented it of two ingredients, which are gall and copperas, by its bitterness and venom to suit in some degree, as well as to foment the genius of the combatants.'

Ink, then, was the only fluid Alice could find in Looking-glass House. It will be remembered also that Alice found (in Wonderland) a new kind of rule by which pepper made people bad-tempered, and vinegar made them sour, and camomile made them bitter. Kingsley had copied the prickliness of the porcupines in *The Water Babies*, where Tom, who had been naughty, looked at himself and he was all over prickles, just like a sea-egg:

Which was quite natural: for you must know and believe that people's souls make their bodies, just as a snail makes its shell (I am not joking, my little man, I am in serious solemn earnest). And therefore, when Tom's soul grew all prickly with naughty tempers, his body could not help growing prickly too, so that nobody would cuddle him, or play with him, or even like to look at him.

In *Sylvie and Bruno Concluded* Prince Uggug, a naughty and therefore ugly little spirit ('Loveless, loveless!') becomes more and more prickly and eventually turns into a porcupine. That is why Dodgson's Red Queen is 'thorny' and his White Queen 'all over pins'. The allegory in *Sylvie and Bruno* is transparent, and many of the ideas openly discussed. In *Through the Looking-glass* the ideas are roughly the same but they are cunningly hidden and 'things flow about so', from ink to the White King's memorandum-book, from that to the Looking-glass book and thence back to ink again.

There was a book lying near Alice on the table and while she sat watching the White King (for she was still a little anxious about him, and had the ink all ready to throw over him in case he fainted again) she turned over the leaves.

And found Jabberwocky, which was Controversy. The little White King was the King of Controversy, or Protesting, and ink, as the chief missive weapon in all the battles of the learned, was the fluid best calculated to revive him. This nothing's more than matter.

On the other hand, a deluge of ink from a Superior Being like Alice might have changed his colour—if it was red ink, to red—just as the spoonful of ink in the letter to the Hughes children turned a white cat black. There was a point when Alice was about to put the black kitten out into the snow, which would have turned it white, and it was the gentle snow which made the boys leave off building the bonfire. Moreover, the white kitten was called Snowdrop. Like Alice on the Looking-glass paths, we are walking in at the front door again.

One thing was certain, that the *white* kitten had nothing to do with it: it was the black kitten's fault entirely.

Through the Looking-glass, each of the kittens became a Queen, and Dodgson is at great pains to make us believe that the black kitten became the Red Queen.

'And as for *you*,' Alice went on, turning fiercely upon the Red Queen, whom she considered as the cause of all the mischief . . . 'I'll shake you into a kitten, that I will.'

The process occupies two short chapters, each with its illustration. 'Shaking' has two paragraphs and ends in the Red Queen's growing 'shorter—and fatter—and softer—and rounder —and—'. 'Waking' consists of the words: '—and it really *was* a kitten, after all'.

Tenniel's illustration makes it the black kitten, but that was merely the kitten Alice had in her hands before and after the dream. The words, and the words demand the closest attention, are 'a kitten'. Perhaps it is a small point—one kitten after all is very like another kitten—but it was the black kitten that un-ravelled the wool and spread it out in knots and tangles on the hearth-rug, and it is the white side which represents the con-troversial or protestant side of the University or the Church or the human mind. It seems natural to suppose that Through the Looking-glass the black kitten became the White Queen.

The substitution of Red for Black in the other transformation is also curious. Chess-men are sometimes made in that colour and it is a more attractive colour than black, but the opposition of snow and bonfire must not be forgotten. It seems to me that Through the Looking-glass the white kitten became the Red

Queen (instead of the Black Queen) because of the association of ideas set up by the bonfire. It was the dogmatic side after all which insisted, as was wittily said, on its right to eternal damnation; the Athanasian Creed and the everlasting bonfire.

At all events, while Alice is exploring the fantastic world of chess and struggling with the mysteries of time, she is also passing serenely through the Battle of the Books, Sermons and Speeches which raged about Dodgson himself during the 1860's. Of this there is a general view on the Sixth Square, where Alice met the White King:

> The next moment, soldiers came running through the wood, at first in twos and threes, then ten or twenty together, and at last in such crowds that they seemed to fill the whole forest. Alice got behind a tree, for fear of being run over, and watched them go by.

> She thought that in all her life she had never seen soldiers so uncertain on their feet: they were always tripping over something or other, and whenever one went down, several more always fell over him, so that the ground was soon covered with little heaps of men.

Alice's attitude here is exactly that of Dodgson as he describes it himself in 1856. The awkward squad of soldiers replaces the Babel of voices in which nothing was done and the irresistible Juggernaut before which the young tutor saw no reason to prostrate himself.[1] He, too, 'got behind a tree, for fear of being run over, and watched them go by'.

In an open space Alice discovered the White King 'seated on the ground and busily writing in his memorandum-book'. '"I've sent them all!" the King cried in a tone of delight.'

The combat of the Knights was typical of the 'fighting', in which the Rules of Battle were not easy to discover:

> 'One Rule seems to be that, if one Knight hits the other, he knocks him off his horse, and if he misses, he tumbles off himself.'

It is the age-old conflict of Science and Religion, of which Kant said in his coarse German fashion, 'One side seems to be milking a he-goat and the other to be holding a sieve.'

Nobody really won, of course:

> Another Rule of Battle, that Alice had not noticed, seemed to be that they always fell on their heads, and the battle ended with their both falling off in this way, side by side: when they got up again, they shook hands, and then the Red Knight mounted and galloped off.

[1] Coll., pp. 65–6.

Shane Leslie relates this combat to the clash at Oxford in 1860 of Wilberforce and Huxley and it is a tempting identification. It would be wrong, however, to say that the White Knight was Huxley or the Red Knight Wilberforce. The allegory is more general than that. The combat may be abstracted from the Huxley-Wilberforce incident. It is certainly abstracted from the general controversy about science and religion.

Where were the soldiers going when Alice saw them running through the wood? They were going to put Humpty Dumpty together again—or to make the attempt. The fall of Humpty Dumpty ('at this moment a heavy crash shook the forest from end to end') is the immediate occasion of the Battle of the Books. I think there can be no doubt that the Rev. Ronald Knox was right in suggesting to Shane Leslie that Humpty Dumpty represents Verbal Inspiration sitting on the wall of scripture, and his fall the acquittal of Wilson and Williams by the Privy Council in 1864. 'When I use a word,' says Humpty Dumpty, 'it means just what I choose it to mean—neither more or less.' Verbal Inspiration was the Protestant substitute for Catholic dogma. Every word of the Bible was true because directly inspired by God. The task of reconciling the Scriptures with common-sense or the most elementary principles of justice had just proved superhuman.

In addition, Dodgson certainly owes something to Fechner here, for Fechner had said of philosophy: 'But I consider the world as a fat hen of which philosophy in general is just a hollow egg' (literally, a 'wind-egg').

Humpty Dumpty was of course a riddle with the answer first—an egg:

However, the egg only got larger and larger, and more and more human: when she had come within a few yards of it, she saw that it had eyes and a nose and mouth; and when she had come close to it, she saw clearly that it was HUMPTY DUMPTY himself.

His shape—'and a good handsome shape it is too'—is like that of the mushroom in Wonderland, and after she woke up Alice asked, 'Tell me, Dinah, did you turn to Humpty Dumpty? I *think* you did—however, you'd better not mention it to your friends just yet, for I'm not sure.' Dinah, as has been remarked, partook of the nature of both sides and so did the mushroom in 'Wonderland'.

Again, there is the word 'Impenetrability', which for a mathematician and a friend of the Rev. Bartholomew Price had a special significance. 'Matter,' says Price, 'exists in space and time: all matter, even the minutest particle, occupies space. No two particles of matter and, also, no two bodies can occupy the same space at the same time; this property of matter is called its *impenetrability*.'

' "Impenetrability! That's what I say!" said Humpty Dumpty', and soon afterwards, 'a heavy crash shook the forest from end to end'.

Not everything Humpty Dumpty said can be related to Verbal Inspiration or to allegory of any kind. Occasionally *Through the Looking-glass* is just what it was all intended to seem, bewildering and amusing. Ideas, successful with actual children, are worked in, sometimes merged so skilfully with the mathematical-theological ideas that no line of demarcation can be drawn, sometimes quite openly.

Humpty Dumpty's explanations of the 'hard words' in the first verse of Jabberwocky are different from the *Misch-Masch* explanations but most of them are still just clever and amusing. At one point Alice is made to speak quite out of character:

'And "*the wabe*" is the grass plot round a sun-dial, I suppose?' said Alice, surprised at her own ingenuity.
'Of course it is. It's called "*wabe*", you know, because it goes a long way before it, and a long way behind it—'
'And a long way beyond it on each side,' Alice added.
'Exactly so.'

Alice seems to be brought in here merely to break up the explanation, which has, however, a deeper significance than the others. A sun-dial marks 'the present moment'. The 'wabe' which extends before and behind that moment and beyond it on each side is the time-board across which Alice, like Everyman, has to travel.

''Tis all a Chequer-board of Nights and Days . . .'

Next moment we are back among the green pigs and live mops.

Humpty Dumpty's poem is a masterpiece of inconclusiveness, with every action incomplete, unexplained, absurd, and sentences broken off in the middle:

And when I found the door was shut,
I tried to turn the handle, but—
There was a long pause.
'Is that all?' Alice timidly asked.
'That's all,' said Humpty Dumpty. 'Good-bye.'

And yet Humpty Dumpty has a story to tell. It is all about a kettle of fish, 'a pretty kettle of fish', more trouble, or perhaps the same old trouble in still another disguise, controversy again. Humpty Dumpty went out of his way to stir up trouble. He filled the kettle at the pump, went to wake the sleeping fishes and created a scene.

Later, in the Eighth Square but before the three Queens entered the palace, the White Queen referred to this incident. It was *à propos* of a thunderstorm they had had—one of the last sets of Tuesdays—

'Humpty Dumpty saw it too,' the White Queen went on in a low voice, more as if she were talking to herself. 'He came to the door with a corkscrew in his hand—'

'What for?' said the Red Queen.

'He said he *would* come in,' the White Queen went on, 'because he was looking for a hippopotamus . . .'

'I know what he came for,' said Alice, 'he wanted to punish the fish, because—'[1]

Here the White Queen began again. 'It was *such* a thunderstorm, you can't think!' ('She *never* could, you know,' said the Red Queen.) 'And part of the roof came off, and ever so much thunder got in—and it went rolling round the room in great lumps—and knocking over the tables and things—till I was so frightened, I couldn't remember my own name!'

Why a hippopotamus?

In *The Water Babies* Kingsley had introduced a professor who was Huxley, thinly disguised. 'He had even got up once at the British Association, and declared that apes had hippopotamus majors in their brains, just as men have, which was a shocking thing to say; for if that were so, what would become of the faith, hope and charity of immortal millions?' That looks like our hippopotamus, a malapropism for 'hippocampus major' (part of the brain). If so, Humpty Dumpty was creating a scene over the intrusion of ideas taken from Darwin into English Church

---

[1] i.e. to punish them for the sake of punishing them:
' "I'll be judge, I'll be jury"
Said cunning old *Fury*',
'Off with their heads!', etc.

affairs; the *Essays and Reviews* controversy is the thunderstorm where part of the roof came off and ever so much thunder got in.

On the other hand, there was a hippopotamus in 'Wonderland', or at any rate Alice thought there was:

Just then she heard something splashing about in the pool a little way off, and she swam nearer to make out what it was: at first she thought it must be a walrus or hippopotamus, but then she remembered how small she was now, and she soon made out that it was only a mouse that had slipped in like herself.

Perhaps Humpty Dumpty had made the same mistake and was making a hippopotamus out of a mouse—a mountain out of a molehill. It would be idle to pretend that it is always possible to say exactly what Dodgson means. In the 'hyaline of drifting glooms', meaning emerges as veiled allusion and loses itself in vague innuendo. The general impression is more trustworthy than a too curious examination of the detail and one has a general impression that Dodgson regarded the Church controversy of the time as a rather regrettable storm in a teacup.

There is a dreamy resemblance between the thunder rolling round the room in great lumps and the rolling about of the ball of wool by the black kitten. It is all, one feels, a matter of scale. To those involved in a controversy how large and serious everything looms; to the detached observer, how 'small and undistinguishable'!

It was the Old Sheep who set the egg upright on a shelf at the dark end of the little dark shop, and the Old Sheep had been the White Queen. That does come back to the ball of wool which the black kitten had been unwinding on the hearth-rug. The White Queen's shawl was the covering hidden within the ordinances of the Church in Archdeacon Dodgson's sermon, or the coat in Swift's *Tale of a Tub*. The transformation of the White Queen into an old sheep cannot be described as an improvement, yet as her shawl becomes a fleece, what is she saying?

'Oh, much better!' cried the Queen, her voice rising into a squeak as she went on. 'Much be-etter! Be-etter! Be-e-e-etter! Be-e-ehh!' The last word ended in a long bleat, so like a sheep that Alice quite started.

She looked at the Queen who seemed to have suddenly wrapped herself up in wool,

just as the black kitten had done in the drawing-room before the dream began.

This is, for Dodgson, quite a savage caricature of the trans-formation that seemed to him to have come over the Protestant Church. The little dark shop is 'a confusedly furnished second-hand symbol-shop', as the Athenaeum said of George Mac-Donald's *Phantastes*. Alice could see nothing on any particular shelf, though the others round it were crowded as full as they could be. There was nothing in the jar labelled 'Orange Mar-malade' either. The Old Sheep meantime was busily knitting with fourteen pairs of needles and Alice couldn't help looking at her in great astonishment.

'How *can* she knit with so many?' the puzzled child thought to herself. 'She gets more and more like a porcupine every minute!'

The significance of porcupines in this kind of writing has already been demonstrated. The old sheep was loveless, loveless!

The water-scene into which and out of which the shop scene flows dreamily is made up chiefly of puns used by Dodgson him-self when he was teaching Alice to row. In themselves they are not very amusing but they cloak such apparently casual asides as 'the Sheep cried again, taking more needles' and 'said the Sheep, sticking some of the needles into her hair, as her hands were full'. Tenniel's drawing shows the Old Sheep, her hair and hands bristling with needles, half-transformed into a porcupine. The shop he drew from one which can still be seen at 83 St. Aldate's, Oxford, reversing the position of door and window, no doubt on Dodgson's instructions.

Shane Leslie regards the Old Sheep as 'Dr Pusey knitting his interminable sermons and pamphlets in the Anglican shop' and it will be recalled that in *The New Method* Pusey's Patristic Catenary contained 'many multiple points'. Probably he did sit, though not alone, for this portrait. It might be thought that as leader of the High Church party his place was on the Red side, but as a Tractarian he was indulging in argument, protesting. He belonged to the White or Protestant side.

It is noteworthy that all the articles in the little dark shop turned into separate trees, except the egg, which turned into Humpty Dumpty.

'Aren't you sometimes frightened at being planted out here,' Alice asked the Live Flowers, 'with nobody to take care of you?'

'There's the tree in the middle,' said the Rose. 'What else is it good for?'

The tree is their Church, and like the Church in Dodgson's time it barked, it said, 'Bough-wough' and under it 'the air seemed full of little shrill voices'. The tree is one of Dodgson's recurrent symbols, like bread-and-butter and 'off with his head'. When Alice found herself 'back on earth' after her train journey she was sitting quietly under a tree. When Tweedledum and Tweedledee were about to fight and the Crow was flapping overhead, 'Alice ran a little way into the wood, and stopped under a large tree. "It can never get me *here*," she thought.' When all the king's soldiers came running through the wood, 'Alice got behind a tree'. She got behind a tree when the Red and White Knights joined battle. When the White Knight sang his song, 'she leant against a tree'. But on the Eighth Square, it was an old Frog who was sitting under a tree. Alice was a Queen and had got beyond the tree. She had got somewhere else, as the Red Queen said she would, if she moved fast enough.

The little dark shop turned into a whole forest. 'Let me see, is this a chair? Why, it's got branches I declare! How very odd to find trees growing here!' I think he meant that each nonconformist sect seized on some aspect or other of the Church and made a separate Church out of it.

Strife is the key-note throughout, strife in and about the Church; the spirit of Guy Fawkes' Day is symbolized in the first chapter by the bonfire of sticks and the nursery rhymes were chosen to fit into the strife-pattern. Humpty Dumpty's fall was the signal for the general engagement, and both Tweedledum and Tweedledee and the Lion and the Unicorn were already locked in combat before they found their way on to Dodgson's chess-board. They have of course no business there, and like Humpty Dumpty are not really chess-pieces at all. They appear in the Dramatis Personae but not in the key to the chess-problem.

They were standing under a tree, each with an arm round the other's neck, and Alice knew which was which in a moment, because one of them had 'Dum' embroidered on his collar and the other 'Dee'. 'I suppose they've each got "Tweedle" round at the back of the collar,' she said to herself.

They were standing under a tree, that is, in the protection of the Church. They lived in the same house and Shane Leslie is correct in identifying them as High Church and Low Church.

Compare them with Swift's caricature in *Gulliver's Travels*.

You are to understand that, for above seventy moons past, there have been two struggling parties in this empire, under the name of Tramecksan and Slamecksan, from the high and low heels of their shoes, by which they distinguish themselves. It is alleged indeed, that the high heels are most agreeable to our ancient constitution; but, however this be, his Majesty hath determined to make use of only low heels in the administration of the government . . .

The High Heels are the High Church or Tory Party of Swift's day; Low Heels are the Low Church or Whig. George I is the emperor who favoured the Low Heels and the heir to the throne with his High Heel leanings is the Prince of Wales. Swift's satire is direct, pungent and uncompromising. Note that the names Tramecksan and Slamecksan are identical but for the first syllable. Tweedledum and Tweedledee are identical but for the last. But Swift has definitely identified his imaginary parties with High and Low Church by means of the high and low heels of their shoes. Can the same be said of Dodgson?

It can, but, as usual, he has been more ingenious in his efforts to cover his tracks.

'To tweedle,' says the Oxford Companion to Literature, 'is to produce a succession of shrill musical sounds, to whistle or pipe. The original contest is between the sounds of high- and low-pitched musical instruments.' The original contest was between Handel and Buonocini in the 1720's.

> Some say, compared to Buonocini
> That Mynheer Handel's but a ninny,
> Others aver that he to Handel
> Is scarcely fit to hold a candle.
> Strange all this difference should be
> Twixt tweedle-dum and tweedle-dee.

The lines have been attributed to various eighteenth-century poets, including Swift and Pope.

Dodgson uses the familiar nursery rhyme, which he did not invent, as it can be found in *The Nursery Rhymes of England*, edited by Halliwell-Phillips (5th ed. 1853).

> Tweedledum and Tweedledee
> Agreed to have a battle
> For Tweedledum said Tweedledee
> Had spoiled his nice new rattle.

K

'Rattle' and 'ritual' are almost the same word and, unsympathetically regarded, meant much the same thing. But it was Low Church which spoiled High Church's rattle or ritual (or wanted to spoil it), whereas the rattle seemed to belong to Tweedledum (low note). We are, of course, Through the Looking-glass, where that kind of thing is to be expected.

The monstrous crow which ended their mock-heroics Shane Leslie regards as the threat of disestablishment which certainly did cause the English Church to sink its differences.

> Just then flew down a monstrous crow,
> As black as a tar-barrel;
> Which frightened both the heroes so,
> They quite forgot their quarrel.

This chapter is full of most exquisite satire.

'We must have a bit of a fight, but I don't care about going on long,' said Tweedledum. 'What's the time now?'
Tweedledee looked at his watch, and said 'Half-past four.'
'Let's fight till six, and then have dinner,' said Tweedledum.

The bolsters, blankets, hearth-rugs, table-cloths, dish-covers and coal-scuttles are irrelevancies and the trouble they gave Alice in tying strings and fastening buttons—'Really they'll be more like bundles of old clothes than anything else by the time they're ready!'—once more recalls the coats in Swift's *Tale of a Tub*. Tweedledee is greatly concerned in case his head is cut off and Tweedledum smiles with satisfaction as he remarks:

'I don't suppose there'll be a tree left standing for ever so far round, by the time we're finished!'
'And all about a rattle!' said Alice, still hoping to make them a *little* ashamed of fighting for such a trifle.

This is an indulgent caricature, the theme of which is 'Here we go round the mulberry bush', to which melody, played 'by the branches rubbing one across the other',[1] Alice suddenly found herself dancing with the brothers. She didn't know when they began but it had been going on a long, long time. It had indeed.

The sword is probably the Sword of Scripture, since they only had one. Tweedledum offers his brother the umbrella (of doctrine?) with the remark 'It's quite as sharp'. Tweedledee had

---

[1] Children can enjoy this without understanding, but for adults surely it adds depth and significance to realize that the 'branches' were branches of the Church.

folded himself up in that umbrella, and earlier the brothers had stood under it when rain threatened.

Tweedledum spread a large umbrella over himself and his brother, and looked up into it. 'No, I don't think it is,' he said: 'at least—not under *here*. Nohow.'
'But it may rain outside?'
'It may—if it chooses,' said Tweedledee. 'We've no objection. Contrariwise.'

Probably Dodgson was thinking of the view complacently held by the English Church (apart from the Essayists, Reviewers, Dodgson and other heretics) that the heathen would all go to hell. ' "Selfish things!" thought Alice', pointing the moral.

Just before the battle actually commenced, a thunderstorm seemed to be blowing up.

'It's the crow!' Tweedledum cried out in a shrill voice of alarm: and the two brothers took to their heels and were out of sight in a moment.

'The Walrus and the Carpenter', the poem recited by Tweedledee with the full approval of his brother, is to some extent a parody of Hood's 'Eugene Aram', but like most of Dodgson's parodies has become a new poem in the same stanza. According to Harry Furniss (whose evidence is not, however, completely reliable) Tenniel thought the Walrus and the Carpenter 'a hopeless combination'.[1] They are two of his happiest (and also unhappiest) Looking-glass figures and have passed into folk-lore.

So far as I know, they are Dodgson's own invention. The Walrus may be the one that the mouse in the pool of tears turned out not to be. The Carpenter, as befits one who saws up wood, which comes from trees (tree being a Dodgson symbol for Church), is the more materialistic and sceptical of the two, but the tears and sobs of the Walrus are certainly related to those of the crocodile.

We first meet these 'very unpleasant characters' walking on the dry sand beside the wet sea. They are in a sad mood and the cause of their melancholy is the amount of sand they see around them.

> 'If seven maids with seven mops
>   Swept it for half a year,
>   Do you suppose,' the Walrus said,

[1] Frances Sarzano: *Sir John Tenniel*, p. 18.

> 'That they would get it clear?'
> 'I doubt it,' said the Carpenter,
> And shed a bitter tear.

There were seven essayists and reviewers and this looks like an allusion to them.

Addressing themselves next to a bed of oysters, the Walrus and the Carpenter invited them to take a walk along the briny beach. A wily old oyster, rightly suspicious of their motives, declined, as Pusey had declined Stanley's invitation to preach in Westminster Abbey.

> But four young oysters hurried up
> All eager for the treat,
> Their coats were brushed, their faces washed,
> Their shoes were clean and neat.

These certainly look like the confiding young clergy led astray, as Shane Leslie suggests, by higher critics such as Stanley and Colenso.[1]

As a variant reading to the last three lines of the famous verse: 'The time has come, the Walrus said', Leslie suggests:

> Of Genesis and Kings
> And whether hell is boiling hot
> Or Angel-folks have wings.

I like the first and second of these but not the third. 'Whether pigs have wings' is, I think, the old query which Ferrovius expressed, 'Have animals got souls or have they not?'

At all events, once a few oysters had been persuaded to walk with the Walrus and the Carpenter many more followed. Alas, they were being lured to their destruction. A grisly tone crept into the Walrus's voice as he mentioned bread, pepper and vinegar, while the Carpenter thought there was too much butter. These are all familiar Dodgson symbols.

'I like the Walrus best,' said Alice, 'because, you see, he was a *little* sorry for the poor oysters.'

'He ate more than the Carpenter, though,' said Tweedledee. 'You see, he held his handkerchief in front so that the Carpenter couldn't count how many he took: contrariwise.'

The out-and-out sceptic, we may translate (however loosely), does less harm to the faithful Anglican than the hypocritical churchman who is a sceptic or a Roman Catholic at heart.

[1] *London Mercury*, 1933.

In an attempt to justify the presence of Tweedledum and Tweedledee on the chess-board, Dodgson made them things in the Red King's dream, chimeras like those in Brueghel's 'St James and his Persecutors'.

'If that there King was to wake,' added Tweedledum, 'You'd go out—bang!—just like a candle!'
'I shouldn't!' Alice exclaimed, indignantly. 'Besides, if I'm only a sort of thing in his dream, what are *you*, I should like to know?'
'Ditto,' said Tweedledum.
'Ditto, ditto!' cried Tweedledee.

They were only things in his dream, yet they claimed to know what he was dreaming about. Alice said, 'Nobody can guess that,' and later, 'I know they're talking nonsense,' but she was worried about it even after she woke up:

'Now Kitty, let's consider who it was that dreamed it all. You see, Kitty, it *must* have been either me or the Red King. He was part of my dream, of course—but then I was part of his dream too.'

It would be fatally easy to read into this all sorts of profundities culled from Berkeley, Hume and Kant, and perhaps Dodgson meant them, but only as overtones.

'Isn't he a *lovely* sight?' said Tweedledum.
Alice couldn't say honestly that he was. He had a tall red night-cap on, with a tassel, and he was lying crumpled up into a sort of untidy heap, and snoring loud—'fit to snore his head off!' as Tweedledum remarked.

Perhaps he was 'sunk in dogmatic slumber', like Kant before he read Hume. Perhaps his tall red night-cap was a flame of the everlasting bonfire on which his party insisted.

'I'm afraid he'll catch cold with lying on the wet grass,' said Alice, who was a very thoughtful little girl.

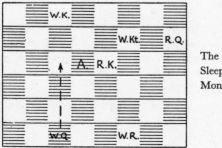

The
Sleeping
Monarch.

Alice has no suspicion of the danger she is in, yet if that there king was to wake, she would certainly leave the board. This is probably the root idea: by virtue of his chess situation, the Red King cannot wake. Unknown to Alice, she passes him under the protection of the White Knight, who hands her over to the White Queen. The Red King's powers are dormant.

One last group of conflicting figures remains to be noticed: the White King, the Lion and the Unicorn.

> The Lion and the Unicorn were fighting for the crown;
> The Lion beat the Unicorn all round the town.
> Some gave them white bread and some gave them brown;
> Some gave them plum-cake and drummed them out of town.

The White King was not asleep. On the contrary, he was busily engaged in sending his troops into action. He had two messengers, one to come and one to go: Haigha, the March Hare, and Hatta, the Mad Hatter.

Haigha is tricked out in antique costume and striking Anglo-Saxon attitudes like those of the Primitive Church ritual so dear to the hearts of soi-disant Catholic rectors. He gives the White King a ham sandwich (a good, meaty argument?) and then has nothing to offer but hay (dry stuff at the best of times).

Alice had no more breath for talking, so they trotted on in silence, till they came in sight of a great crowd in the middle of which the Lion and Unicorn were fighting. They were in such a cloud of dust, that at first Alice could not make out which was which: but she soon managed to distinguish the Unicorn by his horn.

Hatta joined them, Hatta, in whom we can just recognize our old friend the Mad Hatter still munching his bread-and-butter and drinking his tea (twinkling, or weak, with cream in it?). He, too, has been Anglo-Saxonized, is eating a bit of the bread-and-butter that the Lion and the Unicorn are to be offered and is eventually sent to start the drums beating. He has also been in prison, sentenced before his trial for a crime he has not committed, and is probably the Essayists and Reviewers again, whose arguments were proved not to contain the element of novelty (in *The New Method*). Hence the antique garb, to match Haigha's.

In the 'ten minutes allowed for refreshments' Alice tried the bread which Haigha and Hatta carried round on trays but it was *very* dry. Then Hatta bounded away to start the drums and while Alice was watching him she suddenly saw the White Queen 'running across the country'.

As the White King was explaining how useless it was to do anything but make a memorandum about her, the Unicorn 'sauntered by them, with his hands in his pockets'. He had always thought children were fabulous monsters, but agreed to believe in Alice if she would believe in him. The Lion took charge of the situation.

'Then hand round the plum-cake, Monster,' the Lion said, lying down and putting his chin on his paws. 'And sit down both of you' (to the King and the Unicorn): 'fair play with the cake, you know!'

His idea of fair play is well known, but his attitude is also significant: 'his chin on his paws'. Compare Alice with 'her chin pressed so closely against her foot that there was hardly room to open her mouth'. This is a very materialistic attitude.

Seated between the two great creatures, the King represents the Erastian principle, with the Unicorn as Convocation and the Lion as Parliament.

'What a fight we might have for the crown now!' the Unicorn said, looking slyly up at the crown, which the poor King was nearly shaking off his head, he trembled so much.

Tenniel made the Unicorn resemble Disraeli and the Lion Gladstone, which would suggest political strife; no doubt Dodgson intended that meaning also, for he did not believe in party politics and thought the idea of an opposition farcical.

'All round the town?' said the White King. 'That's a good long way. Did you go by the old bridge, or the market place? You get the best view by the old bridge.'

The market-place is commerce, one way to power and reward; the old bridge, I suggest, the Asses' Bridge from public school to university. But it no longer made any difference. Either way, 'there was too much dust to see anything'.

It is astonishing how the eye can pass smoothly over the little devices by which Dodgson kept the atmosphere of strife alive. The words throb with strife as an impressionist sky throbs with heat. Look once more at 'the Crown, which the poor King was nearly shaking off his head'. 'Off his head' is no accident. If Humpty Dumpty had smiled any more his mouth might have met behind and 'then I don't know what would happen to his head! I'm afraid it would come off!' The Red King was snoring loud—'fit to snore his head off!' as Tweedledum remarked. The crowning—or perhaps one should say uncrowning—example occurs when the two Queens fall asleep and 'first one round head, and then the other, rolled down from her shoulder, and lay like a heavy lump in her lap'.

There is no doubt whatever that he is fooling us to the top of our bent. It is a little late to be expressing our appreciation, but better late than never.

Brown bread and white bread (copper and silver?) are rewards like the comfits after the caucus-race. Alice tried a bit herself, but it was *very* dry. The Lion and the Unicorn wanted something better—plum-cake. A 'plum' has meant an important, lucrative position at least since the days of Henry VIII when the original Sir John Horner pulled his plum out of the dissolution of the monasteries. Dodgson had used the symbol in his caricature of Jowett pulling £500 a year out of the Oxford pie. The Lion and the Unicorn were as churchmen and statesmen seeking power and wealth, as Church and State fighting for the power and the glory which properly belonged to the King.

And so it goes on, satire, pun and leg-pull, all subdued to the Looking-glass lapse and flow.

Alice had seated herself on the bank of a little brook, with the great dish on her knees and was sawing away diligently with the knife.

'It's very provoking!' she said, in reply to the Lion (she was getting quite used to being called 'the Monster'). 'I've cut off several slices already, but they will always join on again!'

'You don't know how to manage Looking-glass cake,' the Unicorn remarked. 'Hand it round first and cut it afterwards.'

It sounded nonsense, but it worked, and it often happens that rewards are shared out in advance. This is an improvement on the caucus-race.

'*Now* cut it up,' said the Lion, as she returned to her place with the empty dish.

'She's kept none for herself, anyhow,' commented the Lion a moment later. 'Do you like plum-cake, Monster?'

But before Alice could answer him, the drums began.

Where the noise came from, she couldn't make out; the air seemed full of it and it rang through and through her head till she felt quite deafened. She started to her feet, and in her terror, she sprang across

```
*       *       *       *
    *       *       *
*       *       *       *
```

the brook and had just time to see the Lion and Unicorn rise to their feet with angry looks at being interrupted in their feast, before she dropped to her knees, and put her hands over her ears, vainly trying to shut out the dreadful uproar.

There is a faint suggestion of divine retribution in the drums. Notice that Alice 'dropped to her knees', another significant attitude. Yet the drums are started by the orders of the little King of Controversy, so perhaps it is only the Battle that is commencing—and that certainly will not drive the Lion and the Unicorn out of town. Tenniel's drawing consists of shadowy drums, hands and drumsticks, with Alice on her knees and beside her an empty plate and knife. Dodgson does not mention the knife again, but the dish was there and was promptly 'collected' by the White Knight in case they found any plum-cake. To do him justice, he was not looking for plum-cake.

It is a kind of metaphor Dodgson is using, a metaphor so elaborate and far-fetched that if found in the work of Donne or Herrick it would be called 'conceit'. And this is the truth of the matter: in his serious verse Dodgson was a minor nineteenth-century romantic, but in his prose he was the latest, and greatest, of the metaphysical poets. The book is not so much an allegory as a kind of plastic fable or parable, the same symbols, even Alice, being used in different ways at different times in the way that a phrase is used in music or an expression in algebra.

Alice herself is our observer throughout. We see and hear by means of her eyes and ears and judge by her childish and, in important matters, trustworthy standards. Such details as her relative size at any particular moment we are left to infer, and Dodgson makes great play with relative sizes. In the Wonder-land story he told us Alice's size each time it changed, and only once left us to make a deduction from it. When Alice approached the house of the March Hare

She thought it must be the right house, because the chimneys were shaped like ears and the roof was thatched with fur. It was so large a house, that she did not like to go nearer till she had nibbled some more of the left-hand bit of mushroom, and raised herself to about two feet high: even then she walked up towards it rather timidly, saying to herself, 'Suppose it should be raving mad after all!'

'It' was the March Hare, which she had mistaken for a house when she was nine inches high.

In *Through the Looking-glass* it is assumed that we are familiar with such obvious changes in the point of view as must follow a reduction or increase in our own (or Alice's) stature. More subtle variations are in store for us. The Red Queen, we are told, was three inches in height and, in the garden, Alice half-a-head shorter. That no doubt was why Humpty Dumpty looked so large to her (though he was only an egg after all) 'when she had come close to it', whereas 'when she had come within a few yards of it' she could just distinguish the eyes, nose and mouth. A few yards is a considerable distance if you are only a couple of inches in height.

But why then did she see the bees 'a mile off' the size of elephants and the flowers 'something like cottages with the roofs taken off, and stalks put to them'? Perspective, too, seems to be reversed and things appear larger the further away they are—or perhaps we are in a 'world before perspective' like that which Lamb saw in a china tea-cup. 'Those little, lawless azure tinctured grotesques . . . whom distance cannot diminish . . . a cow and rabbit couchant and apparently co-extensive . . . thus objects show seen through the lucid atmosphere of fine Cathay.'

Apparently Dodgson meant her to go down among the insects, for Alice decided to go down the other way, which would take her towards them. But at this point Tenniel rebelled and refused to draw a wasp wearing a wig. Disclaiming any wish to be brutal, he felt bound to point out that the 'wasp' chapter lacked interest, at least for him, and suggested that if Dodgson wished to shorten the book (there is no reason to suppose that he did) *there* was his opportunity.[1]

A wasp wearing a wig, in view of the recent Church trials, was surely not entirely without interest. However, a curiously submissive Dodgson cut out the chapter and adopted Tenniel's further suggestion that Alice should seize the Goat's beard 'instead of the old lady's hair' when the train jumped the brook between the Third and Fourth Squares. Alice's 'seizing the old

---

[1] Coll., p. 148 (facsimile of Tenniel's letter dated 1 June, 1870).

lady's hair' in a moment of emergency must surely have been intended to correspond in some way with the White Queen's action at the very end of the game.

'Take care of yourself!' screamed the White Queen, seizing Alice's hair with both her hands. 'Something's going to happen.'

Tenniel's reactions reminded Dodgson that most of his subtleties would be completely lost on his readers and it must have been with an almost cynical shrug that he made the alterations Tenniel suggested.

The train journey symbolizes Alice's rapid transit through the Third Square in 'a pawn's first move' and at the same time casts doubt on the reality of progress. 'You're travelling the wrong way,' says the Guard.

Ideas derived from Alice's extraordinary smallness as a pawn and extraordinary largeness as a Human Being are mixed up with ideas about the city and real train journeys. The tickets are the same size as the people and even the smoke is worth a thousand pounds a puff. The Guard has to look at her through a telescope, a microscope and a pair of binoculars, yet one of the passengers suggests that she should draw the train the rest of the way herself, as Gulliver did the enemy fleet. Back on the board, Alice's size becomes more stable again, for the Gnat is 'about the size of a chicken', which is how that mournful insect with his sorrowful jokes would appear to a chess pawn.

It does not matter that Alice understands nothing of what is happening to her. She 'keeps her head', whereas the people she meets seem in danger of losing theirs in one way or another. Even in the wood where things have no names she remains herself, though she thinks her name begins with an L. ' "L, I *know* it begins with L!" '

Love begins with L.[1]

Sometimes the book seems to be of the stuff of fable or parable. At other times it might be a lyric by Blake or one of Donne's metaphysical rhapsodies. Alice's meeting with the Fawn in the wood where things have no names is poetry which rhyme or rhythm would only spoil.

Just then a Fawn came wandering by: it looked at Alice with its large gentle eyes, but didn't seem at all frightened. 'Here then!

[1] So, of course, do Lily and Liddell.

Here then!' Alice said, as she held out her hand and tried to stroke it; but it only started back a little and then stood looking at her again.

'What do you call yourself?' the Fawn said at last. Such a soft sweet voice it had!

'I wish I knew!' thought poor Alice. She answered, rather sadly, 'Nothing, just now.'

'Think again,' it said: 'that won't do.'

Alice thought, but nothing came of it. 'Please would you tell me what *you* call yourself?' she said timidly. 'I think that might help a little.'

'I'll tell you if you'll come a little further on,' the Fawn said. 'I can't remember here.'

So they walked together through the wood, Alice with her arms clasped lovingly round the soft neck of the Fawn, till they came out into another open field, and here the Fawn gave a sudden bound into the air, and shook itself free from Alice's arms. 'I'm a Fawn!' it cried out in a voice of delight. 'And dear me, you're a human child!' A sudden look of alarm came into its beautiful brown eyes and in another moment it had darted away at full speed.

Blake's 'Piping down the valleys wild' is no more perfect.

The dialogue with the Gnat, on the other hand, in which Alice is warned about the wood, is loaded.

'What sort of insects do you rejoice in, where *you* come from?' the Gnat inquired.

'I don't *rejoice* in insects at all,' Alice explained, 'because I'm rather afraid of them—at least the large kinds. But I can tell you the names of some of them.'

'Of course they answer to their names?' the Gnat remarked carelessly.

'I never knew them do it.'

'What's the use of their having names,' the Gnat said, 'if they won't answer to them?'

'No use to *them*,' said Alice; 'but it's useful to the people that name them, I suppose. If not, why do things have names at all?'

'I can't say,' said the Gnat. 'In the wood down there, they've got no names—however, go on with your list of insects.'

It is because these words are informed with meaning that they produce in the receptive mind a feeling of exquisite pleasure. We join for the moment with Dodgson in glorious revolt against the whole wearisome business of classification and nomenclature.

And then he switches to Looking-glass insects, 'insects' being another surreptitious pun which I think Shane Leslie has missed, though he identifies the 'sects' more definitely than I care to do. The Rocking-horse-fly, for example, which he takes as a

'Methodist on circuit' may 'swing itself from branch to branch' because it has changed over to suit the religious temper of the times. It has just been repainted, like the roses in the Garden of Preferment, and lives on sap and sawdust (symbols as obvious as pepper and treacle, but derived from trees). Its brightness and stickiness refer, I think, to the bonfire, as well as to the paint. The Snap-dragon-fly, a creature made of plum-pudding (rewards), holly-leaves (prickliness) and a raisin burning in brandy, he regards as 'the extinct two-bottle Orthodox' and he may be right, though it seems to me there is a touch of Rationalism about the 'raisin'.

My own favourite is the Bread-and-butter-fly, whose wings are 'thin slices of bread-and-butter, its body is a crust, and its head a lump of sugar'.

'And what does *it* live on?'
'Weak tea with cream in it.'
A new difficulty came into Alice's head. 'Supposing it couldn't find any?' she suggested.
'Then it would die, of course.'
'But that must happen very often,' Alice remarked thoughtfully.
'It always happens,' said the Gnat.
After this, Alice was silent for a minute or two, pondering.

We all know the Bread-and-butter-fly.

Sometimes the thought is turgid, the words packed with many meanings; sometimes it flows blandly along like good conversation.

Alice is sometimes a human child, sometimes a pawn, sometimes the quality of love or faith, sometimes all three. Inevitably Dodgson wrote himself into Alice, pushed Alice Liddell out, as it were, and took her place, but inevitably also he wrote himself into the White Knight and for a moment Alice Liddell returned to wave him goodbye.

'I hope it encouraged him,' she said, as she turned to run down the hill: 'and now for the last brook, and to be a Queen! How grand it sounds!'

For some squares now her powers have been developing. On square six, for example, she sees the White Queen, 'running across the country', and the White Queen is on the eighth rank. At the beginning of square seven she has a momentary glimpse, behind her, of the Lion and Unicorn rising with angry looks

—on square six. A more sinister development is the little
scream of laughter she gives as the White Knight falls off his
horse while explaining the art of staying on. The White Queen's
screams sound like the whistle of a steam engine. Not Alice,
surely! Yet Alice could not escape entirely the consequences of
chess-life. White she is, and shrill she is becoming.

But at the end of square seven she is nearing the end of her
journey. The sun is setting—or rising—who can say which?
She has to go 'down the hill' and across the last brook. If he had
wished to do so, Dodgson could not have avoided symbolism
here, and he had no wish to avoid it. Eagerly Alice leaps across,
into the unknown.

The end of the game is another point at which it seems to me
Shane Leslie has gone very wide of the mark. He thinks that
Alice's becoming a Queen denotes her conversion to Roman
Catholicism.[1] Dodgson's 'grand finale' is much more subtle and
magnificent than that. All the ideas mingle and merge in one
glorious crescendo; chess and theology flow together towards
the climax.

To the Queens all solid objects are of equal importance, and
of equal importance with Alice herself. To the Red Queen, all
are supernatural, just as to the ritualist even church vestments
and other externals were supernatural. To the White Queen,
none are supernatural, as to the rationalist there were no
miracles and (almost) no Superior Being.

'You ought to return thanks in a neat speech,' the Red Queen
said, frowning at Alice as she spoke.

Despite her whispered protest the Queens insisted upon sup-
porting her.

('And they did push so!' she said afterwards, when she was telling
her sister the history of the feast. 'You would have thought they
wanted to squeeze me flat!')

They wanted to reduce her to their own level, which was that of
the surface.

'I rise to return thanks—' Alice began: and she really *did* rise as
she spoke, several inches . . .

'Take care of yourself!' screamed the White Queen, seizing Alice's
hair with both her hands. 'Something's going to happen!'

The end of the game is going to happen. To the chess-men, it is

---

[1] *London Mercury*, 1933.

the end of the world. A new world is breaking in on them, a
world of which they know nothing, in which they are 'less than
nothing and dreams'.

And then (as Alice afterwards described it) all sorts of things
happened in a moment. The candles all grew up to the ceiling,
looking something like a bed of rushes with fireworks at the top. As
to the bottles, they each took a pair of plates which they hastily
fitted on as wings, and so, with forks for legs, went fluttering about:
'and very like birds they look,' Alice thought to herself, as well as she
could in the dreadful confusion that was beginning.

After Judgment Day ('Examination'), Kingdom Come—or
Creation. It is the Twilight of the Chess-men, the last confusion.
The Leg of Mutton sits in the Queen's chair and even the Soup-
ladle comes 'walking up the table to Alice and signing to her to
get out of its way'. Matter is triumphing over mind. The last
shall be first, with a vengeance! The White Queen vanishes into
the soup. 'In the soup' means trouble again, just as her last
words to Alice were 'Take care of yourself'—the motto of the
self-seeker. Alice pulls the table-cloth and brings 'plates, dishes,
guests and candles crashing in a heap on the floor', which looks
like the end of a good many things dear to the heart of the
Catholic.

Alice, you see, is a White Queen now, and, like Hamlet in the
last act, an instrument of fate. She has just brought about
the downfall of the Catholic style of service. Now she turns on
the Red Queen:

'And as for *you*—' but the Red Queen had suddenly dwindled
down to the size of a little doll and was now on the table, merrily
running round after her own shawl, which was trailing behind her.

But it is nothing very terrible Alice intends towards the Red
Queen:

  'I'll shake you into a kitten, that I will!'

She will shake some softness and roundness into it.

The text of *Through the Looking-glass* will be found in 'Maud',
where the poet is said to be

  Dowered with the hate of hate, the scorn of scorn,
  The love of love.[1]

When Alice begins to move the game is nearly over. White
is all over the board and Red, though still smouldering, doomed

---

[1] Lines which Dodgson asked Tennyson to interpret. See Coll., p. 71.

to extinction. Red is reduced to three pieces, none of which intervenes effectively. The Red Queen vanishes before Alice makes her first move as a pawn and only reappears to be captured. The Red Knight is quickly disposed of.

Most of the satire is directed against the Protestant aspect of the Church, by means of White and the various chimeras and fabulous monsters brought in to augment the chess-men and to represent various subtle shades of non-conformist and Anglo-Catholic opinion. Alice starts off, as Dodgson himself had done, very much under the influence of dogma (Red Queen) but in the game she is made to belong to the White side. She meets two things in the Red King's dream, Tweedledum and Tweedledee, who are High Church and Low Church. In the poem they warn her against Broad Church. Presently she meets the White Queen and is helpful to that flustered and dishevelled lady, though declining to think of herself as her servant.

Meanwhile, the White Queen or Protestant aspect of the Church has turned into an old sheep and almost into a porcupine, that is has become both woolly and prickly. She has also laid an egg, which is Verbal Inspiration or Protestant Orthodoxy (Humpty Dumpty). It is the shattering of this orthodoxy which has produced, as it has been produced by, the Battle of the Books, through which, and so far as possible remaining neutral, Alice, in all her different 'meanings', must make her way towards Queendom. The Red Knight, who is Blind Faith, claims to have captured her, and the White Knight, who is Science or Pure Reason, to have set her free, but it is noticeable that she is of much more help to the White Knight than he is to her. She is gentle, patient, unselfish, does everything that is asked of her cheerfully and to the best of her ability and, sure enough, her empty plate turns into a queenly crown.

How can such work be assessed? Resemblances to different branches of art and literature have been noted. It is a form of caricature, containing satire and burlesque, wisdom and speculation and mischief. In some ways it resembles *Gulliver's Travels* or *Erewhon*, in others the fables of Aesop or the parables of Jesus. It is the nothing that is more than matter on the lips of distracted Ophelia, the assumed madness of Hamlet or Edgar, the professional madness of the court fool. It is entirely unlike the contemporary nonsense of Edward Lear; nor is it in the least

Gilbertian. It has more in common with the theories of non-Euclidean geometry or with the poetry of Donne or Blake.

But in the aggregate it is unlike anything else, a separate and distinct form of art. It is not mere ingenuity, for of that we would tire, and we never tire of it. It is as 'full of quotations' as Hamlet or the Bible. Familiarity with its symbols is expected of educated people, though the literary convention is to misapply and the parliamentary tradition to misquote. It has provided countless books with titles and illumined the profundities of modern physics at least for those who write them. One meets Alice wandering, puzzled but not downhearted, through sermons, treatises on relativity or psychology, examination papers —and invariably one experiences a sudden lifting of the load as at the sight of a known face in a strange city, 'a white sail on a windy sea, a green tree in a solitary place'.

For such a book, Tenniel was the ideal illustrator. His method, too, was a form of metaphor, of which the famous 'Dropping the Pilot' cartoon to mark the dismissal of Bismarck is a good example. Nevertheless, Tenniel was not a great and original artist like Dodgson. He was an illustrator, and few of the ideas even in his *Punch* cartoons were his own. On the contrary, he was given his ideas to illustrate at the Wednesday *Punch* conferences in which he took little part, his political opinions being mildly Conservative, whereas the policy of *Punch* at that time was mildly Liberal.[1]

Altogether, Tenniel did ninety-two illustrations for Dodgson, and Harry Furniss's story that the only one Dodgson liked was Humpty Dumpty is quite incredible. According to Furniss, Tenniel could not tolerate 'that conceited old don' any more, and he quotes Sir John as giving him a week in which to reach the same opinion as himself.[2] There was undoubtedly constant well-bred friction between Dodgson and Tenniel. The latter tried hard to avoid illustrating *Through the Looking-glass*, and when Dodgson wrote to him about a later book (*The Hunting of the Snark*?) declined on the grounds that *Through the Looking-glass* had exhausted his interest in book illustration. This he regarded as 'a curious fact'.[3]

---

[1] Frances Sarzano: *Sir John Tenniel*, p. 31.
[2] Harry Furniss: 'Recollections of Lewis Carroll', *Strand Magazine*, January, 1908.
[3] Coll., p. 146.

Dodgson himself had a pictorial mind and never gave up the practice of making preliminary sketches for his illustrator to copy. He had pictures in his mind which his own hand had not the skill to capture on paper. Tenniel was to do that and the sketches were intended to assist Tenniel. The trouble was that Tenniel brought an alien intelligence to bear on the problem. Of Dodgson's real purposes he had not the smallest inkling, but he saw wonderful opportunities of a quite different kind in Dodgson's queer dream-characters, and, from his point of view, rightly and properly imparted to them his own style of drollery, which he had developed in his work for *Punch*, his illustrations for *Aesop's Fables* and other books. The details of the story were less important to him than the artist's duty to make a good picture at all costs, and the pictures he produced were so good in themselves that Dodgson often had to compromise.

Thus Tenniel's White Knight was nowhere near Dodgson's idea of the White Knight. 'The White Knight must not have whiskers,' wrote Dodgson. 'He must not be made to look old.'[1] Tenniel paid no attention. 'Wait till he sees the finished picture,' we may imagine him saying. We know what the White Knight looks like now, not as Dodgson saw him but as Tenniel saw him, old and with whiskers, bearing, as his *Punch* colleagues were quick to detect, a considerable resemblance to one of their number, 'Ponny' Mayhew; Tenniel would not admit that this was intentional.[2]

When Tenniel made the drawing of Alice as a Queen he not unnaturally gave Alice a corrugated chess-dress like those of the other Queens. Dodgson made him change that. Alice was not of the nature of the chess-men at all, and in the drawing as published she appears in her best party frock with only the chess crown to mark her new status.[3]

Perhaps if Dodgson had taken Tenniel into his confidence there would have been less friction. As it was, Dodgson had no reason to be dissatisfied. Tenniel tried his best to reconcile the demands of his author with those of his medium, and it must be remembered that to him many of Dodgson's requirements must have seemed capricious and unreasonable. Only very

[1] Frances Sarzano: *Sir John Tenniel*, p. 17.
[2] For this and others of Tenniel's originals see F.S.: *Sir John Tenniel*, p. 21.
[3] See Tenniel's original sketch in Frances Sarzano's *Sir John Tenniel*, p. 68.

occasionally did he kick over the traces, as in the case of the 'wasp in a wig', which he declared was 'beyond the appliances of art'.

There have been, as Frances Sarzano declares in her study of Sir John Tenniel, better drawings but no better illustrations. In fact, they are simply the illustrations to the *Alice* books and nobody else need try.

CHAPTER SEVEN

Chasms and Crags

IT was a greatly changed Dodgson who emerged from the
writing and publication of *Through the Looking-glass*. In that
work he had made it clear to himself, if to nobody else, that his
God was a God of Love and a God of Mystery, the world vastly
stranger than the churchmen or the scientists realized, the great
controversies infinitely petty and ridiculous. He was not understood, nor had he meant to be. Nevertheless, the publication of
the book in December, 1871, brought him a measure of adult
appreciation, and 'Jabberwocky' was at once recognized as a
new and original use of language.

Another important consequence was that Macmillan and
Company could not keep pace with the orders from the book-
sellers.[1] Dodgson did not worship money. He was liberal in his
gifts to hospitals and other charities. But he rejoiced in his
power to earn money by his pen and there is no doubt that he
benefited enormously by the freedom and independence which
his secure financial position gave him. This is clearly seen in the
new batch of skits on local affairs which flowed from his pen in
the next three years. In these, the chief quarry he hunts is no
longer Jowett but the Dean of Christ Church himself. Dodgson
hated his surroundings to be disturbed. Once he was used to a
place it was impossible to improve it for him. He wanted it left
alone. No doubt it disturbed his thoughts to find the skyline of
Christ Church altering, the very quadrangle quaking and
erupting, and he found nothing edifying in the sight of the tall,
austere Liddell emerging from a drain[2] or balancing precariously
on the Cathedral roof.

But Liddell pressed on with the alterations, in the course of
which he found it necessary to pull down the old belfry in which
Great Tom was housed and as a temporary measure, in order to
protect it from the elements, to house the bell in a plain wooden

[1] Coll., p. 143. See also *Handbook*, p. 240.
[2] *Life of Liddell*, p. 196.

box.[1] This drove Dodgson nearly frantic, as did the new entrance to the Cathedral from Tom Quad and the excavations in the quadrangle itself. In 'The New Belfry' (1872) and 'The Vision of the Three T's' (1873) he gave vent to his irritation and with much wit but less humour ridiculed the Dean's efforts to put the House in order.

The best thing in 'The New Belfry' is the burlesque on Shakespeare with the Great Bell as poor Tom: 'Do poor Tom some charity. Tom's a-cold.' The Dean is now Lear, now Hamlet:

> Dean (as King Lear): The little dons and all, Tutor, Reader, Lecturer—see they bark at me!
> Censor: His wits begin to unsettle.
> Dean (as Hamlet): Do you see yonder box, that's almost in the shape of a tea-caddy?
> Censor: By its mass, it is like a tea-caddy, indeed.
> Dean: Methinks it is like a clothes-horse.
> Censor: It is backed like a clothes-horse.
> Dean: Or like a tub.
> Censor: Very like a tub.
> Dean: They fool me to the top of my bent.

But there is no real sting in that. Not so harmless was the suggestion that the Dean had embarked on a scheme of reconstruction without due regard to the cost. Dodgson's opinion, put into the mouth of the Professor of Logic, was that 'when people thus commit a fatal blunder in child-like confidence that money will be forthcoming to enable them to set it right, in ten cases out of nine, the money is *not* forthcoming. This is a large percentage.' In the sequel it is clear that the money had been forthcoming and Dodgson, no doubt nettled at being proved wrong, was not content to let sleeping dogs lie. 'The Three T's' parodies Walton's *Compleat Angler* and Piscator's remarks become indiscreetly topical:

> I will now say somewhat of the Nobler kinds, and chiefly of Goldfish, which is a species highly thought of, and much sought after in these parts, not only by men, but by divers birds, as for example, the King-fishers: and note that wheresoever you shall see those birds assemble, and but few insects about, there shall you ever find the Gold-fish most lively and richest in flavour; but wheresoever you

---

[1] In order to photograph this, Dodgson himself climbed the roof. Helmut Gernsheim, p. 66.

perceive swarms of a certain gray fly, called the Dun-fly, there the
Gold-fish are ever poorer in quality, and the King-fishers seldom
seen.

This hints obscurely at Liddell's friendship with the Prince of
Wales and at the methods by which the money was obtained to
complete the building programme.

Dodgson's chagrin at the contrast between the salaries of
University lecturers and the emoluments of Church dignitaries
also expressed itself in terms of fish:

A good Perch may sometimes be found hereabouts: but for a good
fat Plaice (which is indeed but a magnified Perch) you may search
these waters in vain. They that love such dainties must needs betake
them to some distant Sea.

The 'Three T's' were the Tea-chest (or temporary bell-
housing), the Tunnel (or new entrance to the Cathedral with its
odd double doorway) and the Trench (or excavations in the
quadrangle).

Offence was taken at the Deanery[1] but there was not much
the Dean could do about it. To take action would have been to
admit that the cap fitted and the Dean knew well enough that
his reforming policy was unpopular with the majority of his
Chapter and educational staff. Dodgson's views ran counter
to those of the age, but not to those of the Christ Church
common-room. He may have gone farther than others were
prepared to go, but on the whole he was their mouthpiece.[2]

In May, 1873, he came out into the open with some 'objections', which he submitted to 'the Governing Body of Christ
Church, Oxford' and printed for private circulation. He ob-
jected in this case to the lowering and narrowing of the terrace
and the proposed replacement of a wall by a grass slope. On the
last point his objection was sustained and he may therefore
claim a place, though an unwilling one, among those who have
made Christ Church architecturally what it is.

As to the Dean's approval or disapproval, Dodgson showed
his indifference by bringing out in the following year a collected
edition of *Notes by an Oxford Chiel*: 'Evaluation', 'Dynamics',
'Three T's' and 'The Blank Cheque, a Fable'. The last of these,
which appeared separately earlier in 1874, concerned proposals

---

[1] *Handbook*, p. 54.
[2] See *Life of Liddell*, pp. 134–7.

for building new 'schools' (examination halls) before any estimate had been obtained or plans drawn. Mrs Nivers (the U-NIVERS-ITY) and John (probably the professors, since he has his feet tucked well under his chair) have empowered Susan, the maid, to find a new school for Angela. 'Susan' was the Committee of nine appointed by Convocation on 28 November, 1873, to arrange for the building of the 'schools' and armed with powers which Dodgson thought excessive. The parable had some effect and the terms of reference were revised.

During this period, apart from the *Notes*, Dodgson published nothing but mathematical textbooks for undergraduates and a series of 'Discussions' on the best method of taking votes in elections. Nevertheless, he had already begun collecting material for another nonsense book and we can once more trace the process from the beginning.

Dodgson had met Lord Salisbury in 1870 when the Marquis had come to Oxford to be installed as Lord Chancellor. He photographed him in his robes of office along with his two sons, and partly on this account, partly, no doubt, on account of his growing reputation, was invited to Hatfield at the end of 1872. There was a large party of children and Dodgson, perhaps in response to a suggestion, perhaps on his own initiative, told them the story of 'Bruno's Revenge' which he had contributed in 1867 to *Aunt Judy's Magazine*. It was not a success. Lady Salisbury came in during the telling with 'some new toy or game to amuse her little guests, who with the usual thoughtlessness of children, all rushed off and left Mr Dodgson'.

All but one. Princess Alice, with truly royal good manners, sat down again by his side, at which he was pleased and touched.[1] And yet, it was almost a pity. But for that charming gesture he might have taken the hint, accepted the omen, let well alone. As it was, he spent the next twenty years elaborating that harmless trifle into an eccentric novel in two large volumes.

In the Preface to *Sylvie and Bruno Concluded* (1893) he wrote, correcting his earlier impression that the idea of expanding the story originated in 1874:

It was in 1873 as I *now* believe, that the idea first occurred to me that a little fairy-tale (written in 1867 for *Aunt Judy's Magazine*, under the title 'Bruno's Revenge') might serve as the nucleus for a longer

[1] Coll., p. 156.

story. This I surmise, from having found the original draft of the
last paragraph of Vol. II, dated 1873. So this paragraph has been
waiting twenty years for its chance of emerging into print—more
than twice the period so cautiously recommended by Horace for
'repressing' one's literary efforts.

Here it is:

Sylvie's sweet lips shaped themselves to reply, but her voice
sounded faint and very far away. The vision was fast slipping from
my eager gaze: but it seemed to me, in that last bewildering moment,
that not Sylvie but an angel was looking out through those trustful
brown eyes, and that not Sylvie's but an angel's voice was
whispering:
'It is Love.'

Alice, it will be remembered, was to be 'gentle as a fawn and
loving as a dog'; then trustful, 'ready to accept the wildest
impossibilities with all that eager trust that only dreamers know'.
And in the wood where things had no names she thought her
name began with L.

There was no break in the sequence of ideas, merely a
progressive idealization of the child Alice, while Alice Liddell
herself had come of age. The barrier between Alice and her
adopted uncle became more impassable as the discrepancy in
their ages became relatively less important. Many men have
married girls twenty years younger than themselves, and while
the gap between thirty-two and twelve is the same as that
between forty-two and twenty-two, it does not seem the same. It
is a difficulty, but, with goodwill on both sides, surmountable.
Socially and financially also, the gap had narrowed. On his
part there was diffidence, and perhaps reluctance to alter his
mode of living; there was his now ingrained celibacy; the fear
not only of rebuttal but of acceptance. On hers the probability is that she never thought of him as a possible husband,
that she had no feeling of that kind towards him.

Moreover, her future husband, Reginald Hargreaves, was by
then in residence at Christ Church, having come there from
Eton in 1870 or 1871.[1] Against this handsome youth of exactly
her own age with his impeccable county background the
middle-aged Dodgson with his stammer and his queer notions

[1] See F. B. Lennon: *Lewis Carroll*, Appendix D (p. 331), which gives information
published in the *Sewanee Review*, April–June, 1940.

had no chance at all. Probably Alice would meet young Hargreaves when, according to custom, his turn came to breakfast at the Deanery. On such occasions the Dean preserved complete silence and it was left to his family to entertain the visitor. The Dean himself might well look more favourably upon an old Etonian with prospects than upon a member of the college staff who had publicly accused him of bad taste in architecture and finance.

If, in his innocence, Dodgson had imagined that Alice treasured as he did the love which once undoubtedly existed between them, that she would deprive herself of all that this world had to offer her, wait for him as Charles Cayley waited for Christina Rossetti until the shadow-show was over and the great reality began, he was to be disillusioned. She was no dream-child but a healthy young woman, fully conscious of her beauty and her social position. She fell in love, and in due time went the way of the world.

There was apparently no formal leave-taking, of the kind he had envisaged in 'Faces in the Fire', unless it is preserved in the photograph of 1870, the last he ever took of Alice Liddell,[1] though she remained at Christ Church for ten years more. Alice's expression is extremely sad, and in our day of instantaneous photographs the significance of this expression is apt to be overlooked. The wet-plate process demanded a time-exposure which was long enough to be rather trying for the sitter, so that older people usually had to adopt a restful pose and even in this photograph Alice's hands rest on a cushion on her lap. Her melancholy pose was deliberately chosen, and the probability is that it was chosen by Dodgson. He wanted a sad photograph of her to match his own nostalgia for 'childhood and the happy summer days'.

There were now two Alices, therefore. One, a beautiful but sad young woman, was soon to be called Lady Muriel Orme, and the other, henceforward to be thought of as Sylvie, was abstracted from the gentle, lovable side of the child Alice. There was also the wayward, but, in Dodgson's intention, also lovable, little boy-spirit, Bruno, and a benign, elderly gentleman to do the story-telling and mental tidying up.

---

[1] *Lewis Carroll Picture Book*, also in F. B. Lennon's *Lewis Carroll*, where it is wrongly dated 1874.

Next came the hideous and loveless Uggug, abstracted from
all school bullies and spoilt children, with his foolish and
scheming parents and an allegorical Warden who was allotted
to Sylvie and Bruno as Father. The story of Prince Uggug was
written by the end of 1874. On another visit to Hatfield he had
told it to the children, but with what success Collingwood does
not say.[1]

In the 1889 Preface Dodgson says:

As the years went on I jotted down, at odd moments, all sorts of
odd ideas and fragments of dialogue that occurred to me—who
knows how?—with a transitory suddenness that left me no choice
but either to record them then and there or to abandon them to
oblivion. Sometimes one could trace to their source these random
flashes of thought—as being suggested by the book one was reading,
or struck out from the 'flint' of one's own mind by the 'steel' of a
friend's chance remark—but they had also a way of their own, of
occurring, à propos of nothing—specimens of that hopelessly illogical
phenomenon, 'an effect without a cause'.

One such phenomenon refused to be absorbed into the larger
work and achieved separate publication. This was *The Hunting
of the Snark*, in which for the last time his powers were fused.
Again, though not until the book was far advanced, there was
the stimulus of a young female personality. Again there was
violent reaction to the circumstances of his time. Again there
was an illustrator whose hand was to supply the deficiencies of
his own.

'I was walking on a hillside,' he tells us in the *Theatre* article
of 1887,

one bright summer day, when suddenly there came into my head
one line of verse—one solitary line—'For the Snark was a Boojum,
you see'. I knew not what it meant, then; I know not what it means,
now; but I wrote it down and, some time afterwards, the rest of the
stanza occurred to me, that being its last line: and so by degrees, at
odd moments during the next year or two, the rest of the poem
pieced itself together, that being its last stanza. And since then,
periodically I have received courteous letters from strangers, begging
to know whether 'The Hunting of the Snark' is an allegory, or contains some hidden moral, or is a political satire: and for all such
questions I have but one answer, 'I don't know'.

In the Preface to *The Hunting of the Snark* he points out further
that 'this poem is to some extent connected with the lay of

[1] Coll., p. 165.

the Jabberwock'. In it he uses the vocabulary he invented for 'Jabberwocky'; the Jubjub Bird and the Bandersnatch haunt those chasms and crags, and the Snark itself was conjured into existence (or non-existence) on the portmanteau-principle, since Dodgson told Beatrice Hatch that it was compounded of 'snail' and 'shark'.

We may imagine him on his solitary walk juggling with letters and syllables, reversing, transposing, almost multiplying and dividing them until he hit on a combination that pleased him: snark; boojum—'For the Snark *was* a Boojum, you see!' The line has no meaning but, like music, it expresses a mood, not, in this case, a happy one. It is an alphabetical shrug.

The Snark has been identified with Fortune, Social Advancement, Popularity and the Absolute, to mention only a few. Dodgson himself thought, or said he thought, the best explanation was contained in a letter to a newspaper, written by a lady who regarded the book as 'an allegory on the search after happiness'. This, he pointed out, fitted many of the facts, especially the bathing machines. 'When the people get weary of life and can't find happiness in towns or in books, then they rush off to the seaside, to see what bathing machines will do for them.'[1]

So he won't help us; but the mood in which he is so pointedly unhelpful is again ironical; on the surface, the patter is as amusing and whimsical as ever, but 'weary of life', 'can't find happiness', 'rush off' suggest that his own amusement is sardonic, or rueful.

The 'bathing-machines' occur in the Bellman's Speech, when he is recounting

> The five unmistakable marks
> By which you may know, wheresoever you go,
> The warranted, genuine Snarks.

Of these,

> The fourth is its fondness for bathing-machines
> Which it constantly carries about,
> And believes that they add to the beauty of scenes—
> A sentiment open to doubt.

The first three are its taste ('Which is meagre and hollow but crisp'), its habit of getting up late and its slowness in taking a jest.

---

[1] Coll., p. 173.

The fifth is ambition. It next will be right
    To describe each particular batch:
Distinguishing those that have feathers and bite
    From those that have whiskers and scratch.

Like 'Jabberwocky' it fills our heads with ideas—only we don't exactly know what they are. The 'ones which have feathers and bite' seem to be Jubjubs, abstracted no doubt from militant females with their feather boas, since the Butcher in his lesson on Natural History has this to say:

As to temper the Jubjub's a desperate bird,
    Since it lives in perpetual passion:
Its taste in costume is entirely absurd—
    It is ages ahead of the fashion.

But it knows any friend it has met once before:
    It never will look at a bribe:
And in charity-meetings it stands at the door,
    And collects—though it does not subscribe.

Those that have whiskers and scratch are Bandersnatches, one of which is described in action against the Banker.

But while he was seeking with thimbles and care,
    A Bandersnatch swiftly drew nigh,
And grabbed at the Banker, who shrieked in despair,
    For he knew it was useless to fly.

He offered large discount—he offered a cheque
    (Drawn 'to bearer') for seven-pounds-ten:
But the Bandersnatch merely extended its neck
    And grabbed at the Banker again.

However, the Bandersnatches and Jubjubs are less to be feared than the Boojums, since the Jubjub is merely heard screaming in the distance and 'the Bandersnatch fled when the others appeared'. The Boojums were certainly the worst.

Henry Holiday, the illustrator, had no theory, but supplies some very interesting information in an article he wrote for *The Academy*, 29 January, 1898. He first received three 'fits' to illustrate; the remainder came separately at intervals. The poem, he says, was intended to form part of *Sylvie and Bruno*, but as that work was not to be ready for some time and as the poem had grown far beyond the length originally contemplated for it, Dodgson decided to publish it at once. It was published on 29 March, 1876.

One of Holidays's drawings, and, according to himself, one of his best drawings, was of the Boojum. 'Mr Dodgson wrote that it was a delightful monster, but that it was inadmissible. All his descriptions of the Boojum were quite unimaginable, and he wanted the creature to remain so.' To this Holiday reluctantly consented.

The picture which seems to catch the spirit of the poem most hauntingly is that of the search, in which Hope and Care accompany the Bellman and his crew. Holiday tells us that when he sent Dodgson the sketch of the hunting in which he had introduced personifications of Hope and Care to suit the lines:

> They sought it with thimbles, they sought it with care,
> They pursued it with forks and hope—

he replied that much as he liked the drawings they clashed with his intention, which was to bring out two meanings of the word 'with'. Holiday pointed out that his drawings brought out a third meaning 'in company with' and Dodgson adopted the ladies; surprisingly, I feel, in view of their classical semi-nudity. That he realized the added depth given to his strange group of careful-hopeful searchers for something they knew not what is shown by the fact that he asked for their heads (only) to be used in the cover design. He also suggested that Hope should be surrounded by a border of interlaced forks and Care by one of thimbles, while that other significant symbol, the bell, was to decorate the corners.

Care and hope are the two qualities displayed by the bewildered band—hope leading to care. We can see the association of care and thimbles, but if hope is associated with forks, it must be hope of food, a selfish kind of hope reminiscent of 'Bread-and-butter' and the Tumtum tree.

It may be taken as axiomatic that whatever Dodgson was thinking and feeling at the time found its way into his 'nonsense'. We owe it to his new confidence in his opinions that we can tell what he was thinking and feeling at the time when *The Hunting* was being composed—or composing itself, as he wants us to believe.

He was far from happy about the way of the world, and the trigger which released his views was a letter in *The Spectator* of February, 1875, on the subject of vivisection. In the following week a long letter by Dodgson appeared in *The Pall Mall Gazette*, referring to this under the significant title, 'Vivisection as a Sign of the Times'.[1] This letter is by no means confined to the subject of vivisection. Its real subject is the new secular education brought into existence, or at least made possible, by the Education Act of 1870, and incidentally by the University Tests Act of the following year.

How far, he asked could vivisection be considered a sign of the times? The new secular state education was to give us not only knowledge but a high morality. Was the practice of vivisection an example of this or an exception to it? Dodgson himself had taken up the study of anatomy (from textbooks) in 1872 after looking on helplessly at a man in a fit, and he was referring to this when he asked how a man who had studied the brain and the nerves could deliberately inflict pain on any living creature? He was forced to the conclusion that secular education could only lead to 'the purest and most unmitigated selfishness'. (' "Take care of yourself!" screamed the White Queen.') The worship of Nature, of Reason and Humanity had been tried. For the nineteenth century had been reserved the worship of Self. The future was indeed glorious. Religion would disappear, chemistry and biology provide the new ABC and the scientists who ruled the earth would rejoice that it had become 'if not a heaven for man, at least a hell for animals'.

Shortly afterwards Dodgson treated the subject rather differently in an article 'Some Popular Fallacies about Vivisection', which *The Pall Mall Gazette* refused. It appeared in *The Fortnightly Review* dated 1 June, 1875. After considering our right to inflict pain and distinguishing between killing for food and dissecting for knowledge he asserts that the effect upon the operator is worse than that upon the animal. He then compares vivisection with blood-sports, to the detriment of the former, and advocates legislation. His thirteenth fallacy, 'That the practice of vivisection will never be extended so as to include human subjects', is of peculiar interest to a generation which has lived through the Second World War. Dodgson imagines a day when first condemned criminals, then incurables, lunatics, paupers and the weak and unprotected would be regarded as 'legitimate subjects for experiment'. Something like that

[1] Reprinted in Coll., pp. 167–71.

actually did happen in Nazi Germany. However, Dodgson's warning is for Everyman. Let us beware, he says. Our turn might come. And then, to what could we appeal? To the rights of man, to common humanity, to Mercy?

'Ask it rather of the nether millstone.'

It was in this mood of gathering gloom that his mind began, in despite of his invention, to compose a poem of its own. It has apparently escaped notice that the Bellman's bell is an ordinary school-bell of the type used before electric bells came into use. It seems to me that Dodgson quite consciously derived his Bellman from the new secular state education of which so much was hoped.

His crew are simply Tom, Dick and Harry, with the Baker as Everyman, for the framework of the poem is the nursery rhyme:

> Rub-a-dub-dub,
> Three men in a tub,
> A butcher, a baker,
> A candlestick-maker—

but Dodgson limited himself to characters beginning with the letter 'B' and widened the selection as if to let in some of all professions that go the primrose way to the everlasting bonfire. We are all there, all in the same boat, all heading in the wrong direction, going the wrong way, as the Guard said to Alice. We are adrift on unknown seas, not merely rudderless, but with the rudder mixed up with the bowsprit and the ship sailing backwards. Our only chart is a blank with such helpful particulars as equator, nadir and North Pole distributed haphazard round the sides. When we do, in spite of this, reach land, it is an island of chasms and crags in which we must search for something inconceivable, to find which is the worst thing that can happen to us.

And the end, the wild plunge into a chasm, the hope that ended in care:

> 'It's a Snark!' was the sound that first came to their ears,
> And seemed almost too good to be true.
> Then followed a torrent of laughter and cheers:
> Then the ominous words 'It's a Boo—'

> Then silence. Some fancied they heard in the air
> A weary and wandering sigh
> That sounded like '— jum!' but the others declare
> It was only a breeze that went by.

The hunter is caught by his quarry. Everyman, who (like the White Queen in the thunderstorm) has forgotten his own name, is hoist with his own petard. It is the end of 'Some Fallacies about Vivisection' disguised by fantastic dream-imagery.

Much of that imagery can be found in 'The New Belfry' and 'The Vision of the Three T's'. Take, for example, Section VII of 'The New Belfry': 'On the Impetus Given to Art in England by the New Belfry, Ch. Ch.'.

The idea has spread far and wide, and is rapidly pervading all branches of manufacture. Already an enterprising maker of bonnet-boxes is advertising 'the Belfry pattern': two builders of bathing machines at Ramsgate have followed his example: one of the great London houses is supplying 'bar-soap' cut in the same striking and symmetrical form: and we are credibly informed that Borwick's Baking Powder and Thorley's Food for Cattle are now sold in no other shape.

There are the bonnet-maker (or bonnet-box-maker in this case, but the resemblance is obvious enough), the bathing-machines, soap and, if not a baker, at least baking-powder and cattle-cake.

As for the land of chasms and crags, here in 'The Vision of the Three T's' is something very like it:

A darker vision yet! A black gash appeared in the shuddering parapet! Spirits flitted hither and thither with averted face and warning fingers pressed to quivering lips!
Then a wild shriek rang through the air

(The Beaver's Lesson: 'Then a scream, shrill and high, rent the shuddering sky')

as with volcanic roar, two murky chasms burst upon the view, and the ancient College reeled giddily around me! . . .
Stand here with me and gaze. From this thrice-favoured spot, in one rapturous glance gather in, and brand for ever on the tablets of memory, the Vision of the Three T's! To your left frowns the abysmal blackness of the tenebrous Tunnel. To your right yawns the terrible Trench. While far above, away from the sordid aims of Earth and the petty criticisms of Art, soars tetragonal and tremendous, the tintinabulatory Tea-chest! Scholar, the Vision is complete!

Complete it is, chasms and crags and all.

But the danger was past—they had landed at last,
With their boxes, portmanteaus and bags:
Yet at first sight the crew were not pleased with the view,
Which consisted of chasms and crags.

The new generation of secularly educated State schoolboys had arrived in the Christ Church which Dean Liddell had turned (in Dodgson's overheated imagination) into a landscape of nightmare precipices and ravines.

The Hunting of the Snark was not written in a short time but occupied 'a year or two' and in that time Dodgson's mood changed. The discovery that he could still produce his own distinctive work raised his spirits and laughter returned to preside over the filling-out process. Into a form decided upon while he himself was in the doldrums he poured every absurdity that occurred to him, including whole 'fits' which treat old ideas in a new way. The Butcher and the Beaver, for instance, are drawn together by the scream of the Jubjub, just as Tweedledum and Tweedledee forgot their quarrel at the approach of the monstrous crow.

Again, the Barrister's dream is in design identical with the Mouse's Tale.

'I'll be judge, I'll be Jury,'
Said cunning old Fury.

So is the Snark—and Counsel for the Defence as well as for the Prosecution. There is a link here with the trial-scene which Dodgson, on Tenniel's advice, left out of *Through the Looking-glass*, for Holiday's drawing of the trial is based on one made by Dodgson and containing a small female figure obviously intended to be Alice.

Confronted with the Banker one is tempted to outgribe in despair, but he changes colour, in the Looking-glass manner:

He was black in the face, and they scarcely could trace
The least likeness to what he had been:
While so great was his fright that his waistcoat turned *white*
A wonderful thing to be seen!

Then his chanting in mimsiest tones

Words whose utter inanity proved his insanity,
While he rattled a couple of bones

may be a weird caricature of extravagant church ritual. The Banker may well be an official of one of Butler's 'Musical Banks' (churches) in *Erewhon*. In 'The Vision of the Three T's' there are constant and scathing references to the singing and chanting of the Chapter (and also to their collection of money) in the Services which the Dean had renovated along with everything else. Dodgson, as has been shown, did not make his nonsense

M

out of nothing but used whatever lay nearest, provided only that it could be made to harmonize with the context.

Once more he was writing not for a local and restricted public but for all the world. Once more he was negotiating with an artist about illustrations for his work—and would that more of their correspondence had been preserved!

Again (and whether this was a cause or an effect of his changed mood I do not know, though I suspect both), during the summer of 1875, he made a new child-friend, Gertrude Chataway.

The importance of this kind of stimulus can be seen from an entry in his diary, 24 October, 1875, in which he records that on a sudden impulse he decided to publish *The Hunting*, wrote to Holiday and Macmillan and composed the acrostic to Gertrude Chataway—all within twenty-four hours.[1]

Gertrude records that she first met 'Mr Lewis Carroll' on the seashore at Sandown on the Isle of Wight, in the summer of 1875. In the house next door was 'an old gentleman'—he was forty-three years of age, but Gertrude was 'quite a little child' and to her he seemed elderly. Apparently Dodgson used to come out on his balcony to sniff the sea-breezes. Like Sir Roger de Coverley, he loved to clear his pipes in good air. This roused the child's curiosity and she used to watch for his 'morning hems'. One day to her joy he spoke to her. After that, it was the old story over again. They used to sit on the wooden steps which led from the gardens of the houses on to the beach while he told her stories, illustrating as he went along.

As with the Liddell children, he would take his cue from her childish comments. Her questions altered the direction of the story and made her feel that it belonged to her and her alone, as, indeed, it did. Gertrude, in later life, used to wonder just why he sought her society and never seemed to tire of it. Once she asked him and he replied that 'it was the greatest pleasure he could have to converse freely with a child, and feel the depths of her mind'.

When the holidays were over a correspondence began which Gertrude declares was one of the greatest joys of her childhood.[2] It was to her that he wrote the well-known letter about drinking

---

[1] Helmut Gernsheim, p. 72.
[2] Coll., pp. 379–85.

each other's healths (13 October, 1875) and the parcels of kisses letter (9 December, 1875). And *The Hunting* was dedicated to her, though she had no place in it, as *Alice's Adventures* and *Through the Looking-glass* were dedicated to Alice Liddell.

> Girt with a boyish garb for boyish task,
>   Eager she wields her spade; yet loves as well
> Rest on a friendly knee, intent to ask
>   The tale he loves to tell.
>
> Rude spirits of the seething outer strife
>   Unmeet to read her pure and simple spright,
> Deem, if you list, such hours a waste of life,
>   Empty of all delight.
>
> Chat on, sweet Maid, and rescue from annoy
>   Hearts that by wiser talk are unbeguiled.
> Ah, happy he who owns that tenderest joy,
>   The heart-love of a child!
>
> Away fond thoughts, and vex my soul no more!
>   Work claims my wakeful nights, my busy days—
> Albeit bright memories of that sunlit shore
>   Yet haunt my dreaming gaze!

The poem is a double acrostic, since both the initial letters and the words with which the verses begin form 'Gertrude Chataway'.

The Hunting of the Snark is the most obscure, but neither emotionally nor philosophically the most profound, of Dodgson's works. Such feelings as can be discerned appear to be suppressed irritations, the thoughts of the nature of prejudices. There is nothing in the poem which is not ridiculous, no touchstone of sanity, no love, for even the friendship of the Bearer and the Butcher arose 'merely from nervousness, not from goodwill'. He had, in some way, lost Alice, and Gertrude came too late. It is a strange interlude, an interim report in an unknown language. Again it is written in verse, and it is only in his prose that Dodgson is a true poet. His verse is, at its worst, the work of a competent tradesman, at its best of a skilled craftsman. *The Hunting* is a poem of genius, but not metrically.

As with Tenniel, he was able to get from Holiday work of a kind he never produced elsewhere. The nine illustrations are not only better drawings than Dodgson could have made himself; they are better conceptions of the characters. They are also better than Holiday could have made without Dodgson's text and suggestions to work from.

Two stand out almost as surrealist lyrics in themselves, the Search, into which Holiday so beautifully insinuated his allegorical Hope and Care, and the sinister vanishing, with the last streaks of day behind the distant crags, a black gulf containing the suggestions of trees and tenebrous horrors and in the foreground something which might be rock or a dead Prometheus. High in one corner is a hand clutching the familiar bell which seems to be tolling the knell of humanity. A book with Dodgson was not simply a piece of writing. It was an act of publication.

At this time Christ Church was graced by a number of celebrated men with all of whom Dodgson had dealings of one kind or another. There was Liddon, with whom he had toured the continent, Ruskin, who taught Alice to draw and told Dodgson he had not enough talent to make it worth his while pursuing his artistic studies, and the tall, elegant Dean, lexicographer and renovator of Christ Church buildings. Dr Pusey, who nominated Dodgson to his Studentship and who had come to Christ Church as an undergraduate in the days of George III, was now a spare, bowed figure with silver locks under a large black skull-cap.

And there was Max Müller, friend of kings and emperors, of Weber and Mendelssohn, and an accomplished musician and entertainer himself. Made an M.A. and honorary member of Christ Church in 1851, he had been disappointed in not being elected professor of Sanskrit in 1860. In 1869, however, a chair of Comparative Philology had been created specially for him and this he had filled until the year of *The Hunting* when, to give him more time to devote to his *Sacred Books of the East*, the University proposed to relieve him of the duties of his chair and appoint a deputy at half his salary.

This proposal outraged Dodgson, whose pamphlet on the subject took its stand on what would now be called the rate for the job. The decree was carried in spite of him, but Max remembered and in his essay on Dean Liddell written long afterwards refers, though not by name, to Dodgson in scathing terms.

Wherever he went, the Dean, Max says, 'towered high above the heads of all in the room. He was truly beautiful as a man.' He was not, however, without his detractors.

Even in the University there were those who could not bear his towering high above them as he did, not in stature only, but in character and position. Nasty things were said and written, but everybody knew from what forge those arrows came.[1]

Dodgson should have remembered his own fable: if you take (or try to take) a bone from a dog, its temper remains.

1876 saw the publication of two more curious and revealing items, 'An Easter Greeting to every Child who Loves Alice' and 'Fame's Penny Trumpet'. The first was evidently in reaction to the underlying rancour of *The Snark*, while the second gives open expression to it.

And is not that a Mother's gentle hand that undraws your curtains and a Mother's sweet voice that summons you to rise? To rise and forget, in the bright sunlight, the ugly dreams that frightened you so when all was dark—to rise and enjoy another happy day, first kneeling to thank that unseen Friend, who sends you the beautiful sun? . . .

Do you think He cares to see only kneeling figures, and to hear only tones of prayer—and that He does not also love to see the lambs leaping in the sunlight, and to hear the merry voices of the children, as they roll among the hay? Surely their innocent laughter is as sweet in His ears as the grandest anthem that ever rolled up from the 'dim religious light' of some solemn cathedral?

He looks forward to the time when he will walk through the valley of the shadows consoled by the thought that he has added to the happiness of the children he loves, and bids them, too, look forward to the glorious day 'when all the sadness, and the sin, that darkened life on this little earth, shall be forgotten like the dreams of a night that is past'. It is written in the spirit of the dedicatory poem to Gertrude Chataway, and was no doubt suggested by the happy relationship he had established with that 'baby child'. Apparently he met her again that summer and she visited him at Christ Church in the autumn. The friendship continued after Gertrude had grown into a woman, though he told her she would always be a child to him.

'Fame's Penny Trumpet' is an outburst against scientific research, astonishing and a little ridiculous in its vehemence. 'Affectionately dedicated to all "original researchers" who pant for "endowment"', it begins:

> Blow, blow your trumpets till they crack,
> Ye little men of little souls!
> And bid them huddle at your back—
> Gold-sucking leeches, shoals on shoals.

[1] Max Müller: 'Dean Liddell as I knew him', in *Last Essays*.

> Fill all the air with hungry wails—
>   'Reward us, ere we think or write!
> Without your Gold mere Knowledge fails
>   To sate the swinish appetite!'
>
> And where great Plato paced serene,
>   Or Newton paused with wistful eye,
> Rush to the chase with hoofs unclean
>   And Babel-clamour of the sty.

'Mountebanks', 'vermin', 'idols of a petty clique'—can this be from the pen that invited the children to a world where lovelier sights would meet their eyes than waving trees or rippling waters? These are the two aspects of his mind at this time, disgust and disappointment at what he found to be adult life and escape into a wonderland which is no longer pure mathematics but the freshness and innocence of childhood.

He is still harping on vivisection in the 'Penny Trumpet', on the hypocrites,

> Who preach of Justice—plead with tears
>   That Love and Mercy should abound—
> While marking with complacent ears
>   The moaning of some tortured hound.

Surely there is a suggestion there of the Walrus and his handkerchief as well as an echo from the letter to *The Pall Mall Gazette*, while

> And oil each other's little heads
>   With mutual Flattery's golden slime

seems afar off to imitate

> And pour the waters of the Nile
>   On every golden scale!

Afar off indeed! The direct method never suited Dodgson.

> Then let Fame's banner be unfurled!
>   Sing Paeans for a victory won!
> Ye tapers, that would light the world,
>   And cast a shadow on the Sun—
>
> Who still shall pour His rays sublime,
>   One crystal flood, from East to West,
> When ye have burned your little time
>   And feebly flickered into rest!

In the following year another letter by Dodgson appeared in *The Pall Mall Gazette*. It was on 'Natural Science at Oxford' and was suggested by the approach of a Congregation 'to be holden at Oxford on the 24th inst.' (i.e. 24 May, 1877) 'when it will be proposed to grant, to those who have taken the degrees of bachelor and master in Natural Science only, the same voting powers as in the case of the "M.A." degree'. This proposal Dodgson opposed on the grounds that it meant 'the omission of one of the two classical languages, Latin and Greek, from what has been hitherto understood as the curriculum of an Oxford education'. Soon, he thought, would come the thick end of the wedge, in which Latin and Greek might disappear from the curriculum, logic, philosophy and history follow and the destinies of Oxford be left in the hands of those who had no education other than scientific! He protested his impartiality since he himself taught science, 'for mathematics, though good-humouredly scorned by the biologists on account of the abnormal certainty of its conclusions, is still reckoned among the sciences'.

The best parts of this letter are the three acts of a little fantastic morality play. Natural Science, in Act I, presents her three fair daughters, Chemistry, Biology and Physics, and pleads for bones and sulphuretted hydrogen. Her wishes are granted but the family of Sciences remains unsatisfied. 'They fingered the bones, and thought them dry; they sniffed at the hydrogen and turned away.' In the second act Science asks for boys, not bones—for scholarships, not apparatus; and in the third which was 'yet under rehearsal' was to ask for endowments which would enable the devotees to think instead of teach. It is beautifully done, rich and bizarre in imagery, and though it is founded on prejudice and had no effect on Congregation, it relieved his feelings.

After this he seemed to become resigned to the onward march of science, though he retained his horror of vivisection. Once, much latter, when Collingwood himself was walking with Dodgson in Oxford, a well-known professor passed them.

'I am afraid that man vivisects,' said Dodgson gravely.[1]

He was, as Collingwood put it, 'nothing if not a staunch Conservative' and his conservatism was not merely political. Like the northern poets of pagan days, he thought the old times better than the new; like Mr Hardcastle in *She Stoops to Conquer*, he loved old wine, old books, old ways and never tired of

[1] Coll., p. 166.

saying so. Unfortunately for him he lived in a world which was not merely changing but in which the rate of change was also being accelerated. Not merely Christ Church but all Oxford was being renovated. Horse-trams had been introduced; they were widening Magdalen Bridge. Cowley was not yet but the city was expanding into the green country. And in everything it was the same. Even his beloved photography had lost its savour since the new dry-plate process had made it easy and cheap.[1] Now they were interfering with the order of Euclid's propositions! Nothing, absolutely nothing, was sacred.

Once more his voice was raised in defence of the old order. Hands off Euclid! *Euclid and his Modern Rivals* deserves to be better known than it is, and though in places it becomes too elaborate and complicated, it is on the whole a delightful hybrid —a mathematical thesis in the form of a five-act comedy. The prologue says that

The object of this little book is to furnish evidence, first that it is essential in elementary Geometry, to employ one text-book only; secondly, that there are strong *a priori* reasons for retaining, in all its main features, and especially in its sequence and numbering of propositions and in its treatment of parallels the Manual of Euclid; and thirdly, that no sufficient reasons have yet been shown for abandoning it in favour of any one of the modern Manuals which have been offered as substitutes.

After acknowledging that in adopting a dramatic form and a popular style he risked falling between two stools, he makes various apologies, one of which is highly significant as it gives his own estimate of his position in the mathematical world.

To Mr Wilson especially such apology is due—partly because I have criticized his book at great length and with no sparing hand— partly because it may well be deemed an impertinence in one, whose line of study has been chiefly in the lower branches of Mathematics to dare to pronounce any opinion at all on the work of a Senior Wrangler. Nor should I thus dare, if it entailed my following him up 'yonder mountain height' which *he* has scaled, but which *I* can only gaze at from a distance; it is only when he ceases 'to move so near the heavens', and comes down into the lower regions of Elementary Geometry, which I have been teaching for nearly five-and-twenty years, that I feel sufficiently familiar with the matter in hand to venture to speak.

The style has the flavour of good 'shop'. We do not have to

---

[1] This was not why he gave up photography. See below, p. 175.

understand it all to be fascinated by it, and the opening is a glimpse, distorted or transformed as always, but worth having none-the-less, into Dodgson's rooms in Tom Quad, when he was not entertaining children. Let us eavesdrop upon the Mathematical Lecturer, disguised as Minos, talking to himself as he corrects those interminable examination papers, which we are apt to forget occupied a good deal of his time; they were his 'works', as Charles Lamb said of his ledgers. What we call his works were his play.

ACT I. *Scene i.*
'CONFUSION WORSE CONFOUNDED.'

Scene: A College Study. Time: midnight. MINOS discovered seated between two gigantic piles of manuscripts. Ever and anon he takes a paper from one heap, reads it, makes an entry in a book, and with a weary sigh transfers it to the other heap. His hair, from much running of fingers through it, radiates in all directions, and surrounds his head like a halo of glory, or like the second Corollary of Euc. I. 32. Over one paper he ponders gloomily and at length breaks out in a passionate soliloquy.

Minos: So, my friend! That's the way you prove I. 19, is it? Assuming I. 20? Cool, refreshingly cool! But stop a bit! Perhaps he doesn't 'declare to win' on Euclid. Let's see. Ah, just so! 'Legendre', of course! Well, I suppose I must give him full marks for it: what's the question worth?—Wait a bit, though! Where's his paper of yesterday? I've a very decided impression he was all for 'Euclid' then: and I know the paper had I. 20, in it . . . Ah, here it is! 'I think we do know the sweet Roman hand.' Here's the proposition, as large as life, and proved by I. 19. 'Now, infidel, I have thee on the hip!' You shall have such a sweet thing to do in *viva-voce*, my very dear friend! You shall have the two propositions together, and take them in any order you like. It's my profound conviction that you don't know how to prove either of them without the other. They'll have to introduce each other, like Messrs Pyke and Pluck. But what fearful confusion the whole subject is getting into! (*Knocking heard.*) Come in!

Enter RHADAMANTHUS

Rhad.: I say! Are we bound to mark an answer that's a clear logical fallacy?

Min.: Of course you are—with that peculiar mark which cricketers call 'a duck's egg' and thermometers 'zero'.

Discussion follows of Cooley and Wilson on parallels and they finally decide that full marks must be given. Rhadamanthus takes his leave and Minos just takes forty winks and—snores.

Scene ii.

(Minos sleeping: to him enters the Phantasm of Euclid. Minos opens his eyes and regards him with a blank and stony gaze, without betraying the slightest surprise or even interest.)

Euc.: Now what is it you really require in a Manual of Geometry?

That has the grand manner and only the highly specialized nature of the subject-matter has prevented *Euclid and his Modern Rivals* from joining *Alice*, *Looking-glass* and *Snark* as a popular classic.

The attitude to ghosts and spirits displayed in this work is like that in *Phantasmagoria*, frivolous, yet curiously well-informed. Minos is to review the modern geometries without Euclid's help.

Min.: It will be weary work to do it all alone. And yet, I suppose you cannot, even with *your* supernatural powers, fetch me the authors themselves?

Euc.: I dare not. The living human race is so strangely prejudiced. There is nothing men object to so emphatically as being transferred by ghosts from place to place. I cannot say they are consistent in this matter: they are forever 'raising' or 'laying' us poor ghosts—we cannot even haunt a garret without having the parish at our heels, bent on making us change our quarters: whereas if *I* were to venture to move one single small boy—say to lift him by the hair of his head over only two or three houses, and to set him down safe and sound in a neighbour's garden—why, I give you my word, it would be the talk of the town for the next month!

Compare Alice lifting the White King to the table.

Min.: I can well believe it. But what *can* you do for me? Are their Doppelgänger available?

Euc.: I fear not. The best thing I can do is to send you the Phantasm of a German Professor, a great friend of mine. He has read all books, and is ready to defend any thesis, true or untrue.

Professor Niemand (Nobody) is abstracted from German scholarship in general and a more delightful devil's advocate it would be hard to find.

ACT II.   *Scene i.*

'E FUMO DARE LUCEM.'

(Minos sleeping. To him enter, first a cloud of tobacco-smoke, secondly the bowl, and thirdly the stem of a gigantic meerschaum; fourthly the phantasm of Herr Niemand, carrying a pile of phantom-books, the works of Euclid's Modern Rivals, phantastically bound.)

Surely this entrance is like that of the Cheshire Cat, grin first. It seems to me also that the phantom books are related to those in Fechner's 'Space Has Four Dimensions', each one of which would last for only a short time, thus fulfilling their purpose of making way for new books all the quicker.

The detailed discussion of the books is beautifully managed. Legendre is let down lightly as well suited for advanced students, though not for beginners, but Cooley is soon marched off the table; Cuthbertson follows and then Wilson is brought on, heralded by a quotation from his own preface: 'There is moreover a logic besides that of mere reasoning'.

Niemand: I lay on the table *Elementary Geometry* by J. M. Wilson, M.A., late Fellow of St John's College, Cambridge, late Math. Master of Rugby School, now Headmaster of Clifton College. The second edition, 1869. And I warn you to be careful how you criticize it, as it is already adopted in several schools.

Min.: *Tant pis pour les écoles.* So you and your client deliberately propose to supersede Euclid as a text-book.

Nie.: 'I am of opinion that the time is come for making an effort to supplant Euclid in our schools and universities' (Pref. p. XIV).

Min.: It will be necessary, considering how great a change you are advocating, to examine your book *very* minutely and critically.

Nie.: With all my heart. I hope you will show, in your review, 'the spirit without the prejudices of a geometrician'? (Pref. p. XV).

But after collecting the 'unaxiomatic axioms' and other fallacies, Minos concludes that the Manual 'has no claim whatever to be adopted as *the* Manual for purposes of teaching and examination'.

Dodgson revels in the destruction, for example, of Morell.

Min.: What have you about Lines, to begin with?

Nie.: Here is a definition. 'The place where two surfaces meet is called a line.'

Min.: Really! Let us take two touching spheres, for instance?

Nie.: Ahem! We abandon the definition.

He is also seizing on the meanings of words not intended by the author and producing little fire-crackers of pure fantasy as good in their way as any of his other 'nonsense'.

Min.: Look at p. 36. 'A circumference is generally described in language by one of its radii.' Let us hope that the language is complimentary—at least if the circumference is within hearing! Can't you imagine the radius gracefully rising to his feet, rubbing his lips with his table-napkin? 'Gentlemen! The toast I have the honour to propose is etc, etc. Gentlemen, I give you the *Circumference!*' And then the chorus of excited Lines,

'For he's a jolly good felloe!'

Nie.: (Rapturously) Ha, ha! (checking himself) You are insulting my client.

Min.: Only filling in his suggestive outlines.

In Act III the pièce de résistance is the Syllabus of the Association for the improvement of Geometrical Teaching, 1878. Niemand has to have a new name here and chooses Nostradamus, from *Nostra*, the plural of *Nostrum*, 'a quack remedy', and *damus*, 'we give'.

(Even as he utters the mystic name, the air grows dense around him, and gradually crystallizes into living forms. Enter a phantasmic procession, grouped about a banner, on which is emblazoned in letters of gold the title 'Association for the Improvement of Things in General'. Foremost in the line marches Nero, carrying his unfinished 'Scheme for the Amelioration of Rome': while among the crowd which follows him may be noticed—Guy Fawkes, President of the 'Association for raising the position of Members of Parliament'— The Marchioness de Brinvilliers, Foundress of the 'Association for the Amendment of the Digestive Faculty'—and The Rev. F. Gustrell (the being who cut down Shakespeare's mulberry-tree) leader of the 'Association for the Refinement of Literary Taste'. Afterwards enter, on the other side, Sir Isaac Newton's little dog, 'Diamond', carrying in his mouth a half-burnt roll of manuscript. He pointedly avoids the procession and the banner, and marches past alone, serene in the consciousness that he, single-pawed, conceived and carried out his great 'Scheme for the Advancement of Mathematical Research', without the aid of any association whatever.)

From this point, however, the book becomes increasingly difficult to follow, owing to a system of codifying the various methods of treating parallel lines. Dodgson assumes we can appreciate his subtleties as easily as he himself, but the labour of constantly referring to the key is more than most people, including, I suspect, most mathematicians, are prepared to take, even for the intellectual pleasure such an exercise might conceivably yield. The truth is that the field was too narrow for literature and the treatment too frivolous for mathematics. The general conclusion reached in the book was that only very slight changes were required to make Euclid the best geometry book on the market.

(To the sound of slow music, Euclid and the other ghosts 'heavily vanish', according to Shakespeare's approved stage-direction. Minos wakes with a start and betakes himself to bed, 'a sadder and a wiser man'.)

In an appendix Todhunter is allowed to supply an explanation of the sudden urge to change the order of the propositions and perhaps also of Dodgson's irritation thereat.

The objections against Euclid's order seem to me to spring mainly from an intrusion of natural history into the region of mathematics. It is to the influence of the classificatory sciences that we probably owe this notion that it is desirable or essential in our geometrical course to have all the properties of triangles thrown together, then all the properties of rectangles, then perhaps all the properties of circles, and so on.

And De Morgan in a second appendix links the mathematical with the religious heretics. 'Even Bishop Colenso has written a Euclid.'

Dodgson's outspoken pamphlets and open letters had by this time made him rather unpopular in academic circles. Ruskin was the only eminent member of the House who escaped his censure and how he did so is a mystery, for he was rich, popular and an innovator (at one time he set young Oxford to make roads in the name of progress and the brotherhood of man) but he too had a horror of vivisection and no doubt that cemented their friendship forever. It certainly seems that Dodgson was no longer a visitor at the Deanery, which was then the centre of University social life. Everybody of note called on the Liddells; Ruskin, if he thought the Dean was out, to have tea and muffins with Alice and her sisters; the Prince of Wales and other members of the royal family. Dodgson apparently did not. He went off to London to attend the theatre and meet Ellen and Kate Terry or to draw in the studio of Miss E. Gertrude Thomson.

In *The Gentlewoman* (29 January, 1898) Miss Thomson described the circumstances in which she and Dodgson became acquainted. He had seen some drawings of fairies she had made and wrote under his own name asking to see more of her work. By the same post came a letter from her London publisher telling her that the Rev. C. L. Dodgson was 'Lewis Carroll'. Evidently he was considering her in the light of a possible illustrator for *Sylvie and Bruno*.

Later he wrote asking if she ever came to London and if he might call. In the summer of 1879 she sent him word that she was in town, but when he called she was out. However, he left a card suggesting a meeting in two days' time, at some museum or gallery. Miss Thomson selected 'the South Kensington Museum, by the "Schliemann" collection, at twelve o'clock'. She arrived ahead of time and only then realized that neither knew what the other looked like. However, they recognized each other at sight. She knew him by the two little girls clinging to his hands, by his 'tall slim figure' and 'clean-shaven, delicate, refined face'. He had to rely on his own and the children's ability to detect a friend of the fairies.

When they knew each other better he sent her his drawings to criticize, and often went to her studio to draw child models. He loved the effort to draw, deplored his inability to please even his own eye and hoped that in the next world he would 'not only see lovely forms but be able to draw them'. It was nearly twenty years before she illustrated for him,[1] for he did not after all ask her to do the pictures for *Sylvie and Bruno*.

[1] *Three Sunsets*, published posthumously.

CHAPTER EIGHT

Outland

ON 15 September, 1880, Alice Liddell was married to
Reginald Hargreaves. The wedding was in Westminster
Abbey, where Dean Liddell's old friend, Dean Stanley, conducted the ceremony, and Alice was married from the Deanery,
Westminster. The rank or profession of the bridegroom is
registered as 'Esquire', that of his father, 'Esquire, J.P.', their
residence 'Cuffnells', near Lyndhurst, in the County of South-
ampton'.[1]

Dodgson was not at the wedding or, if he was, he did not
record the fact in his diary, where there is a break from 13 to
17 September. So far as we know, he spent the month of
September at Eastbourne with his sisters, and the entries on 13
and 17 September are about the arrival of another sister and
about Eastbourne friends.[2] Nor is the gap conclusive evidence
of agitation, since such gaps occur all through the diaries.
Nevertheless, his failure to mention the wedding cannot be
attributed to indifference. He must have known of it before-
hand, though he was unlikely to receive an invitation—or to
accept one—and on 17 September, when he has only common-
place events to record, the announcement appeared in *The
Times*.

To all outward appearance he was quite unaffected. During
the rest of the month we find him going to the beach, sketching
children, inventing puzzles and games as if nothing of any
importance was happening.[3] But there are unmistakable signs
that he was profoundly affected and the first of these was that he
gave up photography. The last entry in his diary relating to
this art, or, in his case, substitute for art, which he practised
assiduously for twenty-four years, was made on 15 July, 1880,
There is nothing to show why he dropped it, but the sacrifice fits
into a general pattern of renunciation and self-dedication. As

---

[1] General Register Office, Somerset House, London.
[2] Private letter, Miss F. Menella Dodgson.
[3] There is a long entry for 2 September in Coll., p. 211.

Helmut Gernsheim has pointed out, it has nothing to do with the invention four years earlier of the dry-plate process but was apparently a sudden decision taken during the summer vacation of 1880.[1]

It was a sign that he had begun to feel old, that he wished to conserve his powers, and it was soon to be followed by signs even more obvious. He had never been completely at home with young men and there is evidence that his mathematical lectures were neither inspiring nor well-attended, except on compulsion. In February, 1880, he had made the extraordinary proposal that, as the tutorial work was now lighter, his salary should be reduced from £300 to £200. The gesture was lost, for the proposal was not accepted.[2] Now, in 1881, he determined to resign. The £300 he would surrender had made it easier to provide for his sisters but he hoped to make good its loss by his writing.[3] It is doubtful if he did so by his new writing but the *Alice* sales held steady and could be trusted to pay for all.

A month previously he had held out the olive branch to Dean Liddell by defending him in *The Observer* against a charge of neglecting his duties and displaying favouritism towards highly-connected undergraduates.[4] But when he finally took steps to make his resignation effective, it seems that he was still not on calling terms at the Deanery. On 18 October he wrote to the Dean resigning his lectureship and three days later received a reply regretting the loss of his services but admitting that he had earned the right to retire.[5] He and the Dean lived within a hundred yards of each other, yet when this important step was proposed Dodgson neither called nor was invited to call upon the Dean to discuss the matter. They exchanged notes.

At his last lecture on 30 November, 1881, only two attended. The possible was nine. He felt sad and old; he was not yet fifty.[6] Like the superannuated Lamb he now had his whole time to himself and hoped before his powers failed to write something of worth. He dedicated himself to three causes, mathematical education, the entertainment of children and

[1] Helmut Gernsheim, p. 77.
[2] Coll., p. 210.
[3] Ib., p. 218.
[4] Ib., pp. 214–6.
[5] Ib., p. 218.
[6] Ib., p. 219.

religious thought. The cynic might find his prayer, that God would bless his efforts, ironical.[1] He had already written almost everything of permanent value which he had it in him to write. The rest of the story is of declining powers, waning inspiration, growing eccentricity. An entry in his diary for 1 June, 1882, suggests a symbol. 'Went out with Charsley and did four miles on one of his velocimans, very pleasantly.'[2] The velociman was a large tricycle steered from behind the rider's back by means of a curved bar.[3] Dodgson never attempted to bicycle but produced a typical formula:

> In youth, try a bicycle,
> In age, buy a tricycle.

There he is then, our White Knight, in his frock-coat pedalling away towards the sunset and the dark forest. At the turn in the road he pauses to raise his top-hat in a last precarious gesture, hoping perhaps for the flutter of some responsive handkerchief.

Henceforward, he was in a sense finished with the world. He continued to invent games and puzzles, to make endless suggestions for improving things, including the velociman—improving things like lawn-tennis tournaments and the election of proctors—to devise systems of mnemonics and new theories of parallels, to conduct arguments with circle-squarers and hair-splitting disputes with logicians. He was passing the time.

In 1882, he produced the words of 'Dreamland', to suit an air dreamed by a friend of his, the Rev. C. E. Hutchinson of Chichester. In his dream, Hutchinson was seated in some vast amphitheatre, watching a procession of the heroes of former days. One by one the figures passed across a stage against a dark curtain, turned and gazed upon the silent witnesses and moved away. He knew their names, but remembered only the figure of St. George, his mighty arms and silver shield uncannily blue-lit; and when he awoke could still hear a curious melody and the words 'I see the shadows falling and slowly pass away'.[4] This curious dream of his friend's inspired Dodgson to write his best serious lyric, into which he wrote his own pride in the ancient university and in the history of his country, his perception, not new, but his own, of the transience of earthly things,

---

[1] Coll., p. 218.
[2] Ib., p. 219.
[3] Miss Violet Dodgson, broadcast, Third Programme, 15 September, 1950.
[4] Coll., p. 223.

and the strange thought that in dreams we are closer to reality than in waking life.

> When midnight mists are creeping
> And all the land is sleeping,
> Around me tread the mighty dead
> And slowly pass away.
>
> Lo, warriors, saints and sages
> From out the vanished ages
> With solemn pace and reverend face
> Appear and pass away.
>
> The blaze of noonday splendour
> The twilight soft and tender,
> May charm the eye: yet they shall die,
> Shall die and pass away.
>
> But here, in Dreamland's centre,
> No spoiler's hand may enter,
> These visions fair, this radiance rare,
> Shall never pass away.
>
> I see the shadows falling
> The forms of old recalling;
> Around me tread the mighty dead,
> And slowly pass away.

The lyric, be it said, the product of Dodgson's waking mind, is better than Hutchinson's dream-music, which is a rather sentimental hymn tune.

He became indifferent to the proprieties and did not hesitate to go upon long rambles with unchaperoned ladies. E. L. S., wife of a Student of the House, records that she often went walking with him 'by Mesopotamia, up Headington Hill to Joe Pullen's tree; down to Iffley; round the "4-mile grind", over Folly Bridge, along the towing-path and back by Kensington, he talking all the way'. He told her innumerable stories, but never the same one twice and used his old trick of holding up the point by means of his stammer. When they had to negotiate a stile he went first, turned his head away so as not to see the point of her shoe and held out his hand to help her over.[1]

At the end of the year he was elected Curator of the Common Room, which he thought would take him out of himself a little: 'my life was tending to become too much that of a selfish recluse'.[2] There is abundant evidence that he was not merely a

---

[1] 'Lewis Carroll as Artist', *Cornhill Magazine*, November, 1932, pp. 559–62.
[2] Coll., p. 221.

conscientious official—he published several pamphlets on his tenure of office and on the problems he encountered—but a recognized wit. 'There was always the same mind displayed in his talk,' says Strong, who replaced him ten years later, and adds a penetrating analysis of Dodgson's conversation. He did not excel in anecdote but in the power of 'revealing a new meaning in some ordinary expression, or in developing unexpected consequences from a very ordinary idea'.[1] This is exactly what we should expect from the author of the footnotes in *The Rectory Umbrella* or the story-teller described by Gertrude Chataway.

But in his letters Dodgson reveals the other side of his character:

I find that as life slips away (I am over fifty now) and the life on the other side of the great river becomes more and more the reality, of which *this* is only a shadow, that the petty distinctions of the many creeds of Christianity tend to slip away as well—leaving only the great truths which all Christians believe alike.[2]

The Society for Psychical Research was constituted in February, 1882, and Dodgson's name appears in the first list of members, dated December, 1883. He continued to be a member until the year before his death and in the Dodgson Sale Catalogue are listed eleven volumes of the *Proceedings* and seven of the *Journal* of the Society. Other books on spiritualism and kindred subjects which he possessed are Home's *Lights and Shadows of Spiritualism*, Lee's *Other World*, Wallace's *Miracles and Modern Spiritualism*, Thomson's *Philosophy of Magic*, Christmas's *Phantom World*, Seafield's *Literature and Curiosities of Dreams*, Clodd's *Myths and Dreams* and numerous other works on the occult, among which should perhaps be mentioned Gilchrist's *Life of William Blake*.[3] He had always been interested in ghosts and spirits, but in his writings had invariably treated them flippantly. Now he began to take the subject seriously and this new attitude to the spirit-world affected the form and texture of *Sylvie and Bruno*, material for which was still accumulating.

He was also contributing to *The Monthly Packet*, edited by Charlotte M. Yonge, a series of mathematical puzzles. He had

[1] *Cornhill Magazine*, March, 1898, p. 304.
[2] Coll., p. 340.
[3] *Dodgson Sale Catalogue*, Bodleian.

met this very popular authoress of High Anglican romances in
1866 and, according to Collingwood, before that her novels
'had long delighted him'. From April, 1880, until March, 1885,
he carried on an open correspondence on the problems he set,
classifying and grading the answers that were sent in from all
over the country and thoroughly enjoying himself. The complete set was published in December, 1885, as *A Tangled Tale*,
with illustrations by Arthur B. Frost, who also illustrated *Rhyme?
and Reason?* a collected edition of his humorous verse which
appeared two years earlier.

At the beginning of 1885 he seems to have felt that the time
had come to put *Sylvie and Bruno* into its final shape. Reluctantly
but firmly, even rather abruptly, he terminated the *Tangled Tale*,
declaring: 'My puppets were neither distinctly *in* my life (like
those I now address) nor yet (like Alice and the Mock Turtle)
distinctly *out* of it'. By then, most of the material for both
volumes of the new work was in chaotic existence and on
1 March he wrote to Harry Furniss of the *Punch* staff asking him
to do the illustrations.[1]

On the same day he wrote to Alice asking her consent to the
publication in facsimile of the original *Under Ground* MS. It
is a strange letter, beginning 'My dear Mrs Hargreaves' and
suggesting that his words will come 'like a voice from the
dead, after so many years of silence'. The years have made no
difference, however, to his memory of the days when they *did*
correspond. He calls her his ideal child-friend and dismisses the
scores of child-friends he has had since as 'quite a different
thing'. And so to his request. He has not seen the volume for
'about twenty years', has doubts about the quality of the illustrations, but requests that Alice should send the volume, 'registered
post, I should think'. He could, he realizes, lay himself open to
the charge of 'gross egoism' but knows he has 'no such motive',
and reminds her that more than 120,000 copies of the two
Alice books have been sold. No doubt many people would like
to see the original form of the story. He signs himself always her
friend, C. L. Dodgson.

A great deal might be read between the lines of that letter.
'A voice from the dead . . . quite a different thing . . . we *did*
correspond . . . I have not seen it for about twenty years' (since

[1] Coll., p. 236.

about 1865 that is to say)'. . . My dear Mrs Hargreaves . . . Always your friend.'

Egoism being ruled out we may reasonably feel some curiosity about the motive which led him to publish this rough draft of a book which was already known to the public in a form more complete, better illustrated and less personal. The most probable explanation is that, when about to turn his accumulation of bits and pieces into a new major work, he required some contact, however remote, with Alice and the times with which she was associated. He felt that he had lost the magic touch and hoped thus to recover it.

More than a year later, in a letter to Alice dated 11 November, 1886, he tells the story of this odd edition.[1] He has, he says, had 'almost as many adventures in getting that unfortunate facsimile finished *Above* ground, as your namesake had *Under* it!' The first zincographer he approached insisted on being entrusted with the book, which Dodgson refused, countering with an offer to come to London and turn the pages. He felt that the book ought not to be '*touched* by the workmen's hands'. The offer being declined on the grounds that other authors' works were being photographed and must on no account be seen by the public, and Dodgson's word that he would look at nothing but the *Adventures* not being sufficient, he next applied to a photographer who was willing to come to Oxford. The photographing was accordingly done in his own studio, he turning the pages. Next he made the mistake of paying for the blocks in advance. At first these arrived regularly, but when twenty-two remained to be delivered the photo-zincographer disappeared, taking the negatives with him. Meantime Dodgson had returned the book to Alice, by the hand of one of her sisters, and he had scruples about asking for it a second time, 'to rob her of it again' as he put it, for even registered post was not, in his opinion, absolutely safe.

As nobody then could have had any suspicion that this small volume would one day change hands at nearly £30,000 his anxiety about its safety must have seemed excessive, at any rate to Mrs Liddell, perhaps even to Mrs Hargreaves, but that we cannot certainly know. At all events it was worth treasuring, for in 1928 Alice sold it at Sotheby's for £15,400, thus launching

[1] Coll., pp. 256–8.

it on its own adventures in America. From these it has now returned, gifted generously and unobtrusively to the British Museum by a group of American business-men.

We digress. 'Mr X', as Dodgson called him, came out of hiding in April, 1886, left eight blocks at Macmillan's and again vanished. In the summer of that year Dodgson had to employ a solicitor, take out a summons, appear in court and explain what photo-zincography was. Threatened with actual imprisonment, Mr X produced the fourteen negatives, Mr Dodgson dropped the action, pocketed his loss and had the blocks made elsewhere. The first copies were available on 17 December and Alice received one bound in white vellum.

December saw another recrudescence of the *Alice* story, for Savile Clarke's stage version was then appearing at the Prince of Wales' Theatre with Phoebe Carlo as Alice and Sydney Harcourt as the Mad Hatter. The music was by Walter Slaughter. It met with some success, 'for the first few weeks at least', and in the provinces 'with a fair amount of success'.[1] It also led to the very revealing *Theatre* article of 1887 to which frequent reference has been made.

On 29 March, 1885, Dodgson had noted in his diary: 'Never before have I had so many literary projects on hand at once' and listed fifteen of them besides 'other shadowy ideas'. Not all of these were actually published, but the Supplement and second edition of *Euclid and his Modern Rivals* and *A Tangled Tale* belong to 1885, the *Under Ground* facsimile and *Game of Logic* to 1886. The first part of his *Pillow Problems and other Math. Trifles* appeared in 1888 as *Curiosa Mathematica*, and the *Nursery Alice* in 1889.

In 1889 also was published '(15) The new child's book, which Mr Furniss is to illustrate. I have settled on no name as yet, but it will perhaps be *Sylvie and Bruno*.'[2] In the preface to the first part he explains why he did not adopt the same plan as for his earlier and highly successful books. The *Alice* books had been imitated.

The path I timidly explored—believing myself to be 'the first that ever burst into that silent sea'—is now a beaten high-road: all the way-side flowers have long ago been trampled into the dust: and it would be courting disaster for me to attempt that style again.

[1] Coll., p. 252.
[2] Ib., p. 240.

Hence it is that in *Sylvie and Bruno*, I have striven—with I know not what success—to strike out yet another new path: be it bad or good, it is the best I can do. It is written, not for money, and not for fame, but in the hope of supplying, for the children whom I love, some thoughts that may suit those hours of innocent merriment which are the very life of childhood: and also, in the hope of suggesting, to them and to others, some thoughts that may prove, I would fain hope, not wholly out of harmony with the graver cadences of Life.

Here was the chief cause of failure. In the *Alice* books the solemn thoughts were allowed to come and go, to give rise to the nonsense and to emerge from it again. Now for pages on end we have to consider them on their merits, then for pages on end the kind of nonsense which is not based upon them. It is as if a conjuror, instead of producing a rabbit out of a hat, were to present them both to the audience at the same time.

Let us, however, examine the new plan, which was, as he said himself, the best he could do. In the first place there is a group of human characters among whom is worked out a simple but highly significant little plot. The hero is Arthur Forester, a brilliant young doctor, very much in love with Lady Muriel Orme, the daughter of a kindly old Earl.

'I hadn't meant to tell you anything about her,' he said (naming no names, as if there were only one 'she' in the world!) 'till you had seen more of her, and formed your own judgment of her: but somehow you surprised it out of me. And I've not breathed a word of it to anyone else. But I can trust *you* with a secret, old friend! Yes! It's true of *me*, what I suppose *you* said in jest.'

'In the merest jest, believe me!' I said earnestly. 'Why, man, I'm three times her age!'

(He had said, '*I* quite lost my heart to her!')

'But if she's *your* choice, then I'm sure she's all that is good and—'

'—and sweet,' Arthur went on, 'and pure, and self-denying, and true-hearted, and—' he broke off hastily as if he could not trust himself to say more on a subject so sacred and so precious. Silence followed, and I leaned back drowsily in my easy-chair, filled with bright and beautiful imaginings of Arthur and his lady-love, and of all the peace and happiness in store for them.

But Arthur is at first not over-endowed with worldly goods.

'When I first spoke to you about—' Arthur began after a long and embarrassing silence, 'that is, when we first talked about her—for I think it was *you* that introduced the subject—my own position in life forbade me to do more than worship her from a distance: and

I was turning over plans for leaving this place finally, and settling somewhere out of all chance of meeting her again.'

'Would that have been wise?' I said. 'To leave yourself no hope at all.'

'There *was* no hope to leave,' Arthur firmly replied, though his eyes glittered with tears as he gazed upwards into the midnight sky, from which one solitary star, the glorious 'Vega' blazed out in fitful splendour through the driving clouds. 'She was like that star to me —bright, beautiful and pure, but out of reach, out of reach!'

A letter from his solicitor alters Arthur's financial position and removes that particular obstacle, but still he dares not put the matter to the proof.

'And as for—as for Lady Muriel, try as I may, I *cannot* read her feelings towards me. If there *is* love, she is hiding it! No, I must wait, I must wait!'

The Narrator, older and wiser, advises him to speak.

'But meanwhile,' I pleaded, 'you are running a risk that perhaps you have not thought of. Some other man—'

'No,' said Arthur firmly. 'She is heart-whole. I am sure of that. Yet, if she loves another better than me, so be it! I will not spoil her happiness. The secret shall die with me. But she is my first— and my *only* love!'

Next there is the arrival of a handsome young cousin, the Honourable Eric Lindon, who is waiting for a commission in the army. The telegram which informs him of his posting leads to his formal engagement to Lady Muriel and the end of Arthur's hopes.

'Then the telegram has come!' I said.

'Did you not hear?' (the Earl speaking). 'Oh, I had forgotten, it came in after you left the Station. Yes, it's all right. Eric has got his commission; and, now that he has arranged matters with Muriel, he has business in town that must be seen to at once.'

'What arrangement do you mean?' I asked with a sinking heart, as the thought of Arthur's crushed hopes came to my mind. 'Do you mean that they are *engaged*?'

'They have been engaged—in a sense—for two years,' the old man gently replied: 'that is, he has had my promise to consent to it, so soon as he could secure a permanent and settled line in life. I could never be happy with my child married to a man without an object to live for—without even an object to die for!'

'I hope they will be happy,' a strange voice said. The speaker was evidently in the room, but I had not heard the door open, and I looked round in some astonishment. The Earl seemed to share my surprise. 'Who spoke?' he exclaimed.

'It was I,' said Arthur, looking at us with a worn, haggard face, and eyes from which the light of life seemed suddenly to have faded. 'And let me wish *you* joy also, dear friend,' he added, looking sadly at the Earl, and speaking in the same hollow tones that had startled us so much.

'Thank you,' the old man said, simply and heartily.

A silence followed: then I rose, feeling sure that Arthur would wish to be alone, and bade our gentle host 'Good night': Arthur took his hand, but said nothing: nor did he speak again, as we went home, till we were in the house and had lit our bedroom candles. Then he said more to himself than to me, '*The heart knoweth its own bitterness.* I never understood those words till now.'

Arthur prepares to leave for India where he has been offered a medical appointment.

'Out there, I suppose I shall find something to live for; I can't see *anything* at present. "This life of mine I guard, as God's high gift, from scathe and wrong. Nor greatly care to lose!" '

'Yes,' I said, 'your name-sake bore as heavy a blow, and lived through it.'

'A far heavier one than *mine*,' said Arthur. 'The woman *he* loved proved false. There is no such cloud as *that* on my memory of—of—' He left the name unuttered.

The book ends with a kind of litany: 'Look Eastward!'

'Aye, look Eastward!' Arthur eagerly replied, pausing at the stair-case window, which commanded a fine view of the sea and the eastward horizon. 'The West is the fitting tomb for all the sorrow and the sighing, all the errors and the follies of the Past: for all its withered Hopes and all its buried Loves! From the East comes new strength, new ambition, new Hope, new Life, new Love! Look Eastward! Aye, look Eastward!'

And the Narrator, as he watches the sunrise, concurs.

'So may it be for him, and me and all of us!' I mused. 'All that is evil, and dead, and hopeless, fading with the Night that is past! All that is good, and living, and hopeful, rising with the dawn of Day!

'Fading, with the Night, the chilly mists, and the noxious vapours, and the heavy shadows, and the wailing gusts and the owl's melancholy hootings: rising, with the Day, the darting shafts of light, and wholesome morning breeze, and the warmth of a dawning life, and the mad music of the lark! Look Eastward. ·

'Fading, with the Night, the clouds of ignorance, and the deadly blight of sin, and the silent tears of sorrow! and ever rising higher, higher with the Day, the radiant dawn of knowledge and the sweet breath of purity, and the throb of a world's ecstasy! Look Eastward!

'Fading, with the Night, the memory of a dead love, and the

withered leaves of a blighted hope, and the sickly repinings and moody regrets that numb the best energies of the soul: and rising, broadening, rolling upward like a living flood, the manly resolve, and the dauntless will, and the heavenward gaze of faith—*the sub-stance of things hoped for, the evidence of things not seen!*

'Look Eastward! Aye, look Eastward!'

This is not fiction but autobiography. Arthur and the Narrator are projections of Dodgson himself, the latter older than Dodgson ever became ('three score years and ten, baldness and spectacles'), Arthur apparently younger but, in the passages quoted above, not really to be distinguished as a character.

What Dodgson meant his characters to look like in Harry Furniss's illustrations can be seen from his criticisms of the preliminary sketches.[1] The doctor would not do at all! He was too much the popular London type, too old at forty and could have had 'no love-affair for the last fifteen years'. Dodgson wanted him to be 'about twenty-five, powerful in frame and poetical in face'; and, rather surprisingly, capable of being a passionate lover. As a model he suggested 'King Arthur when he first met Guinevere'. Eric was better but his face suggested the 'masher', which meant that it must be re-drawn, and his hair must not be short, as that fashion could not be expected to last! Lady Muriel was even less satisfactory. He did not think he would enjoy talking to her and would be quite unable to fall in love with her. Nor was the Earl acceptable. He looked, said Dodgson, as if he would be proud of his title, too formal and distant (one thinks at once of the Red Queen) and too tall. What was required was 'a gentle, genial old man with whom one would feel at one's ease in a moment'.

Furniss's 'Earl' was, in fact, too like Dean Liddell. Dodgson was writing plastic autobiography and gave Lady Muriel the characteristics he thought Alice had or should have had, in-cluding a very different father and no mother! Her age in the story is 'scarcely over twenty', about the age, that is, of the 'sad' photograph of 1870. But Arthur's age is 'about twenty-five' and he is identical with Dodgson and with the Narrator. He is the age Dodgson would have liked to be when Alice was 'scarcely over twenty', that is to say, young enough to have a chance (about twenty-five), just as the Narrator is much too old (about seventy), and therefore not expected to compete.

[1] Coll., p. 260.

In *Sylvie and Bruno Concluded* (1893) there is a 'wish-fulfilment' ending with Lady Muriel breaking off her engagement on theological grounds.

'I would like to tell you how it happened,' Lady Muriel remarks to the Narrator, who has again arrived at Elveston station.

'I had long realized that we were not in sympathy in religious belief. His ideas of Christianity are very shadowy; and even as to the existence of a God, he lives in a sort of dreamland. But it has not affected his life! I feel sure, now, that the most absolute Atheist *may* be leading, though walking blindfold, a pure and noble life.'

Eric, it seems, has released her unconditionally, though the ethics of accepting his self-sacrifice have to be debated at length before she can be convinced that she is entitled to her freedom. The next task is to bring Arthur and Lady Muriel together, which, with a little sylph-like assistance from the invisible Sylvie and Bruno, is at length accomplished.

'And what sort of meeting was it?' I wondered, as I paced dreamily on.

'They shooked hands,' said Bruno, who was trotting at my side, in answer to the unspoken question.

'And they looked *ever* so pleased!' Sylvie added from the other side.

> 'Ah Love! Could thou and I with Fate conspire
> To grasp this sorry Scheme of Things entire,
> Would we not shatter it to bits—and then
> Re-mould it nearer to the Heart's desire!'

About these sprites a whole world has grown up, a realm called Outland, governed by a Warden who absents himself in order to go upon a journey disguised as a beggar. The Sub-Warden and his fat wife conspire with the Chancellor to usurp his authority. He visits them in disguise, is spurned and insulted by their ugly son, Uggug, and eventually returns in thunder and storm to discipline the guilty and proclaim the Empire of Love.

The system by which the two worlds are brought into contact has already been explained. The Narrator himself is the chief 'medium', since he suffers from heart-trouble which produces states of semi-consciousness (or eerieness) and sometimes trances in which he visits Outland. All the permutations and combinations are exhibited, and still further complicated by the fact that Arthur, Lady Muriel, the Earl and even the sceptical Eric are also subject to various degrees of eerieness and thus make the acquaintance of visitants from Outland.

Allegory freely invades our everyday world, in the person of an aged man in a smock frock who is roughly cleared out of the way by the Station-master at Fayfield Junction ('change here for Elveston') in order to make way for Lady Muriel. That was in Part I. Part II takes us again to the Junction,

and, to make this repetition of it stranger still, there was the same old man, whom I remembered seeing so roughly ordered off, by the Station-master, to make room for his titled passenger. The same, but 'with a difference': no longer tottering feebly along the platform, but actually seated at Lady Muriel's side, and in conversation with her! 'Yes, put it in your purse,' she was saying ... Rather than disturb the poor old man at her side, she rose from her seat, and joined me in my walk up and down the platform . . .

In the words of the old Gaelic poet,

> Often, often, often
> Goes the Christ in the stranger's guise.

The characters in the Outland story are also used to demonstrate a system of punishments and rewards in the hereafter similar in some respects to that devised by Kingsley in *The Water Babies*.

On his departure to Elfland, the Warden gives to Sylvie a locket, which has the curious optical property of being transparent, yet red on one side and blue on the other. When rubbed in the correct manner, the Outland scenery opens to reveal Elfland. But when the locket is wrongly handled, our world begins to break through in the most alarming fashion and a mouse finds its way into Outland. Here it turns into a lion, but a gentle, loving lion, without any earthly fierceness. Perhaps, on earth, it was a good mouse, the mouse that set the lion free in Aesop's fable?

The reverse process is exhibited when the Professor is delivering his long-promised lecture. By means of a 'Megaloscope' he reduces an elephant to the size of a mouse. He then 'reverses the tubes' and turns a flea into a monster, the size of a horse. It escapes.

The monster gathered its legs together, and in one tremendous bound vanished into the sky.

'Where is it?' said the Emperor, rubbing his eyes.

'In the next Province, I fancy,' the Professor replied.

No doubt it has entered our world, where relative to ourselves it will be of the normal, inconvenient size. The application of this idea to Prince Uggug reveals Dodgson's purpose. This 'boy', ugly in nature as in appearance, 'Loveless, loveless!', turns into a porcupine and is sent into our world to be disciplined, as the mouse went into Outland to be rewarded. The 'philosophy' is, in fact, a modified form of Platonism.

Puzzles, jokes and riddles are set, told or posed by the Professor, whose counterpart, the Other Professor, always has his back to us, and by Mein Herr, but though some of these are amusing and all are ingenious, there is nothing of the *Wonderland* or *Looking-glass* quality in them. The contrast is greatest when, as he frequently does, he uses *Wonderland* or *Looking-glass* ideas remade as problems or whimsical discussions.

There is, for example Mein Herr's gravity-trains which require only 'machinery to stop them with'.

'But that would need a railway going *down-hill*,' the Earl remarked. 'You can't have all your railways going down-hill?'
'They *all* do,' said Mein Herr.
'Not from *both* ends?'
'From *both* ends.'
'Then I give it up!' said the Earl.
'Can you explain the process?' said Lady Muriel. 'Without using that language, that I can't speak fluently?'
'Easily,' said Mein Herr. 'Each railway is in a long tunnel, perfectly straight: so of course the *middle* of it is nearer the centre of the globe than the two ends: so every train runs half-way *down*-hill, and that gives it force enough to run the *other* half *up*-hill.'
'Thank you. I understand that perfectly,' said Lady Muriel. 'But the velocity in the *middle* of the tunnel, must be something *fearful*!'

Mein Herr was evidently much gratified at the intelligent interest Lady Muriel took in his remarks.

This is the kind of use made of dynamics in contriving Alice's fall to the centre of the earth, though the strict application of the principle would, as she half-suspected, have landed her at the 'antipathies'. But in the *Wonderland* story we are not asked to admire the cleverness of the idea. We are presented with the consequences in the form of Alice's experiences and share her bewilderment. That was 'nonsense'. This is merely a stray 'knot' from *A Tangled Tale*.

Another gravity problem is expounded by Arthur:

'How convenient it would be,' Lady Muriel laughingly remarked, *à propos* of my having insisted on saving her the trouble of carrying a cup of tea across the room to the Earl, 'if cups of tea had no weight at all! Then perhaps ladies would *sometimes* be permitted to carry them for short distances!'

'One can easily imagine a situation,' said Arthur, 'where things would necessarily have no weight, relatively to each other, though each would have its own weight, looked at by itself.'

'Some desperate paradox!' said the Earl. 'Tell us how it could be. We shall never guess it.'

'Well, suppose this house, just as it is, placed a few billion miles above a planet, and with nothing else near enough to disturb it: of course it falls *to* the planet?'

The Earl nodded. 'Of course—though it might take some centuries to do it.'

'And is five o'clock tea to be going on all the while?' said Lady Muriel.

Compare with this the Mad Hatter's remark: 'It's always six o'clock now'. Conditions have been devised which affect not only the law of gravity but time, and these are factors which would also be affected at the centre of the earth. Arthur goes on to develop the little scientific fantasy but only in conversation. H. G. Wells, whose *Time Machine* was already on the market, went back to Dodgson's earlier method of demonstration in action and used the very same idea in *The First Men in the Moon* and 'The Truth about Pyecraft', with far more striking effect.

In his treatment of time Dodgson does use the old baffling technique, but mere ingenuity has replaced the exquisite simplicity of the earlier works. There is, for instance, an 'Outlandish Watch' which makes everything happen backwards in a manner calculated to the last tedious detail. The White Queen living backwards on the chess-board Through the Looking-glass was one thing. An ordinary humdrum family sewing and eating backwards is another. Nor does it seem to matter that the Narrator can have a multitude of outlandish experiences in 'the space of a single comma in Lady Muriel's speech! A single comma, for which grammarians tell us to "count *one*"!' We accept the fact that in his trances he is out of our time and space, but if it is only to meet the Professor, or the Mad Gardener, he might just as well stay in the drawing-room with Lady Muriel, Arthur and the Earl.

Even there, however, he is by no means isolated from the other world. Sylvie and Bruno come and go, bringing flowers from Central India which disappear from a locked room and performing other 'miracles', all in a manner irresistibly suggestive of spiritualism. More interesting is the system of identifications, for we are certainly led to suppose that Sylvie and Lady Muriel, and Bruno and Arthur, are somehow the same. There is a further, disturbing possibility that Lady Muriel is one with the wife of the Sub-Warden, and that Uggug, the hideous boy, is her son. Here a curious dream, recorded by Dodgson on 15 May, 1879, may provide a clue. It was about Marion ('Polly') Terry. He seemed to be staying with his sisters in a suburb of London and went to call on the Terrys who lived near. Mrs Terry told him that Polly was playing in the 'Water House'.

'In that case,' said Dodgson in his dream, 'I'll go on there at once, and see the performance—and may I take Polly with me?'

'Certainly,' said Mrs Terry.

He felt no surprise, he says, at being about to take the ten-year-old Polly to see her grown-up self on the stage. He had two clear pictures of Polly in his mind and in his dream had given them separate and simultaneous existence.[1] This is what he has contrived to do in the case of Lady Muriel and Sylvie, Arthur and Bruno, and he has carried the process a step further by adding the Narrator, his possible older self, and the Sub-Warden's wife, a creature of nightmare when thought of as related to Lady Muriel or her prototype, Alice Liddell. As for Prince Uggug, he seems to embody the side of boyhood repugnant to Dodgson, the bullying, gloating, greedy little beast who is not and never was us, but whom we remember as just too large to tackle successfully. He cannot in his origin have had anything whatever to do with Alice, her marriage or children, but he probably explains why Dodgson, who had confidently expected another little Alice, ignored an invitation to be godfather to a young male Hargreaves.

The whole book is of interest only in so far as it throws light on the creator of the *Alice* books. In itself, as literature, it has no claim on our attention. It is a web spun out of his suppressed desire for a happy married life, out of his jealousy and his dreams. It is a sad book and the saddest part of it is the happy ending.

[1] Coll., p. 200.

One more aspect of *Sylvie and Bruno* remains to be considered. Besides figuring in the story, the human characters are used to air Dodgson's views on a variety of subjects. Thus we have Socratic discussions of Art Criticism and Church Services, drama in life and in the theatre, how to read, observation of Sunday, Prayer and fatalism, alcoholism and teetotalism, eternity, whether animals can reason or have souls, sin and socialism. It is impossible to do justice to all these opinions here. Briefly it may be said that Dodgson believed in free-will and individual responsibility to a personal God. He thought that animals had rudimentary souls and some reasoning powers, that all life consisted in progress and that progress was its own reward. After death there would be neither heaven nor hell in the ordinary sense but simply progress again towards ever richer and fuller experience.

In *Sylvie and Bruno Concluded*, Chapter XVI, the Earl is feeling a little despondent. Life is slipping away from him and he envies the younger men their opportunities and interests.

'Yet surely many human interests *survive* human life?' I said . . .
'Many do, no doubt. And *some* forms of Science; but only *some*, I think. Mathematics, for instance; *that* seems to possess an endless interest: one can't imagine *any* form of life, or *any* race of intelligent beings, where Mathematical truth would lose its meaning. But I fear Medicine stands on a different footing.'

And he points out that in a life where there are no material bodies, there will be no disease. Arthur, who is a doctor, is bound to agree.

'*Military* science is a yet stronger instance,' says the Earl. Wellington, he thinks, will have to find himself some other congenial line of work hereafter. But he is still troubled.

'The one idea,' the Earl resumed, 'that has seemed to me to over-shadow all the rest, is that of *Eternity*—involving as it seems to do, the necessary *exhaustion* of all subjects of human interest. Take Pure Mathematics, for instance—a Science independent of our present surroundings. I have studied it, myself, a little. Take the subject of circles and ellipses—what we call "curves of the second degree". In a future Life, it would only be a question of so many years (or *hundreds* of years, if you like), for a man to work out *all* their properties . . . And when I transport myself, in thought, through some thousands or millions of years, and fancy myself possessed of as much Science as one created reason can carry, I ask myself "What then? With nothing more to learn, can one rest content on *knowledge* for the eternity yet to be lived through?" It has been a very wearying thought to me. I have sometimes fancied one *might* in that event, say "It is better *not* to be," and pray for personal *annihilation*—the Nirvana of the Buddhists.'

'I know that weary feeling,' said the young Doctor. 'I have gone through it all more than once. Now let me tell you how I have put it to myself. I have imagined a little child playing with toys on his nursery floor and yet able to *reason* and to look on thirty years ahead. Might he not say to himself, "By that time I shall have had enough of bricks and ninepins. How weary life will be!" Yet if we look forward through these thirty years, we find him a great statesman, full of interests and joys far more intense than his baby-life could give —joys wholly inconceivable to his baby mind—joys such as no baby-language could in the faintest degree describe. Now may not our life, a million years hence have the same relation to our life now that the man's life has to the child's? And, just as one might try, all in vain, to express to that child in the language of bricks and ninepins, the meaning of "politics", so perhaps all those descriptions of Heaven, with its music and its feasts and its streets of gold, may be only attempts to describe in *our* words, things for which we *really* have no words at all. Don't you think that in *your* picture of another life, you are in fact transplanting that child into political life, without making any allowance for his growing up?'

So may the Dodgsons, father and son, have conversed in the old days at Croft.

The failure of *Sylvie and Bruno* was not entirely due to the plan on which it was written. Another cause was certainly Dodgson's bee-in-the-bonnet about drawing from life, for he transcribed a good deal of the childish prattle straight from real children and made much more to conform. Real children, however, supple-ment words by gesture, tone, facial expressions and other evidences of intention less easy to define, shorn of which their grammatical (and other) eccentricities are more irritating than amusing.

An example will show how far Dodgson was from realizing this simple truth. In the Preface to *Sylvie and Bruno Concluded* he says,

I once found two very small boys in a garden playing a micro-scopic game of 'Single Wicket'. The bat was, I think, about the size of a table-spoon; and the utmost distance attained by the ball, in its most daring flights, was some four or five yards. The *exact* length was of course a matter of *supreme* importance; and it was always care-fully measured out (the batsman and the bowler amicably sharing the toil) with a dead mouse!

o

As an anecdote, nothing could be more delightful. Now see what he made of it in *Sylvie and Bruno*.

'What do you keep that mouse for?' I said. 'You should either bury it, or else throw it into the brook.'

'Why, it's to measure with!' cried Bruno. 'How ever would oo do a garden without one? We make each bed three mouses and a half long, and two mouses wide.'

It is almost cruel to compare this kind of thing with Dodgson's earlier dialogue. We open the book at random.

'I can't explain *myself*, I'm afraid, sir,' said Alice, 'because I'm not myself, you see.'

'I don't see,' said the Caterpillar.

That he could no longer do.

But even yet we have not plumbed the depths to which had sunk this master of ruthless rhyme and trenchant prose. There is still the maudlin lovingness of the Fairy Duet, with its chorus:

'For I think it is Love,
For I feel it is Love,
For I'm sure it is nothing but Love!'

There is worse. There is the supreme bathos of Bruno's Last Words:

'God's own sky,' the little fellow repeated, as they stood, lovingly clinging together, and looking out into the night. 'But oh, Sylvie, what makes the sky such a *darling* blue?'

The awful thing is the complete sincerity.

He had always been an odd character and as the years wore on, he became 'difficult'. His friends were warned not to tell improper stories, particularly about the Bible, in his presence. In the middle of a theatrical performance he would walk out if something indelicate were said or done on the stage. Most of his friends forgave him his goodness cheerfully but once he carried his prudery a step too far and incurred the formidable displeasure of Ellen Terry. He taken a little girl to see her in *Faust* (it must have been in 1885) and he wrote to her afterwards that when Margaret began to undress the child had said, 'Where is it going to stop?' As it had affected a mere child disagreeably, he thought she ought to alter her 'business'. 'I thought you only knew nice children,' was Ellen's devastating answer.[1] But he had succeeded in making her feel 'ashamed and shy' and she

[1] Ellen Terry: *Memoirs*, p. 142.

had no such success with him, as can be seen from the Preface to
Sylvie and Bruno, where he improves the occasion by warning
his readers of the risk to their immortal souls of watching plays
with 'risky' situations, strong dialogue or suggestive 'business'.
'Be sure,' he says, 'the safest rule is that we should not dare to
live in any scene in which we dare not die,' which, he assures us
cheerfully, may happen to us tonight.

His attitude to his own literary reputation was odd. When he
made a new child friend he invariably presented a copy of *Alice*
or *Looking-glass* or both, yet any reference to his authorship of
these works by friends or acquaintances caused his instant
departure. Autograph-hunting he regarded as an impertinence
and also as tending to make him vain. He delighted in passing
off his friends' forgeries of his signature as his own, and he only
called where he was not invited.[1]

Harry Furniss, who illustrated *Sylvie and Bruno*, summed him
up as 'a clergyman, an Oxford man, an orthodox cleric and a
typical Don to boot'. He also expressed the opinion, the converse
of Bishop Strong's, that 'his humour was not spontaneous; in
himself he was a dull man; his jokes, elaborate and designed,
were feeble'.[2] Perhaps that was so when Furniss knew him. It
was not always so. Also, Furniss was a more spiteful character
than either Tenniel, that other White Knight, or Holiday, and
Dodgson was never renowned for tact. According to Furniss,
Dodgson used to count the lines in a square inch of one of his
drawings and compare the total with that in a similar area of
one made by Tenniel.[3]

The artistic temperament takes that kind of thing very hard.

On another occasion Dodgson called at Harry Furniss's
studio to see the illustrations in the making. Furniss invited him
in but warned him that if he criticized any of the drawings they
would have to be destroyed. Dodgson retired in haste. Furniss
rather spoils the story by adding that the illustrations had not
been started. On the whole, I think that Furniss is a rather
unreliable witness and that both his estimate of Dodgson and his
account of Tenniel's estimate of Dodgson should be taken with a
pinch of salt.[4]

[1] Coll., p. 273, p. 335, etc.
[2] *Strand Magazine*, January, 1908.
[3] Ib.
[4] F.M. in *Handbook*, p. 126.

o*

The truth is probably that, having a reputation as a wit, Dodgson occasionally displayed a little too much ingenuity in his efforts to justify it. But this does not detract from such successful sallies as that recorded by Falconer Madan. Somebody in Congregation stated that it was the chief function of Universities to turn out Professors. In a pause which followed Dodgson rose and with his curious hesitating speech exclaimed: 'Quite right! Quite right! Turn them out! Turn them out!'[1]

From his rooms in Christ Church was emitted a continuous flow of pillow-problems, indoor-games, circulars, letters to the press and private correspondence. The last of these activities he took seriously. He summarized every letter he received from 1 January, 1861, to 8 January, 1898, numbered them, crossreferenced them and could trace correspondences which lasted for years through the various registers. Altogether there were 98,721 entries. It is not to be wondered at that there were generally seventy or eighty names on his list of unanswered correspondents.[2]

His child-friends were legion, almost always little girls, whom he met on the beach or in trains. He carried safety-pins in case they needed anything pinned up and toys and puzzles as bait. He sketched them, told them stories, illustrating as he went, gave them copies of his books and as a rule dropped them before the dangerous age. 'He always used to say,' Ethel Arnold remarks, 'that when the time came for him to take off his hat when he met one of his quondam child friends in the street, it was time for the friendship to cease.'[3] But the rule was not invariable. Gertrude Chataway and Ethel Arnold herself were exceptions and he had several good friends among women he had not known as children.

Isa Bowman, who played Alice in the 1888 revival of the Operetta, became an especial favourite and records that Dodgson not merely entertained her but provided her with the best education that money and influence could obtain, including elocution lessons from his friend Ellen Terry, swimming lessons, and lessons in singing and languages; and he himself undertook geography, arithmetic, Euclid and the Bible. Her 'course'

---

[1] F.M. in *Handbook*, Intro., p. xv.
[2] Coll., pp. 265–6.
[3] *Atlantic Monthly*, June, 1929, pp. 782–9.

lasted for about three hours, six days a week, and was extended over a period of years. When she went to America his own part of the instruction continued by post. She faithfully played her part in this, for a child-actress in those days, wonderful opportunity.[1] *Sylvie and Bruno* was dedicated to her, and *Sylvie and Bruno Concluded* to Enid Stevens, a pastel study of whom hung above his mantelpiece in the 90's.[2] But they were all 'a very different thing' and quite enough attention has been paid to them.

His last meeting with Alice Liddell was, according to her son, in 1891, and as Dean Liddell retired in that year and the family left Christ Church, it would probably be the last opportunity for such a meeting. The note of invitation which he sent round to the Deanery, where he had heard Alice was paying her parents a visit, is a study in constraint and embarrassment. He realized that she would 'probably prefer to bring a companion' but left the choice to her, adding that her husband would be ('most' crossed out and 'very' substituted) 'welcome'.

He had met Reginald Hargreaves not long before in the Christ Church Common Room. In mentioning this fact to Alice he remarked that he found it strange to think of him as married to one he still thought of as seven years of age.[3] That does not ring true. Alice was ten in the boat, thirteen when the book was published and twenty-eight when she left Christ Church to be married. Perhaps he had disciplined himself to think of her only as a little girl or as a character in his books.

About ten years before his death he wrote to his friend, the Rev. F. H. Atkinson, comparing single and married blessedness. He not only was, but intended to remain 'a lonely old bachelor'. College life, he reminded his friend, was 'by no means unmixed misery', though he realized that marriage had 'no doubt many charms' unknown to himself.[4]

The other side of the picture appears in his preface to *Pillow Problems*, where he says it is no use trying not to think of so-and-so. It is, however, possible to think of something else, which has the effect of banishing, or almost banishing, 'the worrying subject'. 'There are,' he says,

---

[1] Isa Bowman: *The Story of Lewis Carroll.*
[2] F. B. Lennon: *Lewis Carroll*, p. 205. Dodgson's relations with his later child-friends are very fully covered in the chapter called 'Matilda Jane'.
[3] *New York Times*, 1 May, 1932; quoted in F. B. Lennon: *Lewis Carroll*, p. 195.
[4] Coll., p. 231.

sceptical thoughts, which seem for the moment to uproot the firmest faith: there are blasphemous thoughts, which dart unbidden into the most reverent souls; there are unholy thoughts, which torture, with their hateful presence, the fancy that would fain be pure. Against all these, some real mental work is a most helpful ally.

The ceaseless and multifarious activity with which he filled his waking hours tells the same story. There is no reason to believe that he was incapable of forming an adult sex-relationship, though he did not in fact do so. Very few people are incapable of marrying. We all know men who, having seemed less likely to marry than C. L. Dodgson, have yet married and to all appearances happily. Dodgson was for much of his life a very eligible bachelor; he remained unmarried from choice, not because he could not fall in love but because he had fallen in love once and finally—

> But either it was different in blood . . .
> Or else misgraffèd in respect of years . . .
> Or else it stood upon the choice of friends—

or else Alice simply preferred Reginald Hargreaves.

Dodgson started off his relationship with Alice as adopted uncle to adopted niece at a time when he felt repugnance towards the physical aspect of love, probably due to fear and inexperience. (His very sheltered upbringing, preoccupation with independence and cloistered life at Oxford must be remembered.) There was a time when that relationship might have developed into the kind of love which leads to marriage, but at that critical time something happened which threw him back upon his loneliness. Perhaps he was waiting until Alice was old enough to be capable of choosing for herself, as a man twenty years her senior was bound in honour to do, but by the time she was old enough to choose she had met Reginald Hargreaves; her parents approved of him and disapproved of Dodgson. The older man accepted the loser's part without putting the matter to the test and his loneliness was permanent. Then, like Arthur in *Sylvie and Bruno*, he determined that the secret should die with him, except that he told Collingwood, who respected his confidence and left it out of his biography.

There was once a slave who whispered a secret to the earth, and when he passed again, the reeds were telling it.

The importance of Alice is that she acted upon Dodgson as a

powerful stimulus and catalyst. She made him put forth all his powers at once in her service, and rewarded him with a smile. Their love was an irrelevance in both their lives, yet its by-products were two masterpieces. Without her, he floundered along for a time, and even produced a lesser masterpiece, in *The Hunting of the Snark*, and, diminuendo, a work touched here and there with genius, *Euclid and his Modern Rivals*. And then his powers disintegrated. The elements of *Sylvie and Bruno* are not fused at all but arranged according to a mathematical formula.

The rest of the story is soon told. Collingwood assures us that the resignation of Dean Liddell 'came as a great blow to Mr Dodgson',[1] but there was nothing personal about this regret. The Dean stood for everything that Dodgson resented. He was a Liberal where Dodgson was a Conservative, Broad Church as opposed to High Church, the friend of Stanley, the Champion of Jowett, the man who thought Oxford had disgraced itself by not re-electing Gladstone. Dodgson hated change and the Dean had been the instrument of change at Christ Church. He had altered the shape of the buildings, the system of administration, the composition of the College hymn-book. He was cold, reserved, proud and implacable. He was the only man in Christ Church who occupied better quarters than Dodgson himself, and he had put them tacitly out-of-bounds.

With Mrs Liddell, Dodgson was on scarcely better terms, though she sometimes forgot to be cold to him, which always pleased him greatly.[2] But they were part of the past and it was like the end of an old song when there was no longer a Liddell at the Deanery. Still, the new Dean, Dr Paget, was a close personal friend of Dodgson's and the last years of 'Lewis Carroll' were passed in something like the tranquillity in which it used to be thought he had passed all his life.

In 1892 he resigned as Curator of the Common Room, thus severing his last link with University affairs.[3] He lived on at Tom Quad, a celebrity whom scarcely anybody knew, though there are many people alive who can remember his rather melancholy appearance. He rose early and attended College Service, but seldom dined in hall; he still went for long walks and often

[1] Coll., p. 297.
[2] Private letter: Miss F. Menella Dodgson.
[3] Coll., p. 303.

worked, standing at his tall writing-desk, until four in the morning. He also worked in bed without light, using an instrument of his own invention called the 'nyctograph'. He became deaf in one ear and suffered from the form of hallucination known as 'moving fortifications' but his general health was excellent.

The summer vacations were generally spent at Eastbourne and at other times between terms he went to Guildford, where no fewer than five of his sisters had lived at 'The Chestnuts' since the death of the Archdeacon. There, too, repaired a numerous tribe of young nephews and nieces to be given gold watches and instructed in Symbolic Logic. He was always a wonderful uncle.[1]

And there, on 6 January, 1898, he contracted influenza, took to his bed and died some eight days later.[2]

[1] Miss Violet Dodgson, broadcast, Third Programme, 15 September, 1950.
[2] Coll., pp. 345-8.

BIBLIOGRAPHY

I. WORKS BY C. L. DODGSON (LEWIS CARROLL)

1. *The Rectory Umbrella and Misch-Masch*, ed. Mrs Florence Milner, Cassell, 1932.

2. 'A Visit to Tennyson', *Strand Magazine*, May, 1901. (A letter written to William (Edward Wilcox) on 11 May, 1859.) Reprinted, *Handbook*, pp. 195–8.

3. *Alice's Adventures Under Ground* (facsimile of the original MS. book with Dodgson's illustrations), London, Macmillan & Co., 1886.

4. *Notes by an Oxford Chiel*, James Parker & Co. (1865–74); reprinted with valuable explanatory notes in *The Lewis Carroll Picture Book*, London, T. Fisher Unwin, 1899; also in *Complete Works* without Notes.

5. *Alice's Adventures in Wonderland*, London, Macmillan & Co., 1st ed. 1865. Any standard edition with Tenniel's illustrations.

6. 'Condensation of Determinants', *Proceedings of the Royal Society*, Vol. XV, 1866.

7. 'Enigma and Explication of the Enigma', two single leaflets printed for private circulation, 1866; see *Handbook*, pp. 29, 30.

8. *Russian Journal*, Dutton, 1935 (Continental tour with Liddon).

9. Telegraph-Cipher and Alphabet-Cipher, both privately printed, 1868; see *Handbook*, pp. 33, 34.

10. *Phantasmagoria and Other Poems*, London, Macmillan & Co., 1869; reprinted in *Collected Poems* and *Complete Works*.

11. *Through the Looking-glass*, London, Macmillan & Co., 1st ed. 1872. Any standard edition subsequent to 1887, with key and preface.

12. 'Vivisection as a Sign of the Times', Letter in *The Pall Mall Gazette*, 12 February, 1875, reprinted in Collingwood's *Life* (pp. 167–71).

13. 'Fallacies about Vivisection' (1875), printed for private circulation; reprinted in *Complete Works*.

14. *The Hunting of the Snark*, London, Macmillan & Co., 1876.

15. 'An Easter Greeting to Every Child who loves *Alice*', Oxford, 1876; reprinted in the People's Edition of *Alice* and *Looking-glass*.

16. 'Professorship of Comparative Philology', Oxford, printed for private circulation, 1876, Bodleian.

17. 'Natural Science at Oxford': A Letter to the Editor of *The Pall Mall Gazette*, 17 May, 1877. Reprinted in Collingwood's *Life*, pp. 187–91.

18. *Euclid and his Modern Rivals*, London, Macmillan & Co., 1879.

19. 'Dreamland', Oxford University Press, 1882, reprinted in Collingwood's *Life*.

20. 'A Tangled Tale', London, Macmillan & Co., 1885, reprinted in *Complete Works*.

21. *The Theatre*, April, 1887, '*Alice* on the Stage'; reprinted in *The Picture Book*.

22. *Curiosa Mathematica, Part I, A New Theory of Parallels*, London, Macmillan & Co., 1888.

23. *Sylvie and Bruno*, London, Macmillan & Co., and New York, 1889, reprinted in *Complete Works*.

24. *Sylvie and Bruno Concluded*, London, Macmillan & Co., and New York, 1893, reprinted in *Complete Works*.

25. *Curiosa Mathematica, Part II, Pillow Problems*, London, Macmillan & Co., 1893.

26. *Symbolic Logic, Part I, Elementary;* London, Macmillan & Co., and New York, 1896; reprinted in *Complete Works*.

27. *Three Sunsets and Other Poems*, Macmillan, 1898; see also *Collected Verse* and *Complete Works*.

28. *The Collected Verse of Lewis Carroll*, with introduction by John Francis McDermott, E. P. Dutton, 1929.

29. *Selections from the Letters of Lewis Carroll to his Child Friends*, ed. E. M. Hatch, Macmillan, 1933.

30. *The Complete Works of Lewis Carroll*, with a Preface by Alexander Woollcott, Random House, 1937.

II. BIOGRAPHIES, MEMOIRS, ETC.

1. *The Dodgson Sale Catalogue*, Oxford, 1898. Bodleian.

2. STUART DODGSON COLLINGWOOD: *Life and Letters of Lewis Carroll*, London, T. Fisher Unwin, 1898.

3. STUART DODGSON COLLINGWOOD: *The Lewis Carroll Picture Book*, London, T. Fisher Unwin, 1899.

4. LIONEL TOLLEMACHE: 'Reminiscences of "Lewis Carroll"', *Literature*, 1898.

5. BISHOP STRONG: 'Lewis Carroll', *Cornhill Magazine*, March, 1898.

6. BEATRICE HATCH: 'Lewis Carroll', *Strand Magazine*, April, 1898.

7. HENRY HOLIDAY: *Academy*, 29 January, 1898.

8. ARTHUR FURNISS: 'Recollections of "Lewis Carroll"', *Strand Magazine*, January, 1908.

9. ETHEL ARNOLD: 'Reminiscences of "Lewis Carroll"', *Atlantic Monthly*, June, 1929.

10. WALTER DE LA MARE: *Lewis Carroll*, London, 1930.

11. *Handbook of the Literature of C. L. Dodgson (Lewis Carroll)*, by SIDNEY HERBERT WILLIAMS, F.S.A., and FALCONER MADAN, M.A., Oxford University Press, 1931.

12. CARYL HARGREAVES: 'Alice's Recollections of Carrollian Days', *Cornhill Magazine*, July, 1932.

13. E.L.S.: 'Lewis Carroll as Artist', *Cornhill Magazine*, November, 1932.

14. LANGFORD REED: *Lewis Carroll*, London, Foyle, 1932.

15. SHANE LESLIE: 'Lewis Carroll and the Oxford Movement', *London Mercury*, July, 1933.

16. FLORENCE BECKER LENNON: *Lewis Carroll, a Biography*, Cassell & Co., 1947.

17. FRANCES SARZANO: *Sir John Tenniel*, London, Art and Technics, 1948.

18. HELMUT GERNSHEIM: *Lewis Carroll, Photographer*, London, Max Parrish & Co. Ltd, 1949.

III. BACKGROUND MATERIAL

1. ABBOTT, EDWIN: *Flatland, A Romance of Many Dimensions*, London, 1884.

2. AESOP: *Fables*, ed. Thomas James, with illustrations by Tenniel and Wolf, London, John Murray, 1928 (1st ed. with illustrations by Tenniel alone, 1848).

3. BELL, E. T.: *Men of Mathematics*, London, Victor Gollancz, 1937; *Development of Mathematics*, New York and London, McGraw-Hill Book Company Inc., 1940.

4. BERKELEY, GEORGE: *Works*, ed. G. N. Wright, London, Thomas Tegg, Cheapside, 1843.

5. BUTLER, SAMUEL: *Erewhon*, London, Trubner & Co., 1872.

6. CHURCH, RICHARD WILLIAM: *Life and Letters*, by Mary C. Church, London, Macmillan, 1894.

7. COLENSO, JOHN WILLIAM: *Life*, by the Rev. Sir George Cox, Bart., M.A. (2 vols), London, W. Ridgeway, 1888.

8. CRUSE, AMY: *The Victorians and their Books*, London, Allen & Unwin, 1935.

9. DARWIN, CHARLES: *Origin of Species*, London, John Murray, 1859, 6th ed. 1875. *Descent of Man*, London, John Murray, 1871.
   Life and Letters, by FRANCIS DARWIN (3 vols), London, John Murray, 1887.

10. DE MORGAN, MRS SOPHIA ELIZ.: *From Matter to Spirit*, London, Longmans Green, 1863.

11. DODGSON, CHARLES (Archdeacon): Sermon, *Ritual Worship*, 1852. *Letter to the Lord Bishop of Ripon*, 1852. *Tertullian*, trans. for the Library of the Fathers, ed. E. B. Pusey.

12. DOYLE, ARTHUR CONAN: *History of Spiritualism* (2 vols), London, Cassell & Co., 1926.

13. *Essays and Reviews:* Jowett, Pattison, Wilson, Williams, Goodwin, Baden-Powell and Temple, 1860.

14. FECHNER, GUSTAV THEODOR: Kleine Schriften, 'Space Has Four Dimensions', *Vier Paradoxe*, No. 2, 1846.

15. FIRTH, C. G.: 'Political Significance of Gulliver's Travels', *Proceedings of the British Academy*, Vol. IX, 1919.

16. GLADSTONE, WILLIAM EWART: *Life*, by John Morley (3 vols), London, Macmillan, 1903.

17. HALLIWELL-PHILLIPS (JAMES ORCHARD HALLIWELL): *The Nursery Rhymes of England*, London, Percy Soc., 1842.

18. HAMMOND, J. L. and B.: *The Age of the Chartists*, London, Longmans Green, 1930.

19. HARVEY, SIR PAUL: *The Oxford Companion to English Literature*, Oxford, Clarendon Press, 1932.

20. HERSCHEL, SIR JOHN: *Popular Lectures on Scientific Subjects*, London, W. H. Allen, New Ed., 1895.

21. HOOKER, C. W. R.: *What is the Fourth Dimension?* (*Reflections inspired by a pair of Gloves*), London, A. and C. Black, Ltd, 1934.

22. HUME, DAVID: *A Treatise of Human Nature* (3 vols), London, Thomas Longman, 1740.

23. HUXLEY, THOMAS HENRY: *Life*, by P. Chalmers Mitchell, New York and London, G. B. Putnam's Sons, 1900.

24. JOWETT, BENJAMIN: *Life and Letters*, by Evelyn Abbott and Lewis Campbell (2 vols), London, J. Murray, 1897.

25. KANT, IMMANUEL: *Inaugural Dissertation and Early Writings on Space*, trans. John Handyside, London, Open Court, 1929.

26. KEBLE, JOHN: *The Christian Year*, Oxford, 1827. Sermon, *The National Apostasy*, Oxford, 1833.

27. KENDALL, GUY: *Charles Kingsley and his Ideas*, London, Hutchinson & Co., 1947.

28. KINGSLEY, CHARLES: *The Water Babies*, London, Macmillan, 1863.

29. KITCHIN, GEORGE: *A Survey of Burlesque and Parody in English*, Oliver & Boyd, Edinburgh and London, 1931.

30. LIDDELL, HENRY GEORGE: *Memoir*, by Rev. Henry L. Thompson, M.A., London, John Murray, 1899.

31. LIDDON, HENRY PARRY: *Life and Letters*, by John Octavius Johnson, M.A., London, Longmans Green, 1904.

32. MACDONALD, GEORGE: *Orts*, London, Sampson Low, Marston, Searle & Rivington, 1882.

33. MACDONALD, GREVILLE: *George Macdonald and his Wife*, London, Allen & Unwin, 1924.

34. MANNING, HENRY EDWARD: *Life*, by Edmund Sheridan Purcell (2 vols), London, Macmillan, 1896.

35. MORRIS, WILLIAM: *Life*, by J. W. Mackail, London, Longmans Green, 1899.

36. MÜLLER, F. MAX: 'Dean Liddell as I Knew Him', in *Last Essays*, London, Longmans Green, 1901.

37. NEWMAN, JOHN HENRY: *Apologia pro Vita Sua*, London, Longmans Green, 1864. *Letters and Correspondence* (2 vols), ed. Anne Mozeley, London, Longmans Green, 1892. *Tracts for the Times*, No. I and No. XC.

38. PAGET, SIR JAMES: *Memoirs and Letters*, ed. by Stephen Paget, London, Longmans Green, 1902.

39. PASTEUR, LOUIS: *The Life of Pasteur*, by Rene Vallery-Radot, translated by Lady Claud Hamilton, London, Longmans Green, 1885. *Proceedings of the Royal Soc.*, Vol. 8.

40. PRICE, THE REV. BARTHOLOMEW: *An Essay on Mathematical Science*, Oxford, Thomas Combe (for the Ashmolean Soc.), 1849. *A Treatise on the Differential Calculus*, London, 1848. *A Treatise on the Infinitesimal Calculus* (4 vols), Oxford, Clarendon Press, 1852–89, especially Vol. III, *Statics and Dynamics of Material Particles*.

41. PSYCHICAL SOCIETY: *Proceedings* (1882–96).

42. PUSEY, EDWARD BOUVERIE: *Life* (4 vols), by H. P. Liddon.

43. SPENCER, HERBERT: *Principles of Psychology*, London, Longman, 1855.

44. STANLEY, ARTHUR PENRHYN: *Life and Correspondence*, by Roland E. Prothero and C. G. Bradley (2 vols), London, John Murray, 1893.

45. STRACHEY, LYTTON: *Queen Victoria*, London, Chatto & Windus, 1921.

46. SWIFT, JONATHAN: *A Tale of a Tub, The Battle of the Books and the Mechanical Operation of the Human Spirit*, ed. A. C. Guthkelch and D. Nichol Smith, Oxford, Clarendon Press, 1922.

47. WARD, WILLIAM GEORGE: *The Ideal of a Christian Church Considered*, 1844.

48. WILBERFORCE, SAMUEL: *Life*, by A. R. Ashwell (3 vols), London, John Murray, 1880. *Bishop Wilberforce*, by G. W. Daniel, London, Methuen, 1891.

49. WILSON, P. W.: *The Romance of the Calendar*, London, Allen & Unwin, 1937.

50. WRIGHT, THOMAS: *History of Caricature and the Grotesque in Literature and Art*, London, Chatto & Windus, 1865.

INDEX